Contents

Sincere thanks are due to my students for all their helpful comments, and to Valerie, my wife, for her considerable proofreading help.

Building Your Own
Business

HOW TO BE YOUR OWN BOSS BY CREATING YOUR OWN BUSINESS OR GOING FREELANCE

JOHN HAWKINS

The Crowood Press

First published in 2003 by
The Crowood Press Ltd
Ramsbury, Marlborough
Wiltshire SN8 2HR

www.crowood.com

British Library Cataloguing-in-Publication Data
A catalogue record for this book is available from the British Library.

ISBN 1 86126 647 2

Typeset by Jean Cussons Typesetting, Diss, Norfolk

Printed and bound in Great Britain by Antony Rowe Ltd, Chippenham

1
Introducing the Subject

Occasionally, many of us think about turning our hobbies into a business, giving up work for the perceived good life! With employment prospects for some looking uncertain these days, it can be prudent to have more than one basket for the eggs.

WHO WILL BENEFIT FROM THIS BOOK?

Anyone considering starting, running or building their own business ... which means:

- Virtually anybody contemplating going freelance and being their own boss.
- Working people, employed at the moment, considering 'going it alone'.
- People, although not yet ready to take the plunge, considering setting up their own business in the future.
- Employed people finding themselves suddenly redundant, and not knowing which way to turn.
- Redundant people (ex-employees) fearing another redundancy in new employment – hedging their bets.
- People, not yet convinced that a business is for them, who want more information so as to convince those who are trying to rush them unprepared into business.
- People, without previous suitable experience, who find themselves suddenly thrown into running an existing business through family succession or whatever.
- Managers and directors of existing businesses, considering buying the business from the present owners – management buyouts.
- People tied to their home wanting to generate valuable income or interest from a suitable home-based business.
- Those wanting to convert their hobbies into a viable business (to make money, or to have a much stronger or disciplined motivation).
- Serious and low-key hobbyists wanting to 'upgrade' the status of their hobby.
- Foreigners wishing to set up a business in the UK, with its various conventions and customs.

HOW THIS BOOK HELPS YOU

This book provides practical hands-on guidance, *dos* and *don't*s, tips, experiences and knowledge, covering all aspects of planning and building a business – whether migrating from paid employment and going freelance, turning a hobby into a business or simply deciding in principle to start your own business without, initially, having a concept in mind; it primarily applies to full-time operations, but the thoughts are broadly applicable to part-time activities as well.

It is positive and encouraging; but urges caution and the need for professional advice before you embark. It can be read through in sequence the first time; and thereafter used as a reference book and series of checklists. It:

- looks at the entire subject, including the hard business aspects, commitment and soul-searching
- sorts out the reality and feasibility from the pipe dreams
- adopts a top-level down, sequenced approach to the detailed practicalities
- analyses the resources and risks
- produces a reasoned and rational approach
- emphasizes the cons as well as the pros.

The text covers a very wide range of business interests, with a broad appeal and applicability, ranging from a nominal annual turnover between £500 and £5,000,000 or more. The sentiments and precise starting point in your thinking should be guided by your individual circumstances; and the contents of this book selectively interpreted to suit.

WHAT THIS BOOK COVERS

- Clarifying what you want out of life
- family and personal commitment
- personal and family matters
- relationships and support
- understanding personality, attitudes and qualifications
- contemplating experience, expertise and knowledge
- evaluating your own limitations
- appreciating joys and pitfalls
- coming to terms with creating and building a business
- deciding what business to embark on
- sorting out the fundamental concepts
- thinking out the outline for the overall business
- clarifying realistic and practical expectations
- understanding success yardsticks, risks, liabilities
- deciding whether you still want to start a business
- getting down to the detailed planning clarifying the broad concepts
- obtaining the necessary resources
- handling customers
- getting and sustaining business, marketing, sales

- creating business plans
- preparing the business plan
- checking viability
- establishing success yardsticks
- fundamental financial and other business matters (such as legal points, regulation, taxation, VAT, business type)
- working to the final checklist
- planning the whole venture
- getting underway and launch
- knowing where and when to seek professional help.

Example 1
An entrepreneur whose main focus is on financial aspects when trying to establish a thriving business but who has not the slightest knowledge about the product at the heart of the business and its marketplace – or engages someone who is not sufficiently knowledgeable – is in danger of seeing the business doomed from the outset.

Example 2
A real technical expert (so-called boffin), blindly going ahead alone with a venture, will probably fail because of his or her lack of business acumen generally, and disinterest, or lack of ability, in gaining orders.

WHAT YOU WILL GET OUT OF IT

- A solid understanding of how to set up a business – from a practical point of view, with minimum initial risk and cost exposure.
- An ability to analyse your own business ideas, and estimate the related resources and risks.
- An ability to converse authoritatively, from a position of informed strength and understanding.
- Solid confidence in the venture, as a result of methodically analysing and confirming what is required.
- An ability to develop overall business thoughts and plans with reasoned argument, facts and figures.
- An ability to develop supporting marketing, sales and export plans (if applicable), budgets, purchasing plans and all forecast material.
- An ability to anticipate and answer the points that the professional advisers will raise.
- An ability to construct a businesslike professional case – culminating in the so-called Business Plan.

To appreciate this last and interim objective better and set you thinking along the right lines as you read the book, turn briefly to Chapter 8 where the content and reasoning behind the Business Plan is described.

PHILOSOPHY

The book will:

- help you decide whether a business really is for you
- help stimulate your mind on *what* business venture is appropriate for you
- impart sufficient detailed knowledge to show you *how* to set the business up.

The weighted evaluation of several factors gives the most promising start to a long-term thriving business:

- personal – those connected with the individual generally
- social – contribution to the community at large
- impact on your family or close friends
- business development – being able and willing to get sales
- technical – anything relating to fundamental core matters like the design, build, manufacture, creation, features and benefits of the actual product or service itself (and the consequential ability to use this expertise for furthering the business by getting sales) – not necessarily *technical* in an engineering sense
- financial.

Not only is *How to set up a business* spelled out, but also *What business should I go for* is discussed. The outcome will be a meaningful, constructive exploration of your initial intuition that may demonstrate:

- an endorsement – to go for it
- realistic proof that the venture will probably not be worthwhile, rewarding or successful
- a provisional desire – a preference to await certain developments, or to gain further training.

If you intend to plan and run your own business sometime, you should be sufficiently organized to draw up the List of Actions at the end of each chapter as applicable to your own business and implement the Action List. It is strongly suggested that you shadow each applicable topic with a similar exercise for your own venture; you are often prompted by occasional explicit exercises.

Training and support in running you own business can be provided by enterprise agencies, business links and banks; the Welsh, Scottish and other regional organizations; universities, training colleges generally and other specialist training bodies. If you intend to submit your business creating and planning work for NVQ/SVQ or similar assessment, you will find this reference book invaluable and informative. There are several other books, videos, compact disks, Internet information, broadcasts, and so on that could be consulted, as well as more detailed specialist books.

Apart from the exercises reinforcing your understanding of the whole subject (as comprehensively expounded in this book), you are deliberately made to stop and think about how much and what you are absorbing. Each chapter concludes by presenting revision questions of the salient points, to maximize the benefit derived.

Finally, you should obviously consider the prospects carefully, but essentially strike whilst the iron is hot for maximum benefit – before the broad idea goes off the boil and your enthusiasm diminishes. Generally, planning your business takes between one week and six months, depending how serious you are and what is involved.

The author has detected varying degrees of real commitment when talking casually with adult students with whom he was working on this subject, to the point where some of them would never end up attempting to build their own business although they were clearly (at one time) sufficiently interested in finding out more by enrolling and paying course fees. This result was only to be expected statistically of course; nevertheless, most of them did complete the course.

On the other hand, several of them have thoroughly considered it, have taken the plunge and are enjoying it. Their enthusiasm and questions indicate their quest for knowledge and a desperate need to get under way – but minimizing the risks.

WHAT HAVE YOU LEARNT IN THIS CHAPTER?

★ Who will benefit from reading this book?
★ What will you gain from reading this book?
★ How will you gain from reading this book?
★ What are the three main 'objectives' of this book?

2
Coming To Terms
With the Idea

As an absolute prerequisite, think about your:

- real motivation
- practical options
- personal qualities
- longer-term aspirations
- business ideas.

WHY GO FREELANCE?

Some of the common reasons mentioned are:

- I am fed up with the rat race.
- I am tired of not being recognized and rewarded.
- I am frustrated with being tied to the home every day.
- I want to make the decisions.
- I want the power and kudos.
- My colleague runs his or her own business: I see this as the accepted route to follow.
- I see this as a way to make loads of easy money.
- I've come into some money which means I can afford to go freelance.

These examples are seen primarily as an escape route – not the ideal reason for creating a business. Deep unquestionable motivation is missing and that is crucial for success.

There are some more positive reasons:

- I've always wanted to go freelance, but never had the means – until now. I've come into some money.
- I had this brilliant idea – I've piloted it elsewhere and want to try it myself.
- I've proved that I can do it for someone else: so now I want to do it for myself.
- I've got this brilliant invention that I want to exploit to make money for myself.
- I've created a demand and know there is a business opportunity.
- I've seen a genuine opportunity window: I've devised a proven viable solution

12

(for example, Year 2000 bug problem, or salesmen selling tills when decimalization was introduced in the early 1970s).

- I'm a born salesman! I've already done something similar before.
- I know I can make a success of it, because I've worked for several years in the same business, managing it for someone else. I've got the business know-how, contacts and customer base.

It doesn't really matter *why* you want to go freelance, although it usually helps to consolidate your wider thinking. However, it is very important that your personal attributes are appropriate (*see* later in this chapter).

For many people, buying a car and/or buying or renting a house or apartment is the most involved transaction that will have been encountered thus far in life; so the idea of 'gambling' another (possibly larger) sum on a business as well needs very careful thought. Recklessly going ahead without proper consideration is foolish and even dangerous from the point of view of your responsibilities and risk. Chapter 4 elaborates on this topic.

EXERCISE

Why do *you* want to build your own business, and why now in particular?

INVESTMENT OPPORTUNITIES

A reason often encountered for having your own business is that you have suddenly acquired spare money. It may take the pressure off, but from a purely financial point of view, there is a world of difference between investing money generally, and investing in your own venture. There are often tax benefits and conditions associated with investments that tend to vary from time to time. So clarify them at the appropriate time with professional advisors. Which of the following two options would you be seeking?

1. Merely a solid haven to invest your money (whether derived from savings, lottery winnings, inheritances, windfalls, redundancy payments, and so on) with the three *primary* objectives of security, maximum return and possible access. Generally these investments are made in any sound stocks, shares, gilt-edged securities, unit trusts, ISAs, bonds, savings accounts, and so on – with professional financial advice.
2. Support for your own venture that will probably need some amount of investment anyway. It constitutes a much higher risk, appealing to a sense of adventure; but security, maximum return and access have been severely relegated to *secondary* objectives.

ADVANTAGES AND DISADVANTAGES OF GOING FREELANCE

There are both advantages and disadvantages that might be real or just perceived:

- You fancy the thrill and adventure.
- You want to have, and show off, the prestige, pride, kudos, power and authority.
- You visualize the freedom of work pattern.
- You would welcome the freedom to make decisions by being your own boss.
- You desperately want to be in far more control of what is going on.
- You would appreciate the flexibility of working hours and holidays.
- You would revel in the lifestyle generally.
- You see attractive financial and taxation options.
- You envisage somewhere to keep your savings under close scrutiny.
- You see an opportunity to aid other business or personal interests.
- You might gain more visibility, or standing and reputation in the community.
- You see your own business as a stepping stone to greater things.
- You are astute enough to appreciate the absence of middlemen.
- You realize that any rewards for personal hard work are returned directly to you (the profit generator), rather than going to shareholders, faceless managers and 'fat cats'.

Similarly, there are disadvantages that may be genuine or just imagined, of which you will recognize:

- You don't have the best personality profile or right attitudes.
- You are not sufficiently outgoing.
- Your haven't got the right temperament.
- You find the full responsibility too awesome.
- You are not able to accept the financial, family and other risks.
- It would be incompatible with family or social needs.
- It's effectively a commission-only job.
- There is no-one else to blame when things go wrong.
- You might lose standing as a result of a business failing.
- You might be working longer hours – which may not appeal.
- You can't resource the venture.
- You haven't got and don't know an accountant.
- There's nothing that you can seem to do.
- You don't have or trust any colleagues who could help.
- You are not good at handling customers.
- You haven't tried it before – so you don't really know.
- You don't have sufficient confidence in what you are doing.

SWOT ANALYSIS AND EXAMPLES

Techniques and tools have been devised to sort the wood from the trees, and clarify your thinking. One such technique is known as SWOT analysis that is a very neat way of documenting and assessing personal or business situations –

particularly applicable in this soul-searching arena. The acronym stands for Strengths, Weaknesses, Opportunities and Threats.

A rectangular sheet of paper is divided into its natural four quadrants by drawing one vertical and one horizontal line through its centre, with the four words entered in the top left-hand corners of each quadrant.

For example, as individuals, we all have *strengths* and *weaknesses*. There are also *threats* to our existence and well-being, and positive *opportunities* for us all to capitalize on.

A given quality might seem relevant to two or more quadrants, dependent on the phraseology or perception: a positive strength could be construed as an opposite weakness, for example: *like working with people* (strength) or *don't like working alone* (weakness). Also, emotional, unhelpful or inapplicable thoughts are generated.

Study the SWOT information and transfer items between quadrants if necessary (with suitable wording amendments), crossing out those comments that are irrelevant, or confuse the issues. Be objective. Don't write false or forced comments. Steer towards natural answers: be honest, not too generous, but not too modest. Think how others might complete the diagram, with you specifically in mind. Get someone familiar with you to arbitrate.

It is more practical to consider each of the four quadrants sequentially; but in practice, the four quadrants aren't usually completed neatly – one quadrant at a time; but rather in a *random* order, as various points occur; and additional comments might be added later.

Budding Freelance Photographer
Imagine the responses in relation to a budding photographer contemplating going freelance.

Strengths
Usually the most prolific and easiest to complete, but keep the comments strictly relevant:

- good at photography
- good at science and maths
- have got and can use a quality camera, darkroom and all relevant equipment
- have done some professional assignments already
- have got a small portfolio of own work
- am technically competent
- have got contacts in the trade for special photographic items
- have got patience
- can visualize a good picture
- good at arranging people and things for photographs
- in the photographic club and have won prizes
- physically fit
- available Saturdays for weddings [on top of day job].

Weaknesses

These are a little harder to complete, because people don't like to admit to any personal weaknesses:

- find it hard to work with people for prolonged periods
- haven't got a car or any other form of transport,
- not very good at 'paperwork'
- can't manage daytime in the week.

Opportunities

Positive thoughts about what opportunities there could be in the circumstances (in this case, *If I became a professional photographer, what other opportunities might there be to enhance my success?*):

- chance to go freelance and break away
- chance to give up day job, becoming a full-time photographer
- chance to have own business, etc.
- incentive to do some more reading and training, aimed at advanced photographic techniques
- chance to get professionally qualified and recognized in photographic circles
- ability to be available midweek, getting more assignments, if I gave up the day job
- possibility to get some modest transport: ability to accept more assignments
- could have leaflets produced, taking exhibition stands at wedding fairs and industrial exhibitions, to get more business
- could get another camera, and handle assignments in black and white, and colour.

Threats

Thunderclouds of some sort – from anything or anyone who could undermine what you are trying to do (known threats, possible threats or merely anticipated or perceived threats) that might include:

- outdated equipment, although it still works at the moment
- cost of replacing equipment
- colleague thinking of going into freelance photography (effectively creating competition)
- wedding customers who no longer just want photographs, but also videos.

This last one, deliberately included to provoke thought, could be an *opportunity* in another SWOT – about getting into the video market.

Undecided Individual

Here is another 'completed' SWOT relating to an individual at a turning point in her life; she feels restless and wants to do something, but is genuinely confused as to what to do. She's just simply mulling over some random and vague ideas that just might concentrate her thoughts.

Strengths:

- has typing skills
- has computer knowledge
- is good at art, painting, drawing, maths, golf, tennis
- likes working under people (that is, not as leader)
- gets on with people
- can talk to other people and be a good listener
- serves as an ordinary committee person
- likes arranging flowers
- has a 'welcoming' home
- likes cooking and entertaining
- likes travel and reading
- has a wealth of experience about people and places
- has plenty of time.

Weaknesses:

- is not keen on taking the lead
- doesn't like animals
- doesn't drive
- prefers to finish projects, rather than to mastermind and initiate new schemes
- is getting older; not as physically fit.

Opportunities:

- could go to evening classes to learn a new subject and meet other people
- could go on escorted travel holidays
- could write a book
- could get actively into more advanced cookery and gardening
- could move to new area to be closer to grown-up son-in-law and family.

Threats:

- yet another office reorganization: wants to give up normal secretarial job.
- new houses are being built at back of the garden: might move
- feels slightly insecure as her son lives a long way away
- some arthritis starting to appear.

There is insufficient real detail to draw any firm conclusions, which is often the case; but some ideas must spring out of this SWOT with a bit of encouragement and further exploration.

EXERCISE

Study the above SWOT, making suggestions as to what this person *might* be suited for.

EXERCISE

Produce a similar SWOT about an up-and-coming video photographer.

EXERCISE

Produce your own SWOT to establish whether or not it supports your freelance ideas. If it doesn't, double-check everything with a trusted colleague to improve it and be prepared to change course or even abandon the notion of starting your own business.

BASIC QUESTIONS

You should corroborate your previously completed SWOT with a similar diagram concerned with four other characteristics – *Skills, Skill gaps, Likes* and *Dislikes. You should know your starting point* (the precise skills and knowledge platform) *and build on your assets* (do what you do best).

The skills you possess are fairly straightforward to identify: the gaps could be embarrassingly numerous. Identify *relevant* gaps: the gaps might be to learn Spanish or Italian, if you have French and German language skills, whereas there may be little point in listing some obscure branch of physics.

- What are you really good at, and poor at?
- What do you enjoy doing?
- What do you hate doing?
- What other attributes and facilities would need to be supplied from elsewhere?
- What must you get some help with?
- What opportunities do you see?
- What threats do you see?

The point of all these exercises is simply to get you thinking in a cool, logical way (with the help of a colleague, spouse or partner, if possible) so as to pinpoint the facts, collate all the attributes and characteristics, and draw meaningful consolidated conclusions using all your *Skills, Skill gaps, Likes* and *Dislikes*; and *Strengths, Weaknesses, Opportunities* and *Threats*.

EXERCISE

Produce your own *Skills, Skill gaps, Likes* and *Dislikes* diagram to see how it supports your freelance ideas. Take a colleague's advice.

Your 'Technical' Competence

Almost everybody has a particular talent and can *do something*, to whatever ability, without enhancing their level of skills, knowledge and so on.

With extra commitment to additional study through further reading or training, a few more activities could be identified. At this stage we don't have to be *complete* 'technical' experts, but in the fullness of time, the more knowledge we possess, and the more 'technical' abilities we have at our disposal, the more successful we are likely to be – other things being equal. For the moment, just temporarily concentrate on the 'technical' element or core. A more meaningful interpretation of the word 'technical' in this context is given in Chapter 6.

PERSONAL QUALITIES AND ATTRIBUTES

If you have attributes from the group below, most of them, or even some if they are significant, you are probably going to be a suitable person. If you tend to have the opposite characteristics, it will not usually be such a good idea. It is not absolutely black and white, but certainly caution is urged, supplemented by some independent professional advice:

- enthusiasm
- inspiration
- drive
- leadership
- positive attitude
- determination
- tenacity
- stamina
- motivation
- dedication
- self-discipline
- commitment
- alertness
- shrewdness
- an eye for detail
- accuracy
- strong ability for figurework
- skill for handling people: customers and staff
- trust
- sensitivity
- patience
- outgoing personality
- warm personality
- smiley personality with humour.

There is also another group that are virtually the opposites but under different names that are generally considered counterproductive, because they do not support the typical entrepreneurial profile.

You should also possess:

- significant management skills
- leadership and organization ability
- authority, boldness and assertiveness
- integrity and credibility
- sense of punctuality
- sense of loyalty
- ability to think clearly
- ability to be purposeful
- ability to work to objectives, deadlines and budgets
- ability to keep promises (prompt deliveries, for example)
- willingness to please customers
- willingness to adopt a *can do* attitude
- capacity for hard and possibly heavy work
- attention to quality, beauty and sincerity
- technical ability in the chosen subject.

Both groups of attributes are important because they help to ensure quality and a genuine interest in the product, and business as a whole. You should certainly have qualities and attributes that closely align with their spirit, in order to have the greatest chance of business success. The more of the above characteristics you start with, the better your chances of success: the less you might be dependent on borderline abilities. The big question for you to answer honestly is: *Does this profile broadly fit my personality?*

Conversely, there are examples in history of people with only a very few of the above qualities that have turned out to be very successful. The probability is that they happened to be the beneficiaries of much good fortune or gradually learnt the relevant qualities during their business time. Maybe the pressures were not as great as they are today. Notice that age as such has not been mentioned – until now – because it isn't seen as a possible barrier provided you can still satisfy the attributes criteria, and are in good health. Similarly, if you can satisfy these and other criteria, being male or female doesn't present any problems. It could be a productive way to self-fulfilment.

Shortfalls

Whenever and wherever you notice a shortfall in your technical or other skills, personal qualities and attributes, SWOT Weaknesses or SWOT Threats, ask yourself what you are going to do about them – when?, how? and precisely what? – and whether there are any associated conditions, constraints or risks. There could be strong implications shrieking at you; or merely further training indicated or unrealistic conditions anticipated. Similarly are there any points that must be implemented first in order to realize the full potential of all opportunities and strengths? Once again, carefully and honestly produced lists are called for – with all details shown.

CREATING OR RUNNING YOUR OWN BUSINESS?

Some people want to do one or the other – either create or run their own business; whilst others want to do both. Both are very demanding, but in different ways. Most people are probably capable of running and/or setting up their own business and often do, but nevertheless, you should be aware of your preferences, capabilities, potential and personality. (Equally some people are not cut out for either role.)

Different personality profiles are applicable.

- It is one thing to research and set up the business – a very steep and exciting learning curve.
- It is another thing entirely to operate it on a day-to-day basis – a much flatter and different learning situation.

WHAT DO YOU WANT OUT OF LIFE?

It is essential to have full family backing and commitment (discussed in Chapter 4), where everyone knows what is involved in terms of personal commitment, expectation and risk.

It must also be appreciated that there may be some form of third party *financial* backing (discussed in Chapter 8) to complement the personal money. That party might want a nominal or a major controlling say in the business. In that case, it must be asked whether you are really your own boss after all, or whether you are merely lining the pockets of someone else who is using *your* personal skills, expertise, and so on, as in an 'employed' situation? Is this what you want?

Rough ideas about the business expectations should be considered, too – after all a business without plans, goals, objectives and targets will probably drift aimlessly rather like a ship without an engine, rudder, anchor or navigation charts in the ocean. Ships (and businesses) could so easily end up on the rocks.

Thoughts about the longer-term personal expectations should emerge, even though they might be somewhat vague and tentative at this early stage. They should be firmed up as soon as possible, even if it is not practical to seal them all completely at this stage. Personal and business goals are fundamental to your concerns when building your own business or going freelance: they intimately relate to why you want your own business.

Typical yardsticks for defining a thriving business on a personal basis (which will also be referred to in Chapter 7), might be expressed as:

- an ability to relinquish a full-time salaried position within a year or two – for example, your spouse's or partner's
- an ability to become truly independent of a normal respectable salaried income
- allowing a particular monetary figure to be identified as a personal income target within a certain period of time – typically doubling and maintaining the relinquished daytime job salary within perhaps two, five or ten years, after taking account of inflationary factors
- having a particular lifestyle, cars, yacht, possessions or housing.

EXERCISE

Write down your own personal goals.

EXERCISE

Write down the success criteria for your own venture, including a timescale.

ANOTHER FORM OF RELAXATION?

Remember, if you are migrating from a hobby, that true hobbies are fun and enjoyable but have no real obligations, which means that the hobby can be picked up and subsequently dropped as the personal mood dictates. The current hobby is a true hobby; but when it crosses the line into being a business, it becomes a business. Business means commitment, enthusiasm, determination. Your former hobby will acquire obligations, deadlines, disciplines, responsibilities, risk, time commitments and other commitments to customers and creditors – perhaps contractual ones, and so on.

It is a truism that hobbies are hobbies; and businesses are businesses. You must keep these twin thoughts in your mind. Don't ever attempt to mix them. You must treat your hobby from now on as a *business* all the time; since it will be used to derive very important income: it is a new business and a new lifestyle. It now commands vital wealth generation responsibilities!

Because the original hobby will no longer exist as a hobby, you may need (if there's time to devote to it) *another* hobby. What's your next hobby (or potential business?) or form of relaxation to counterbalance the pressures of the new business world going to be?

EXERCISE

Write down what you really want out of life. What is your 'replacement' hobby?

WHAT HAVE YOU LEARNT IN THIS CHAPTER?

★ What are the advantages and disadvantages of going freelance?

★ What are the advantages and disadvantages of having your own business?

★ How do SWOT (and similar) exercises help you analyse situations?

★ What does the acronym SWOT stand for?

★ What are the personal qualities and attributes conducive to running successful small businesses?

★ What personal qualities would probably be unacceptable – and why?

★ What do you think are the best personal qualities or attributes in order to gain orders, that is, to be able to 'sell' successfully? Put them in order of priority.

★ Why are personal goals established as a prerequisite for the business ones?

3
Understanding Your Venture

You have considered your own suitability, personal qualities, commitment, and (in the next chapter) family support, commitment and risks. Although you will have considered what your own business might be about, this short chapter offers some additional thoughts, if you have not yet decided on the exact nature of your business.

SUGGESTED BUSINESSES

There are very many jobs to be done in the world! This random list (not an exhaustive one) of some freelance activities should stimulate the lateral thinking process. They should provide some nudges: some will derive from hobbies and some will not. Continue to be open-minded: but be realistic.

Look round again – observing and considering. It is essential that you become completely comfortable with the choice: you should also be a *technical* expert – but that should give you a wide enough field. There's always the Yellow Pages, newspapers or the Internet!

Accessories shop
Accountant
Architect
Artist
Author
Baby-sitter
Babywear shop
Bed and breakfast
Car repairer
Carpenter
Central heating installer
Child-minder
Chiropodist
Commission-only salesman
Computer supplier
Consultant
Contract caterer
Counselling

Courier
Dance or aerobics studio
Decorator
Dressmaker
Driving instructor
Electrician
Employment Agency
Farmer
Fashion shop
Financial consultant
Flooring supplier
Flower arranger
Garage mechanic
Gardener
Glassblower
Golfer
Graphic artist
Groceries shop

Hairdresser
Hardware store
Horticulturist
Hotelier
Import/export business
Interpreter
Jewellery maker
Jobbing builder
Knitter
Lecturer
Log merchant
Market trader
Model maker
Model trains dealer
Music teacher
Musician
Newsagent
Office secretarial services
Photographer
Plumber
Post Office
Potter
Publican

Publisher
Reporter
Restaurant
Second-hand clothes shop
Shopkeeper
Soft toy-making
Software services
Solicitor
Sportsman
Tailoring alterations
Taxi driver
Tea shop
Therapist and massage
Tobacconist CTN
Toy shop
Trainer
Tupperware parties, etc.
TV servicing
Van caterer
Washing-machine repairs
Wedding cake supplier
Wholesaler
Woodcarver

Think Positively and Laterally

Mighty oaks from little acorns grow. It may sound a long, long way off but the founder of Marks and Spencer, for example, didn't ever really dream that the empire would be so huge a hundred or so years later. He only saw, at that time, to the end of his nose – and dreamt possibly: there could be a similar germ of an idea waiting to be developed – for you.

The golden rule is just to think openly and laterally: many options should come to mind (however fanciful, for the moment). Many will be discounted. Think also: *why* your venture might be needed, and *why now* in particular?

Think positively about practicalities: think *how* and *when* could it all come about; think about *where* it could happen (there might be several possibilities). Don't reject any ideas at this stage about technology and e-business.

BONFIRE BUSINESS LIMITED

This simple visual philosophy is easy to remember. Three constituents only make a successful bonfire, but they must all be present at the same time to make a good 5 November – heat, combustible material and oxygen. Take any one away, and the bonfire fails.

So too with a successful business, but in this case, the three constituents reappear as:

- *heat* represented by three 'e's (energy, expertise and enthusiasm – hopefully all indigenous and natural)
- *combustible material* represented by the financial and other resources
- *oxygen* represented by customers and orders.

All three constituents must be present simultaneously for success, like the bonfire! There are many successful ventures – most are household names from industry, commerce and the High Street – but there have also been some spectacular crashes (even the mighty Rolls Royce, in the early 1970s). Many started out precariously, growing to their present size and standing, whereas other much smaller examples of successful enterprises can be seen at craft fairs. Why not yours?

FAMILIAR NAMES

The following are names familiar to us all: Bill Gates (Microsoft); Richard Branson (Virgin Group); Rupert Murdoch (News International); Anita Roddick (Body Shop); Laura Ashley; Tesco; Sainsbury; British Telecom; Boots; and so on.
Interesting observations can be made about successful businesses:

- The basic ideas are often very obvious and simple.
- They probably started off as 'bath-time' thoughts evolving from home-based activities, for example, interests or formal hobbies.
- Sometimes, they have migrated from successful employment situations.
- Some are classic opportunist windows, like the Year 2000 bug fixing or decimalization many years back.
- Others have been specially grown to capitalize on existing marketplace demands – for instance, pop drinks.
- Others, particularly in the toy and games spheres, *create* a new demand in the marketplace, typically through television advertising.
- There are generally calculated risks involved – and rewards!

MULTIPLE VENTURES

There is no reason why the activity should just be a single one. Some customers particularly seek 'one-stop' shopping or single information points: your proposed venture could serve several of their needs concurrently.

Are there any secondary businesses that could be considered as an extension to your core business – either directly related, or distinctly separate? All ideas are very welcome and worthwhile at this phase of lateral thinking, but they still have to be fully justified: *what will they cost as 'extras'?*, *will they pay their way?*, *are they interdependent? and what extra percentage contribution do they make?* Reliable answers to these questions will not be available now, but they should be kept at the back of your mind as possibilities.

Here are several examples to illustrate merging related activities: it would not be appropriate for you to discard them at this early stage.

Banks
A classic example of a one-stop organization is the traditional bank – that has now moved into conventional building society operations, insurance, pensions, mortgages, purchase guarantee extensions, estate agency and even building surveying. Different specialist staff might be involved, but from a business point of view, they all belong to the single banking group. The broad commonality is the customer: when the customer wants to move house, to borrow or has money that needs looking after, for example!

Music Shop
A music shop, selling musical instruments, music, CDs, video tapes, theatre tickets, operates an instrument repair and rental service, as well – all broadly related needs as far as the musical customer is concerned.

Design-and-Build Organizations
Design-and-build organizations, perhaps coupled with finance arrangements, and turnkey operations generally that supply, deliver, install and maintain such items as computer hardware and central heating systems.

Bookshop
Yet another example is the store or bookshop that also has a restaurant and/or snack-bar. There are a growing number of such businesses – and cyber cafés, of course.

Airports
Airports are no longer simply interested in handling aircraft schedules and maintenance, and 'processing' passengers: they have moved into retailing, restaurants and car parking, for example, in a big way – all complementary things as far as passengers are concerned. (They even encourage local non-flying shoppers to help balance the books.)

Wedding Arrangements
A young bride and groom plan to get married. Their fundamental requirement is to have a happy and enjoyable wedding day, with all the accepted trimmings. So they sort out the main details, such as where and when the ceremony will take place, and at what time.

They need to book a reception, maybe overnight accommodation for some guests, drinks, food, some spare changing rooms and so on. They also need taxis, other official cars, photographer, video makers, honeymoon, disco. They need to choose, buy or have made dresses and other fine clothes. They will need a florist and church, where clergy, choir, organist and bell-ringers are required. A printer will be needed to print the order of service and invitations.

There are dozens of arrangements to make, all being exciting parts of the fun and experience; but basic information like times, dates, places, names and addresses, is common – repeated at each 'stop'. Each contact follows automatically. Making and coordinating the arrangements for the entire event could conceivably be done with just two or three starting points with a little ingenuity and entrepreneurship, like the reception, church and perhaps one other.

There is certainly food for thought within this happy scene for small groupings of own ventures that could streamline arrangements for the couple. The common denominator is the customer, once again.

Hardware Shop

Being customer-driven was a training film theme, relating to retail shop service and making a valuable point. A customer entered a hardware shop and announced to the narrowly focused assistant that all he wanted was a piece of wood to put up a kitchen shelf. That is precisely what he got!

The scenario was run again with a rather more thoughtful, pleasant and helpful assistant, who tactfully *questioned* the customer about putting up the shelf in the full meaning of the words, including his previous experience – *see* Chapter 11. I have exaggerated the example to make the point – the customer still went away with his piece of wood; but in addition … an electric drill outfit, wall-filling plugs, brackets, screws, a screwdriver, a saw, sandpaper, primer paint, undercoat paint, gloss paint, brushes, and so on.

He presumably put up the shelf, and did a few more jobs besides: the customer was well-pleased, because he could do the job he set out to do really well, primarily because he had been properly attended to by someone who endeavoured to understand his needs; and the proprietor was happy too! The customer would no doubt have patronized the business again as well, pleasing the proprietor even more.

EXERCISE

Write down a brief description of your proposed venture, outlining what you propose to do; where, when and how you hope go about it? How far have you got in your thinking and practicalities?

EXERCISE

Make a list of some of the small businesses that you know. How did they start? How successful are they?

FIVE CATEGORIES OF BUSINESS

This chapter has provided some real pointers and comments about having your own business. You must be constantly looking around to notice what exists – remembering that *someone* had to make and sell them in the first place; it could have been you. You will notice everyday objects like cups, saucers, food, vegetable racks, books, furniture, clothes, light fittings, lampshades, flower arrangements, metalled roads, cars, gates, driveways, buildings, extensions, decorating, stationery, that must have constituted a business for someone, sometime.

Businesses can be broadly categorized in five groups – helping to concentrate the mind when considering suggestions for your own venture. For example:

* *Making* things   builder, dressmaker, manufacturer, wood-turner
* *Doing* things   childminder, flower arranger, gardener, designer
* *Repairing* things   TVs, cars, kitchen appliances, central heating
* *Creating* things   musician, author, artist, designer, software writer
* *Moving* things   milk roundsman, shop, wholesaler, removal firm.

WHAT HAVE YOU LEARNT IN THIS CHAPTER?

★ Restate the underlying principles for a successful business – like Bonfire Business Limited.
★ What is the link between multiple ventures and one stops? Think of some examples from your experiences.
★ What are the five possible activities at the heart of a business?

4
Accepting Total Commitment

This cautionary chapter considers three very sensitive and crucial topics:

- understanding the impact of the business on other peoples' lives
- explaining the project to all parties who are likely to be affected by it
- asking for their corresponding support for both you and the venture – morally and/or financially.

The business rules: OK? still prevails.

You and Your Immediate Family
You (or any other would-be entrepreneur, for that matter) must undergo a critical examination to confirm true commitment, stamina, and so on. The first person to become involved and affected by the business (emotionally and physically) is you, yourself – followed closely by your immediate family (wife, husband or partner; or very close friends or even parents) if this applies to you.

All these people will have a heavy vested interest in the fortunes of the business ranging from a genuine personal desire for success, through to a direct or indirect financial stake. The fallout from the business will manifest itself in impacts of a personal nature, such as:

- stable income
- lifestyle
- fundamental relationships
- general behaviour
- mood swings
- security
- working for the business
- and so on.

Bear in mind that it is not always a good idea to be with the same close people all day and every day – for some it works well and for others it doesn't.

COMMITMENT

The business requires full heart-and-soul commitment. The setting-up and early-running stages consist of immensely interesting and absorbing work that will take every last ounce of effort and stamina. Whilst adrenaline carries you along in front of customers, suppliers and the general public, as soon as you are away from public view, the vast expenditure of effort takes it toll!

This reaction will not be felt to the same degree by everyone, but similar symptoms and behavioural patterns may not be far below the surface. You and your close family should always be looking for signs, so as to take timely remedial action. Stress and breakdown (and ultimately loss of income) are the next stage. What good do they do?

The best personal characteristics to foster and create unsurpassed entrepreneurial qualities often seem to induce unwanted and irritating side effects that become more pronounced when you get away from the business environment – at home, for instance.

The first impact will be felt, sadly, by those closest to you, who should be the last people whose feathers ought to be ruffled. They are experiencing added pressures in their own right, as a result of their own support for the business – and don't need a double helping!

Beyond the immediate family, the business will impact the social life of most of the people associated with it, such as some other relatives and fairly close friends. Interest in other events (committees, business meetings, bridge parties, dinner parties, and so on) must be relegated, at least initially; and some things may have to go completely.

Immediate and more distant neighbours might be affected, too, favourably or adversely – depending on what the business is. Two simple contrasting examples … consider in one case the beneficial effect on the adjacent community of a new, long-needed corner shop in one case, and also the less beneficial effect with associated smells of the opening of a fish and chip shop, or a petrol station, next door, in the other.

The pebble thrown by you into the centre of the hitherto tranquil pond will send out ripples in all directions to affect close family, relatives, friends and neighbours, and so on. The ripple effect travelling out must be complemented by an equivalent measure of solid mutual commitment for the business to succeed. It's like any other commitment we are asked to make; no half measures or maybes are acceptable!

FAMILY CONFERENCE

Immediate Family

Call the immediate family together for concept and implication discussions: be very open and frank. Respond to questions honestly; and if the answers are not known, find them out, reporting back in a follow-up session. These people are effectively the business' first customers: the task is to convince them beyond a shadow of a doubt of the plans, costs and risks. The venture has to be sold!

Explain the social and domestic impact; lay all the cards face up on the table; providing straightforward responses to questions and comments. Have contingency ideas or suggestions ready; identify and crack the support and commitment problems early in the discussions, before any real risks are taken and any money spent. Far better to resolve problems before they get out of hand, or before they become complex and more public – for example after the business has commenced.

In return, and at the right time, ask for *and get* full support and commitment. These matters should not be taken for granted without a full presentation of the open case. Moral support and commitment are often not all that is being sought: material support wll arise, in the form of help, money and other resources.

Close Relatives and Friends

Still within the domestic environment, you must also remember to sound out children, parents, brothers and sisters – not necessarily in as much detail, but certainly the material points as far as *they* are concerned, if relevant. Look from their end of the telescope at the impact on:

- children in terms of free time, being at home, playing, helping with studies
- elderly parents and other relatives, caring ability perhaps, hospital visits
- the social side with spouses, partners, younger parents, brothers, sisters
- conversation, radio, television, further education, other hobbies, jobs about the house
- time availability, generally, weekends, holidays, other obligations, and so on.

Close relatives need to feel comfortable with the venture; they, too, may be able to help in some positive way, if they are genuinely won over. The assistance may only be temporary, but still very useful and to be warmly welcomed during the preliminary planning stages, and post-launch phases. It could merely be mundane help like wielding a paint brush, or fetching, carrying, unpacking and shelf-filling.

It is obvious that the venture must not have any unnecessary hangers-on if the business is to have the best chance of success. Equally, it would be totally selfish for the business to make stringent demands on the individuals as persons in their own right. So these points need careful balancing and honest answers.

Others

Similarly, if external parties to the business are being considered (friends, relatives, straight business arrangements with otherwise unconnected partners), the same broad process must be properly undertaken. Always devote enough time to ensure all obstacles are cleared, one by one.

Friends

Good friends don't make a business thrive and aren't necessarily good customers: they are more likely to want favours.

Offers of Help

Support and commitment are sought, and if the well-prepared case is good enough, tangible support (in the form of additional initial resources – practical help, finance, premises, and so on) may be forthcoming. People *want* to become constructively involved.

The help could be extremely fortunate tangible support; but it could spell disaster as well, if the apparent generosity were accepted without due consideration of all the implications and asking the rhetorical questions:

- Why are they so interested?
- What are they angling for?
- Are they trying to muscle in on the act somehow?
- Who else is potentially being linked to the business?

Consider the long-term implications as well as the short-term bonuses. *Beware of gods bearing gifts?*

Summary

Don't be doggedly dazzled by the prospects of having your own business. Be realistic, and deliberately bring up *all* important matters, especially how much support you can expect from your spouse or partner. Bring everything out into the open. If the maximum chances of launching and running a successful business are to be achieved, there should be no hidden agenda! It could be disastrously too late afterwards.

OBJECTIVE: FULL BACKING AND COMMITMENT

The overall objective of these frank round-table discussions is to gain genuine, realistic backing and commitment from the family. This is most likely to be achieved through straightforward, open and honest talking: you must establish a preliminary case with those from whom moral support is sought.

Family reactions

There are likely to be several types of response that will subdivide into: real problems, imagined problems, misunderstood situations or no-problem areas.

- One clearly unhelpful hand-washing response might be: *Well I won't stop you if that's what you want to do.*
- Beware of the reaction that seems to endorse your proposal without any real underlying thinking and questioning. It could indicate a severe lack of understanding or interest, or another naïve or foolhardy capitulation.
- The hostile reaction is another that can obviously be identified without much difficulty; but even this is worth thinking about, because the other party might see things that are not apparent to you. They might indeed have some very valid points.
- The most positive reaction is one of constructive questioning to test the depth of consideration that has been given to the project. Problems raised can sometimes be construed as positive signs that demonstrate some measure of interest. Isolate the problem areas from the general agreement areas and note them down. Handle them professionally, evaluate them and sort them out one at a time to

everyone's entire satisfaction. More 'off-line' work (necessitating an adjournment and subsequent continuation of the meeting) might be wise, but that's only a minor issue.

Winning over relatives is a very valuable test of one's own *selling* skills, or otherwise. Unless this step is successful, the venture itself may not stand the best chance of success! Successful selling for the long term, not just the short term, is all about making sure both the seller and the buyer are well satisfied with the deal – the so-called *win–win* scenario.

The key point of any selling exercise is to prepare carefully and be prepared to listen! Listen and weigh up all the points raised. Are the uncertainties raised the same as some already considered, or are they subtly different in nature, emphasis or depth? Are they actually raising another point altogether, subtly and obliquely?

EXERCISE

Discuss, analyse and document the commitment and support from family for your particular venture. (Speak to them.)

Other Considerations
Three exceptionally important areas must be covered in the family discussions, in order to be true to yourself and family: health, time, financial risk and its possible consequences.

Health

- Will you be able to stand it, from a health point of view?
- Is everyone involved fit and healthy?
- If not, can the situation be satisfactorily handled without becoming an added burden on the business?
- Is there any recent medical history that might suggest the entrepreneur or key people would need time away from the business, or become a liability themselves?
- How about future operations, hospitalizations, tests, convalescence, caring, children, school runs, and so on?
- How much time has been taken off work by the main players recently?
- What about lifting, physical agility and handling any disabilities – yours and anyone else's?

These must be responsibly and realistically addressed, although they may not necessarily be damaging.

Time
Businesses demand a lot of time, especially in the early stages. It is not easy to

estimate what time they will need, or *when* exactly. But they *will* demand time, sometimes inconveniently which will bite ferociously into family and social life, and any other business or salaried employment time, if applicable.

Maybe, the present salaried job demands high time involvement too: so your own business could appear as a welcome release!

After the business settles down, matters can probably be arranged better, even during the day, which is part of the freedom. It won't happen straightaway. Prepare yourself, spouse, partner, children, other family members, friends and business partners and residual employers (as applicable to your situation) about the extra constraints.

Financial Risks – Relinquishing a Regular Salary

Business financial risks and rewards are inextricably linked; one cannot exist without the other. Otherwise everybody would be rich! Consider the financial risks of having your own business. As a wage-earner or salaried person, certain restrictions and obligations are placed on you in return for financial security to plan ahead.

Resignations, redundancies and other unforeseen circumstances excepted, this supposedly long-term stability (for the next week, one month, three months, six months, one year or whatever notice period, at least) is undoubtedly a tremendous umbrella in the real world of mortgages, holidays, expensive hobbies, second homes, sickness, general family expenditure and so on. 'Regular employment' virtually eliminates financial risk in this respect in personal and family lives, but on the other hand it also shackles us to a job that may not always be enjoyable, sufficiently interesting, rewarding, challenging or frustrating, (to apply but a few polite adjectives).

Having your own business categorically abolishes this apparent anchor or umbrella at a stroke. The twin mechanisms of gradually running down an employment situation and simultaneously building up a business to replace it, can be employed to dramatically reduce the risk, as the changeover is spread in a more controlled way.

Maintaining one or more salaried positions within the family unit is better than losing them all at the same time, so this method could also be used to mitigate the transfer of risk. Also savings, lottery winnings or some other large cash reserve could be used for a once-off similar controlled run-down of salaried work in favour of going freelance.

If the transition from a salaried position is made *gradually* enough and with the umbrella of other salaries in the family there is some further margin. But equally, the self-employed drawings bill could have to support more than one family, if you enter into a business partnership of some sort.

Consider the mortgage on the house and all the monthly repayments (up to several thousand pounds perhaps, for, say, twenty-five years); then consider the effect of a possible second charge taken on the house, or anything else, as bank-security to support the financial loans for the business (perhaps several additional hundreds, thousands or hundreds of thousands of pounds per month).

The business has to support these repayments as well as the other domestic bills, *right from the start*. You've got to live in the meantime! This is a huge financial risk. Also take into account that salaried positions are being relinquished on which these expenditures (and many others) are wholly reliant, and the whole nightmare is plain to see!

The reality is that if and when the business starts to go downhill, you will have *many months' or years'* effective notice: not just the nominal employment period of notice, to give time to sort out an alternative. Another tangible (albeit macabre) 'advantage' of being the boss, is (simplistically) that you should have been actively:

- watching out for potential business disasters
- taking the advanced warnings seriously
- acting to try to prevent decline.

Chapter 21 elaborates on the post-launch situation.

The concept of very careful preparation of a survival budget should the business struggle is mentioned later in this chapter: you can appreciate the objective against this background.

The Real World
- The real business world dictates that your business is not immune from the real world.
- The real business environment is actually a very tough world, where dog can and does eat dog.
- Competition is with the big boys, with so-called market forces.
- It must be plain for all to see that if it *were* so easy, the entire nation would be basking in riches; and it's not quite like that!

WORST-CASE SCENARIO

Doomsday Situation
If the business folded, particularly in the early stages, the spectre of losing everything looms large. The prospects for you, your family, your business colleague, home and family, and all that that represents are awesome. All business assets will have been taken or sold. There may be:

- further personal liabilities to clear the remaining business debts
- the possibility of you and yours being bankrupted
- a possibility of a break-up of relationships and the family
- loss of pride, self-esteem, confidence, health
- loss of all that one has achieved so far in life, and so on.

The chilling summary is that marriages might not be able to withstand the strain; wives, husbands, partners, children, lifestyles, houses, friends, families, savings

... everything could all disappear, including a similar list for any business partner's family and possessions as well!

- What will friends and family members who have invested in the business think or do?
- How will they be pacified and paid back?
- Will you be able to get another salaried job again, at the same level or indeed anything at all?
- Is age or health going to be against you as well?

In real life it's like going down every snake trying to salvage something and then starting again by climbing every ladder, from square one. Visualize scenes on the television of catastrophic earthquake, flood or tornado disasters, starvation and destitution to get an impression of what life might be like!

This scenario is deliberately included to bring home the worst case: not to put you off completely, but for checks and balances. Many successful businesses are created, with mortgages and second charges to be serviced; often they survive and prosper. There are potentially very severe risks that need to be discussed, evaluated, controlled and supported by appropriate contingency plans. Risks are not for everyone, but taken by a great many people.

Take Calculated Risks Only

Risk-takers can, and do, lose money: survivors and winners (also risk-takers) can, and do, make money. Be careful, and ask calmly: *Is an own venture really for me?*

You must acknowledge that there *is* a major risk. The art is to take *controlled* risks, do proper analysis and planning, weigh up the true likelihood of the risk happening in the first place, the value of the outcome if it did, the consequences, tentative remedial escape routes and cost penalties. Risks vary in degree of certainty (very high, high, medium, low, or very low, for example), consequences or effect, and value (for example, from losing a £5 bet; losing a caravan, car, yacht, children's horse; losing all one's house, contents and possessions, and so on; to losing all these things and one's family as well!).

REMUNERATION PACKAGE

The remuneration package you might expect from the business dictates your ability to repay mortgages and other bills (personal or business). Whether the business or the individual actually writes the cheques, ultimately the money has to come from the business.

Suppose your business has an annual turnover of, say, £100,000 – that is the total *takings* of the business whether it be a manufacturer, shop or whatever. It has various miscellaneous bills to pay, stock or raw material to buy, and wages and salaries to honour, and hopefully there is money left over – loosely called profit, but more accurately called net profit.

In no way must you assume that the business therefore has £100,000 to pay out as personal remuneration. Turnover, net profit and personal remuneration are three different things; and must not be confused, although they are interdependent (*see* Chapter 15). Depending on how the business is set up legally (more about this in Chapter 17), you might take your remuneration above or below the net profit line, and in different forms.

Your Pay Cheques
For domestic budgeting purposes as an owner, part owner or employee, you will probably receive a pay cheque periodically (in a similar way to your employed situation); but:

- Cheques will not necessarily be for the same amount each time.
- Drawings or personal remuneration have ultimately to be governed by what the business feels it can afford (if anything!): it may not be regular, or last for ever.
- In bad or cautious times money may have to be held back and in good times more money could be paid – *but the business needs should almost always take precedence.*
- There will be the familiar deductions for items like National Insurance, PAYE, and where applicable, pension, Permanent Health Insurance, Private Health Care.
- The total remuneration package may include a company vehicle or more, mobile telephone, clothes and other 'perks' that are subjected to statutory payments, National Insurance, personal taxation and regulation by the Inland Revenue.

The concept of the total package is similar to that relating to an employed situation, but governed by what the business can afford – and when. In addition, but dependent on how precisely the business is established, loan interest, dividends, repayment of personal loans can be made to yourself (if applicable), subject to certain conditions and rules.

It is comforting to note that some tentative and limited budgeting can therefore still be undertaken on the net pay package personal front. The comparison should be made with any current salaried arrangements, as indicated below.

Five Telling Examples
When you run a small business, simple sums must be carried out, as worst-case scenarios. If *these* figures don't fit, the more complex calculations won't justify the business either!

They provide a rough guide to help keep your feet firmly on the ground. There are millions of successful own-businesses – so don't be scared off. In each case, assume your present gross salary is £25,000 per annum, or approximately £500 per week that you are relinquishing to set up your own business. Although very crude yardsticks, clearly (amongst other criteria) each one has to stack up.

Example 1
Money available from the proposed business (after all other costs, including cost

of stock and all running expenses) for your personal drawing, salary or wages must be at least £500 per week in order to maintain the existing lifestyle and so on. Therefore the minimum sustainable business turnover (even with zero net profit) must be £500 *for each and every week* throughout the year – or £25,000 per annum.

Example 2

This basic calculation relates to time and turnover. Assume a shop business with a turnover of £100,000 per annum, and assume annual opening hours of 2000; the sustainable average takings (or sales) must be a minimum of £50 per hour. £50 must go into the till every working hour, on average, for a whole year! Some hours will produce nothing (perhaps wet, miserable days, holidays, and so on), leaving the remaining hours to produce several hundred pounds.

Whilst these may appear to be tough challenges for your small business, think of the major high street names who might have to target millions of pounds per day to maintain equivalent solvency – not just £50 an hour!

Example 3

Assume that the fixed costs (that is, background costs that do not vary with sales or turnover – *see* Chapter 15 for a fuller explanation) of a manufacturing business are £20,000 per year and that there are approximately 50 weeks in a year (that is, £400 per week).

In other words, the cost of the premises, plant, equipment, vehicles, heating, lighting, rates, and so on, permanently in place will account for the first £400 per week – *whether they are actually being used productively or not*. Therefore the average weekly takings must be at least £400 just to cover fixed costs (for selling absolutely nothing!) – let alone make a respectable profit after paying for items shown in example one.

The combined figure, emanating from Examples 1 and 3, represents a minimum weekly turnover of £500 plus £400, or £45,000 per annum, over and above variable costs, just to support the overhead costs and a minimum personal income equivalent to the original salaried position.

These three simple examples will make you sit up and think! The reality is that there is a vast number of private manufacturing and shop businesses that will have done their sums, accepted the challenge, got on with establishing their businesses and done well at it. In other words, the seemingly large figures need looking at in the true business context – as well as with a crude salary comparison.

Example 4

Consider your proposed venture. Weigh up the time it takes to carry out just one core activity (at the core discipline you contemplate). Suppose it takes 10 hours to complete at a cost of £5 per hour, plus materials priced at £100. Total cost £150.

Suppose you are able to turn round the maximum of 200 a year in the notional 2000 working hours per year; and suppose the market will bear a selling price (*see* Chapter 10) of £200, leaving a nominal unit profit of £50, from which to pay yourself and overheads. This aggregates to only £10,000 – compared to your relinquished £25,000 nominal salary.

Example 5
Prepare a full personal budget showing all personal and domestic expenditure (*all* miscellaneous bills, clothes, food, fuel, phones, subscriptions, council tax, computers, car(s), repairs, petrol, mortgage, insurances, savings, holidays, personal spending, Christmas, birthdays, credit/charge card payments, going out to theatre, and so on) and income (in this case based on £25,000 gross per year). Do you ever have any spare money each month – or shortfall? If you are unclear what is involved, turn to Chapter 14 where budgets are discussed (with an example), albeit in the business rather than domestic context.

Survival Budget
Now prepare a similar *very*, *very* tight budget based on the *minimum acceptable* lifestyle you could sustain, for several years if necessary. This, in its ultimate extreme form, represents a very frugal situation, *the survival* budget – one which you would have to adhere to if the business did very badly. How much money do you need net? Hence, what would have to be the gross salary *each and every* month? Would this exceptionally basic lifestyle be truly acceptable to you and your family?

In all the examples, items like personal and staff holidays, and time spent on non-productive activities (like travelling, buying, managing, administrating) have been temporarily disregarded, although in practice that is totally unrealistic. You may well find the enterprise is not viable on the simple calculations – let alone more accurate and realistic predictions.

Realism

> **EXERCISE**
>
> Do the arithmetic for your own situation to show how your proposed venture stands up to these five tests.

> **EXERCISE**
>
> Produce a survival budget for your personal situation. Is this sustainable and acceptable to you and your dependants?

CAUTIONARY CHAPTER

This chapter is included deliberately as a counter-argument. The tone of the book now changes to being positive again.

Gross National Product Comparisons
When, later in this book, you are asked to consider and project likely sales or business income for your venture, remember the big world and *be realistic* in your

expectations. Do not be either overoptimistic, or overcautious. If the venture is worthwhile, properly set up and run, it ought to be as successful as any other business, if you think rationally about it.

Relate your thinking on projected turnover to the fact that many existing businesses are working well, and their takings generally must exceed their expenditures. Be realistic enough to accept that if your business is *properly established and managed*, it could be as successful as any other small business. Why not?

You should put your 'minute' venture alongside the multitude of businesses, and in the greater context of the country's Gross National Product – that this, the turnover figure for the whole of Great Britain that runs into *hundreds of billions of pounds*. This is the sum of money spent annually in return for the goods and services the country as a whole provides for its own healthy economy.

Then think of the aggregate of all countries' GNPs *for the whole world*. The turnover for your business is only infinitesimal in comparison, and so it looks quite plausible *if the business is handled correctly from the outset*, and has a viable role in society.

So the real challenge is to *ensure that the business is created, founded, organized and operated properly* from the outset: it should look after itself!

WHAT HAVE YOU LEARNT IN THIS CHAPTER?

★ Elaborate on the wider implications of having your own business. Who is involved or likely to be affected?
★ Why is it so important to have the family, if any, behind you when starting your own business?
★ What are the serious risks of going freelance?
★ What three considerations should be taken into account before embarking on your own business?
★ What are the possible consequences for you, your spouse or partner, and the family if the business fails?
★ What must you do about it if the five crude calculations don't match?
★ Why, after all, should you start to feel more confident?

5
Creating a Successful Business

Creating and building a business is analogous to the familiar countdown and lift-off sequence of a space rocket launch, carefully taking one controlled step at a time. There are important parallels. The logical, theoretical and practical stages to launching your own business operate within the seven following guidelines:

- careful planning
- minimum risk
- minimum expenditure
- no premature explosions
- smooth, controlled launch
- no room for failure
- post-launch course adjustments.

The necessary business-building theory is provided to support the basic principles, provoking lateral thinking in the context of *your own* situation with general ideas, concepts and broad issues. Powerful questions are raised. You are given every encouragement – *but with prudent caution.*

COMPLETE PACKAGE

The logical and natural order subject matter expects you to use the information, knowledge and experience intelligently, where helpful and relevant; it can be used as a checklist in the context of your own proposed venture, backed by professional advice when you are serious – whatever your starting point.

The five reasons for this pragmatic approach are:

- maintaining the lowest common denominator whilst imparting the essential principles.
- presenting the *common* business fundamentals whilst the business core ideas are still being considered.
- deliberately directing you to books covering specific businesses (since this particular book is primarily directed at principles common to many potential businesses).
- forcing you to obtain professional advice from the experts, in due course – which is extremely important.

- making you establish the most accurate and current position on legislation (tax and company law, and so on), since information does not remain current for very long – absolutely essential for your business to be guided by the latest information.

The broad process can be considered in four steps – irrespective of the type of business, although their size and complexity could vary considerably, dependent on the depth of interest, degree of seriousness, how much has already been considered and whether or not a business has already been tried.

Each of *four stages* mentioned below should be completed before moving on to the next stage; otherwise, the purposes of treating the whole process in manageable and identifiable stages is lost.

FOUR KEY STAGES

Refer to Figure 1. The main objective of breaking down the creation and establishment of a thriving business into definable stages is to minimize risk and expenditure (especially before it starts to generate its own income). The secondary objective is to create a clear, concise and logical thought platform on which to build the business.

The Four Stages of the Proposed Venture

1. Concept.
2. Outline planning to consolidate and prove the concept.
3. Detailed planning, development and consolidation of the above.
4. Post-launch phase or post-mortem, and future plans.

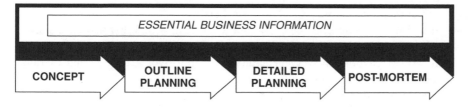

Fig. 1   Process of setting up one's own venture.

The first three stages demonstrate a disciplined and efficient way of establishing the venture for best possible lift-off. Within each stage, there will be a certain amount of intentional reiteration – trying to improve and refine the foundations on which the venture will be founded. By taking enough time to try alternative possibilities, each step will be as robust as it can to withstand rigorous probing and questioning without disintegrating. Essential business management techniques are liberally referenced in the book. The fourth stage concentrates on the post-launch events.

Going freelance is definitely not for everybody, just as the full e-commerce capabilities (*see* Chapter 16) are not for every situation; but you are urged to progress through some of the stages to enable a good decision to be made about what to do. A negative decision could be very prudent and timely: you might be applauded for recognizing appropriate warning signs.

What is the proposed venture all about? Three immediate alternative interpretations:

- You instinctively know that you want to have your own business, in principle, but don't know *what* it will be or what form it will take.
- You are or have been previously employed in a similar business and accepted the challenge as to how to establish your own version.
- An enjoyable hobby already exists: the challenge is *how* to transform it into a viable business.

So one challenge is *what*? (the subject of *Concept*); and the other is *how*? (the subject of the remaining three steps.)

CONCEPT

The *Concept* consists mainly of sitting around, thinking and talking, but not necessarily on home ground: perhaps an ideal time to walk in relative quiet and solitude, in the garden or on holiday, floating ideas and testing the water. Many peoples' fresh ideas and inspiration come to them at night, when unable to sleep, or in the bath!

- It might embrace a lot of lateral thinking – just gazing into bookcases, shops, magazines and generally all around yourself, for ideas.
- Initial thoughts and scope will be very sketchy.
- It will involve bouncing ideas off, and discussing with, other people and close friends.
- It will entail thinking very generally, probably over a long period of time: generalizations are important.
- Be open-minded and positive.
- Constraints of any sort are *not* welcome.
- Don't rule anything in or anything out, yet.
- No gem or possible gem should ever be totally discarded, because it could eventually prove to be useful – particularly in the creating, planning and setting up phase.
- Boundaries in terms of scope, breadth, depth and volume must not be set in concrete, neither must the possibility of wider issues and related products or services be rejected.
- You must loosely note that there might be constraints and conditions, but they should not be actively considered as such for the moment.
- You should get the concept sorted out before moving on.

Part of the concept stage embraces such important topics as:

- self-analysis
- soul-searching
- personal goals
- expectations
- personality

- experience
- expertise
- knowledge
- contacts.

These subjective areas, especially those implied under the general heading of soul-searching, are crucial to a successful venture. They must be taken very seriously and weighed very carefully against the key aspects for the venture. They must be incorporated somehow: either *directly* or *indirectly* in the venture concept.

Incidentally, these embryonic ideas must be exceptionally confidential: they might get to the ear of a potential competitor – so be very careful and sensitive. Be careful when discussions of any sort take place outside the immediate circle – and even then you must be certain where the listeners' respective loyalties really lie! Always assume an efficient grapevine exists. Be very cautious, just in case the embryonic ideas are copied and then protected by others *against* your otherwise legitimate interests, even before the business has started. The effect could be that your proposed business has been stamped on quite legally, before it's even breathed!

Timescales should be considered and provisionally noted – to achieve the individual short-, medium- and long-term goals. 'Milestones' should be indicated to measure progress, and confirm achievement. Financial matters must inevitably be given some priority because of their criticality.

Before leaving the fundamental stage of venture concept, another particularly difficult aspect to contemplate and pin down relates to *special* and *peculiar* considerations pertinent to your own venture that might stem from:

- special knowledge required for working in the industry
- exceptional expertise in the product and its marketing
- industry trading conventions
- technical aspects
- people
- shelf life
- regulations
- legislation
- business generation
- market conditions
- geographical factors.

In summary, the concept stage that actually began in Chapter 1, is deliberately short on detail and long on vague ideas.

Notionally, the *Concept* stage consumes about 5 per cent of the pre-launch activity, calls for very little spending, but a few phone calls and face-to-face research. Very little money needs to be spent, apart from on drinks, eats and green fees. Most of the 'expenditure' will have been on thinking and general discussions, supported by some broad minute taking.

Minutes
Everything discussed, kicked around and thought about should be thoroughly documented during this and the subsequent stages. Making careful notes or taking minutes has six benefits. It:

- assists general understanding and memorizing of the story – a good habit to get into
- forces you to think very carefully, cutting down on generalizations in favour of the specific details, and its implications
- obliges you to be as clear as possible about what is being written down
- provides an unambiguous way of knowing precisely what was agreed, when and by whom
- helps to ensure solid and accurate thinking, saving time and money later on in Stage 3, when the notes are reused, eliminating reinvention of the wheel
- incorporates basic information like contact names, addresses and phone numbers for future reference, all of which will be useful when compiling the business case in due course.

OUTLINE PLANNING

The second stage produces the outline plan for the venture, building on the *Concept* ideas, determining *how* your venture will be established and operated. It fleshes out the initial bones, stopping short of planning the nitty-gritty detail that is dealt with in the third stage.

Producing outline plans goes down to the next layer of thinking within the overall top-down approach. It is concerned with the crystallization and embodiment of the original, subjective and emotional thoughts, proving the validity of the whole concept.

It makes objective sense of the provisional thoughts; all the ideas from the first stage are filtered and re-examined, which might involve trimming, adjustment and possibly major modification. *Outline planning* and *Concept* should be an entity, to be backed now with positive research and fact-finding, leading to planning the broad practicalities.

Questions need to be positively resolved about:

- business and personal goals
- what do you want out of life – power, status, freedom, wealth levels, and so on?
- what's currently missing from your life?
- is your own business the real answer?
- how you will get business
- how much you can and would embrace technology and e-commerce

- what premises you will work from
- how you will keep and grow the business and customer base
- expectations of achievement in turnover and monetary profit terms
- medium-term business development and expansion
- the all-important cash flow (*see* Chapter 15).

The ultimate objective of Stage 2 is proving viability of the proposed venture, with minimal expenditure. However, it could prove to be money well spent if high risks, high expenditure downstream or a non-viable venture were to be identified through a controlled experiment spend at this stage. The proverbial *stitch in time* comes to mind.

Original Policy and Plans
Always keep in total control of your business – don't be unduly deflected. In *running* a business, as well as *creating* it during the planning stages, you should generally keep broadly to the original plans that have been rigorously evolved, minuted and constructively challenged.

Problems must be anticipated and managed: one of your managerial roles is that of pilot and navigator. Be absolutely clear about real objectives – at least until the plans are deliberately reviewed, revised or updated – steering an appropriate heading, whilst constantly watching for the rocks and shallow waters.

Loyalty to the agreed plans is urged, but it is clearly prudent to be constantly looking round and adapting to the circumstances – that's plain common sense, whereas doggedly sticking to a plan that is cracking is just plain stupid! Adapt to the ever-changing world, keeping the main ideas intact.

When working on the outline plans:

- Pinpoint as carefully and precisely as possible, without ambiguity, the outline concept of the proposed business, timescales, and what indigenous resources are available *right now* to support it – resources in a tangible sense (like money, premises, equipment, plant, tools), as well as contacts, possible customers, skills, know-how, expertise, and so on.
- Think about premises, funding shortfalls, technical gaps and any other resources that might be needed – without any of which the business is a non-starter. (Note *non-starter* specifically, as opposed to *non-viable*.)
- Expenditure should be kept to an absolute minimum; but be prepared to spend some effort, money and time for this essential basic research, and for sounding out the next people and contacts in the chain.
- This work represents about 40 per cent of the total pre-launch effort and activities.
- The end result should be more minuted documentation of important meetings and agreements, bolstering credibility of this outline plan.

Minimum Starting Resources
It's the 'minimum equipment' needed before the business can start, analogous to

the similar mandatory list applicable to an aircraft before it can take off. (In a physical safety sense, the passenger-laden aircraft might not *need* all galley or entertainment equipment to be in full working order before it leaves the ground; but the same cannot be said for the engines, navigation instrumentation or wings, for example).

EXERCISE

Compile and consider three lists:

1. What is critical and absolutely vital for the business launch?
2. What is desirable (with rational explanations) for the business launch?
3. What would be nice within the business sometime – a provisional list of longer-term resources and proposed developments, with dates or event triggering points, and rational explanations?

Project Planning

How the various planning activities all interrelate, particularly identifying their triggering or enabling events, their likely duration, and their expected or planned achievements, *their* resource requirements (not those for the business) is extremely important.

Each activity is determined and listed in a column down the left-hand edge of a largish sheet of paper. Against each one is shown a horizontal line, scaled as a time span for each activity. The horizontal axis is divided into time units (representing, say, the next few months), at weekly intervals. The completed sheet looks like a series of horizontal lines, staggered across and down the sheet of paper from top-left to bottom-right, showing every major planning activity – either independently, or sequentially where one activity finishes before another commences. Refer to Chapter 18.

DETAILED PLANNING

There should be two broad 'ticks' against *Concept* and *Outline Planning*. If there aren't, you must re-visit one or both again, before spending real money.

Serious planning begins here: it builds directly on the solid foundations of the previous stage. It assumes a *green Go* signal, or at least a qualified *amber* signal, and that a decision has been made, in principle, to go ahead. It presupposes you have of course decided what sort of business to go for, and that it is likely to be viable in all respects. It recognizes that there is still much to be done, although there does not appear to be anything *insuperable*.

Efficient Use of Time and Money

Someone (perhaps you, but not necessarily so) must have sufficient spare time away from other conflicting priorities (like a normal day job or child-minding, maybe) to undertake detailed thinking, telephoning, preparing plans, and meeting various contacts and professional bodies. This work takes valuable time *directly* associated with the activities above: it also can involve large amounts of travelling time, meals and evenings out, and preparation time.

The total time can mushroom enormously; especially as the initial simple question leads to a whole string of other ports of call – just as in detective stories. You should be highly organized and ruthless: don't get side-tracked into unhelpful and wasteful detours. Good route planning and efficient productivity are pertinent to being a business owner both now, and in running the business later on.

Costs

Time and effort can be wasted, or not used effectively: so too can expenditure – costs associated with:

- travelling
- trips abroad
- taxis
- vehicle running costs
- insurance to include business use of your own car
- meals and snacks on the move
- possible overnight stays
- photocopying
- phone bills
- materials
- stationery
- equipment (however small or seemingly necessary)
- publications like magazines, books and trade journals
- exhibitions
- toe-testing advertisements, possibly, to check the likely interest from customers
- costs of outside help (professional, research, design, clerical, secretarial)
- market research generally.

In the initial, enthusiastic and emotionally charged excitement, you can get carried away on the overspending front, especially when credit cards are accepted virtually everywhere. Several points to keep in mind are:

- The business is not earning revenue: it could be several weeks, months or even years of trading before the money can be recovered (even if the business actually gets to the launch pad and then thrives for a long time).
- Expenses should be logged and receipts obtained, against the possibility of allowing them as legitimate business expenses sometime (this may not always be possible, but you are urged to be disciplined anyway).
- None (or not all) of the money spent may belong to you, but to third parties with agreements to be signed, and certainly money to be repaid.

Check first; but most reputable businesses with whom you are likely to become involved give free estimates: but when legal and financial professionals are engaged, major costs will be incurred.

Arrange meetings at home, or in the evenings, or both, to save your own time, effort and money; and it probably dovetails better with other priorities. Point out that only tentative research is being carried out at this time – and on an implied shoestring.

Take Care – Don't Get Caught Out

You should be careful about any documents, agreements or contracts – an area where extreme diligence is called for. You should be very, very careful not to get involved in signing any deals, even if they do appear to be once-in-a-lifetime offers. Commitments will not be backed by the formal business at this stage, and moneys so expended or agreed to will have to be replaced at some time. A useful get-out when under such pressures is to say honestly that:

* matters are still being explored
* the business has not yet been established
* signatories have not been authorized
* the board or partners need time to study and agree the terms.

Any honest business with whom you are proposing trading will not want to jeopardize a long-term deal, and will always want duly authorized documents (otherwise they are not legally enforceable, if it comes to it!).

Commitments

As the launch date approaches, matters will have to be authorized and signed; but equally, as the launch date approaches, so does the certainty of go-ahead.

Towards the end of this stage, be prepared to sign some formal documents to enable matters to proceed. Read them as carefully as possible making certain every aspect of them is understood – if necessary, get professional help, but be aware that this will usually cost money in itself!

The objective of Stage 3 is to get every loose end sorted out and tied up ready for a launch. The last tasks are to make final preparations – unless, of course, something gets discovered that puts a hold on the project – either a temporary hold (that will need to be cleared) or a permanent stop (effectively killing off the proposed venture).

Be alert to these possibilities and don't go on blindly and in hope! Better to be cautious, once again, minimizing risk, money and general exposure. Work to carefully controlled risks and costs: don't take high-risk chances, which could go wrong and be expensive to sort out through the courts!

These areas can so often be problematic and horrendous, but with careful detailed planning, they need not be. Just take care, taking small steps. As confidence grows, so will the size of the steps.

Thus far we have looked at the first three stages.

Personal Agreements

It is usually a good idea to have inter-personnel agreements when other people are involved, in case things do go wrong – this means more professional money to be spent, but it could be worthwhile. Best intentions and best friends don't last for ever. Potential problems in this area (frequently brushed aside at the outset *as it can never happen to us*) could be clearly unproductive, expensive and acrimonious.

POST-LAUNCH

You will have actually started to build a worthwhile business in the first three stages: but that's not the end. The fourth is just as important, because it proves how well done and on-target the first stages were, or otherwise.

Nothing in life is constant, and it is just the same in business. Stage 4 vitally looks into the post-launch future, to accommodate the moving goal posts: it is ongoing. It can never be thought of as *dealt with* and put to one side: the business must always be alert to changing circumstances if it is to remain successful.

The review can't be commenced in earnest until the business is launched, although items can be pencilled onto the agenda. It reviews and trims the actions prior to launch; it consolidates the steady-state operational details, and looks into the future with realistic projections for growth and expansion plans.

WHAT HAVE YOU LEARNT IN THIS CHAPTER?

★ What is the analogy quoted for the business launch, and its seven guiding principles?
★ Explain the four key stages. Why is this form of 'regimentation' used?
★ What is the vital first question relating to the venture that really summarizes the first stage?
★ What is the second question, the subject of the remaining three stages?
★ Why should each one be answered carefully, and in the right order?
★ Why is keeping a minuted record of discussions important?
★ Why are resource needs segregated into three lists?
★ What resources are involved during the first three stages and why is caution to be observed?
★ Why are interpersonal agreements desirable?

6
Analysing Most Businesses

Before concluding what venture you could undertake, this chapter looks at the precise nature of businesses. The question is asked: *What constitutes a business?* – one to which the answer is both obvious and vague. Ways of starting a business are also considered.

Chapter 3 concluded with the view that a business will be engaged in either making, doing, repairing, creating or moving something, at the heart of its operation and its *raison d'être*. Although the distinction between the categories can be somewhat blurred, it nevertheless implies that something tangible is at the core. But the five simplistic labels mask a vast wealth of additional supporting matter, and this chapter analyses the individual elements that constitute a business.

THE HEART OF A BUSINESS

The Technical Core
Whatever business is being undertaken, core activities imply certain levels of technical ability and excellence, otherwise your business could not be effective. Your customers will assume some or all of the following. They will presume that you will have studied and learnt a trade and gained relevant experience, as a result of which you will have:

- *technical* competence
- extensive intrinsic product knowledge
- considerable expertise
- long-standing skills
- relevant training and formal qualifications
- relevant contacts in the trade or profession
- appropriate reference books, drawings, plans and other documents.

An Expert
In short, if it is not an overworked and glib word, you are *considered in the eyes of your potential customers* to be a true *expert* in your subject – accepting the fact that there are also degrees of expertise that in turn are tempered by degrees of competence and other personal attitudes.

In a literal sense, it is not necessary to actually have all the above attributes, but you certainly must appear to (to the customer) and you don't necessarily need them all simultaneously and right from the start.

When reference was specially made to *technical* (as opposed to personal, social or financial) considerations of a business, in previous chapters, the preceding paragraphs summarize what was meant – but you should take into account that not all characteristics are present in *every* business, nor do they necessarily need to be. The degree of adherence to the embracing range of qualities identified above will vary widely, dependent on the specific core activities.

Customer Expectations

Customer expectations are central to the success of a business: they would expect someone (especially the *boss* or working owner at the very least) to be involved in the core subject; and to be fairly conversant with most (even all) matters associated with the product. Furthermore, the customer would expect to receive reliable and authentic advice, which includes such related information as:

- how and where to use the product
- some historical and anecdotal data
- some technical data
- any special or distinguishing features
- benefits of using the product
- the drawbacks or 'penalties' of not using it
- some cost and price figures
- typical customer profile and marketplace
- competitive information
- health and safety matters
- general features
- optional features
- complementary products and services.

The depth and breadth of the information will not be the same for all types of core activity, but clearly a credible business must be able to impart confidence to its customers. A good way to achieve this is to demonstrate that the business thoroughly understands the subject it is engaged in. Customers will soon learn and filter out the less competent businesses, as well as being drawn to the real top-notch ones. Technical attributes are one measurable ingredient and guide to a probably successful business.

Proof of Technical Qualifications

Certificates to demonstrate achievement and competence, and memberships of learned societies and other similar organizations should be prominently, but tastefully, displayed – whether they relate to the business or individuals. Certain of them should also be reproduced in miniature or referenced on printed leaflets, brochures, notepaper and the like. It's not a case of blowing one's own trumpet as such, but simply imparting additional credibility and confidence to clients and customers.

Rounded Personality and Skills

A deep product technical knowledge is a 'must' in whatever field the business operates, but in isolation it's not enough. All the other relevant personality traits, resources, skills and expertise that the business demands, whether primary or merely supportive, must be identified and provided somehow (but still a cost to the business, of course).

This help could come from outside staff or a potential business partner with a substantial mix of the right complementary skills, experience, expertise, money and so on; but a word of warning, don't be eager to invite or bring in anyone else if they have nothing substantial to bring directly contributing to the business. An embryonic business cannot possibly afford anyone who wants to be paid for their company alone!

MUTUAL SUPPORT IN BUSINESS

Businesses support each other to some extent. Raw materials (loosely abbreviated to INs) for one business are the finished goods (OUTs) for another.

Figure 2 shows five very simple businesses, each making something with 'raw materials' of some sort. Each business depends on another business, or one of its competitors.

The farmer plants seeds to grow wheat for the miller to convert into flour for the baker. The baker uses flour to produce bread for the shop to convert into sandwiches. Finally, the caterer needs sandwiches to produce elementary buffet-style meals, and has to obtain the sandwiches from somewhere, like the shop.

Through a series of businesses, starting from the farmer's seeds there are guests at the wedding reception (for example) able to participate in a buffet meal.

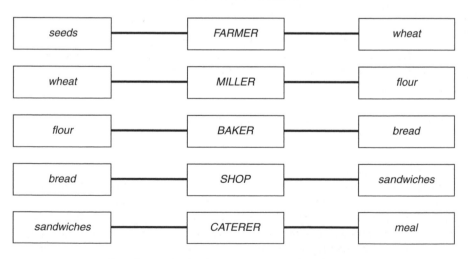

INs and OUTs of business

seeds	FARMER	wheat
wheat	MILLER	flour
flour	BAKER	bread
bread	SHOP	sandwiches
sandwiches	CATERER	meal

Fig. 2   A chain of businesses – INs and OUTs.

ESSENTIAL SUPPORTING FUNCTIONS

Most businesses essentially consist of a core activity with technical expertise, skills, knowledge and a group of peripheral activities that culminate in an ability to make a satisfactory financial return (whatever that is defined as, but refer to Chapter 15). What other complementary features are necessary to create and build an infrastructure for the business as a whole?

- A group of intangible qualities like positive personality and practical communications skills to oil the wheels of the main revenue-generating engine.
- A group of the tangible ones, like an ability to get good profitable business, either from an existing range of customers or by creating new marketplaces, and (ultimately) financial return.

All businesses have common elements as shown in Figure 3, constituting the whole enterprise, although the weight, size, 'added value' and importance of each

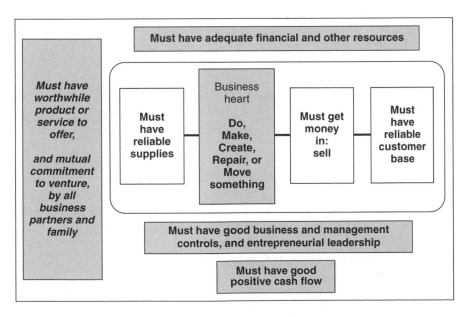

Fig. 3   Common business elements.

55

box will vary, depending on the type of business. The broad principles remain, but the value of stock, plant and equipment, premises, numbers of staff, and so on, will clearly not be the same between businesses. A very small concern will still have only its single creator – but doing other jobs as well.

At the heart of the diagram is the core operation, usually (but not always) founded on a worthwhile product or service. There must be a mechanism for selling the products and getting money into the business, which in turn means having a reliable and healthy customer base. Correspondingly, an otherwise thriving business, without continuous and reliable stock or raw material supplies won't get very far either.

Lubricating the whole operation there must be good management, entrepreneurial leadership, adequate financial and other resources, and a positive cash flow. There must also be commitment in abundance. These crucial subjects are amplified later, so don't go into panic mode.

EXERCISE

Consider the roles that are needed for your business, and rank them in importance.

EXERCISE

What supplies and raw materials will you need? Who can and will be prepared to supply them? How much will they cost?

EXERCISE

What delivery and other terms will apply? How reliable are their products and deliveries?

GETTING STARTED

There are several ways to get started. Here are the main ones:

- The obvious one is to set the business up completely from scratch, and that is probably the most usual.
- You could gradually wean yourself away from an employed situation, by developing a part-time operation of some sort. But check the contract of employment first, to ensure non-contravention of either the letter or even the spirit, particularly regarding setting up in competition, poaching customers or not devoting full-time loyalty. It's worth mentioning that such contracts often contain dubious restrictive clauses which would not hold up in a subsequent court case even if you had previously signed the contract – such clauses are worthless in practice. Take advice first.
- Another possible approach relates to an employed situation, where that concern is being sold (compulsorily or otherwise), or merely going downhill for some reason (like a pending retirement or poor management). *See also* toward the

end of Chapter 21. Some members of an existing management team or other sufficiently interested employees put together a business case for buying the business from the present owners and running it 'under new management'. Often the existing managers, you and/or other employees might genuinely feel there is a better way to run the existing business, or that opportunities are being missed; or you might simply not want to see the business fail through lack of interest or new investment. Clearly there will already exist some valuable technical expertise, a marketplace, a customer base, a publicized business and so on: all these factors will boost the business in its new start. These are known as Management Buyouts (MBOs) and are very worthwhile considering. There are similar routes involving third parties, known as Institutional Buyouts (IBOs).

- Another obvious start is to buy an independent existing business anyway, either on the open market, through the grapevine or from the liquidator of another business for a 'good' price. Because the venturer does not already work for this business, this route is not in the same category as an MBO, but nevertheless a worthwhile option to explore, providing it aligns or *could align* with the original thoughts and carefully reasoned concept from Stage 1.
- You may be fortunate enough to inherit a going concern, even if it is in need of reinvigoration. Whilst this is clearly a way to start, it might represent a sudden jolt start. In which case, you have probably got a considerable amount of 'instant' learning to do – including, possibly the technical core.
- Joint ventures are possibilities: your business operates alongside that of a colleague's – another related or unrelated venture, but both parties share the costs and facilities in appropriate proportion.
- Another option, particularly on the retail front, is the business arrangement of a shop-within-a-shop or store that suits all parties (the current trend for handling some ladies' fashions found in department stores is a good example).

Serious Warning

If you follow a path which is effectively *hostile*, and is perceived to be threatening or competitive to the former owner as a consequence of any of the above, then meetings with colleagues, suppliers, customers, and so on to float ideas and plan forward moves must be held in complete secrecy. If the former owner alleges you have used their time, property or facilities, or otherwise broken your service contract, legal action may follow – whether truly justified or not – against you and the business.

The result will be tremendous additional hassle, with damages and costs awarded against you possibly; especially if you have, or *are assumed* to have, acquired (and/or used) confidential or commercially sensitive information *without permission*. Your home is likely to be searched (with all that extra domestic hurt and disruption) if you are *thought* to have samples, items, documents, figures, future plans, drawings, memos, faxes, e-mails and the like. At the very least, you can expect instant dismissal – and no income!

Now we can examine existing businesses.

How Much Is the Business Worth?

Another very strong word of warning when considering buying all or part of another business. You must ensure that it is absolutely crystal-clear what is being bought and sold. Note the asking price but appraise its *practical worth* to you. Is it beneficial to buy, and worth the investment (and any extra cash injection) in your situation? – it may be, but it may *not* be! The asking price is not necessarily the same as its worth to you of course, although it may reflect the owners' 'published' accounts.

Tangible Assets

Generally an existing business might consist of *tangible* items like premises, equipment, fittings, stock, plant and vehicles. Individually these items will all have a fair and separate market value (price) in relation to their location, condition, age, wear and tear, and so on, and are fairly readily determinable by the professionals who deal regularly with these things.

Intangible Assets

But, there will also be considerably *less tangible* matters to take into account. Even for a professional they are not easy to come to terms with – such things as:

- hidden messages contained in the Accounts
- business reports generally, and prospects for the specific business
- financial and other obligations being inherited
- short leases and rent reviews
- goodwill (more or less similar to reputation and ongoing business prospects)
- hearsay and rumours
- wider economic factors
- trade prospects generally.

As with all selling situations, you will only be told what the seller wants you to hear and questions may arise in your mind to make you nervous, and possibly to try to make you buy in panic. Consider *why* the business is really being sold (it will not necessarily be the same reason as you will be told, of course!).

- Is the business in crisis?
- What's happening next door or in the town's redevelopment plans?
- Is it going to reopen competitively somewhere else nearby?
- How much is the value of the business dependent on the present key people and staff – who might no longer be around?
- How will your plans affect business prospects?

Watch out for employee transfer obligations and for other hidden commitments, too!

What the Asking Price Includes

The total price asked by the vendor should reflect all tangible and intangible assets, although the details may not be explicit. For example, the stock is not usually priced in terms of a precise figure, but simply an unspecified figure referred to as *stock as at valuation* (extra money!). This is often assessed separately by independent third parties.

Opportunities like these are not necessarily bad news, as there might be genuine reasons for the sale; such as:

- The owner might be wanting to retire.
- The business might be ailing, and just ripe for reinvigorating 'under new management'.
- The owner might be trying to raise some money.

Summary

These are *just some* of the ways to start off a business whether shop or non-shop style, but there are also other opportunities based on sharing facilities, costs and customer bases – for example, some business park groupings of similar but complementary businesses.

Whichever option is selected, the concepts, overall plans and detailed plans must always remain completely justified, being viable and workable in practical details. Think long and think hard: but think positively and constructively. Weigh it all up carefully; take professional advice (the fee could well be worth it in the end) and make a business judgement! Your own rational analysis, thought processes, subjective intuition and *considered* advice from family, friends and third parties should all be balanced and taken into account along with the more objective rational arguments from the professionals, before coming to a final decision.

By now, if you are seriously interested in starting a business generally sometime, you will have either made up your mind about what sort of business, or will soon be able to.

WHAT HAVE YOU LEARNT IN THIS CHAPTER?

★ What are the key elements of a business?
★ What are the common denominators and differences?
★ How would you demonstrate technical competence, and why is it so important?
★ What is mutual support in business about?
★ What are the various ways businesses can be commenced?
★ What should you pay for an existing business? What precautions should you take?
★ What messages could be hiding in the published Accounts for another business?
★ How much of another business is really helpful to your business, and what you want? Therefore, how much is it actually worth to you?

7
Convincing You, the Ultimate Resource

KEY PLAYERS

This chapter wraps up the subject of what business you want to go for. It lays on the line (last but not least) *your* responsibilities and commitment, and what the successful business expects of *you*, the ultimate resource in your business. It links with the personal qualities in Chapter 2.

The main resources for the business are discussed in the next chapter, but you are unquestionably the ultimate resource and *key* player – even *the* key player (who binds and holds the business together). In any business, what is a key player, who are the key players, what defines a key and a non-key player and are there any passengers?

Key Players
Successful businesses (from the very large international corporations through to the very small one-person concerns) all have key players – people without whom the business would collapse or virtually collapse unless they were replaced immediately with other people possessing the same broad qualities: people who have a considerable influence on the fortunes of the enterprise, either directly in what they do or in the way they influence others to do things.

Non-Key Players
Not everybody in business is a *key* player, although they may still have a very important role to play somehow. In general all the other employees in a business constitute the *non-key* players – everybody else broadly who works for the organization. They should definitely be made to feel 'wanted', to the point where they are given positive appreciation by the management. It must be acknowledged that they have contributed their bit toward the company's prosperity (since the business is employing and paying them!).

Pure Passengers
A larger successful business may turn out to have a few persons in another category (hopefully a very small minority) close to becoming pure passengers – the sort of person, who would not make any *material* difference to the business if they left and were not replaced. Their workload could either be shuffled about between other staff or discarded.

YOUR ROLE

So, what's your role in this new business? The answer embraces a huge raft of roles of which one or more of the following might be appropriate, depending on the nature, specific legal status and organization of the enterprise: Proprietor; Partner; Director; Managing Director; Chief Executive; Chairman; President; Founder; Head; Boss; Leader.

There's much more to the job than being a pure figurehead (particularly in a small business), since you *are* the business, for all practical purposes. What happens when you're not in, sick or on holiday?

Without you, the business would probably collapse! But don't despair; you may be able to delegate and oversee what is happening although you are ultimately responsible for it – without necessarily being directly involved doing every job, personally.

You'll also have to become virtually all of the following, to some degree or other:

- chief enthusiasm generator and motivator
- chief technical expert
- chief source of inspiration for the product or service: designer, artist, engineer, etc.
- chief point of contact for the customer
- chief salesman/woman
- chief production person
- very versatile multi-talented worker
- chief accountant
- head of personnel, training and security
- multi-skilled leader
- head of public relations
- girl Friday or man Friday
- odd job person
- floor sweeper
- tea maker
- cleaner
- chief dogsbody.

All without getting flustered or acting unprofessionally. Wow! That's a fantastic 'job description' – you've never had one like that before! Sounds great so far.

Image and personal attitude are certainly important, especially *first* impressions where customers, staff and suppliers interact, so you:

- must be reminded that body language speaks loud and clear
- must dress appropriately, instil confidence and leadership, and keep calm
- must maintain the right stance, stature and posture
- must look and feel the part
- must behave and act the part

- must act, listen and speak authoritatively
- are also the navigational pilot steering the safe course through the hidden rocks
- are the ultimate decision-maker.

You will have to live up to this position of power carrying out your responsibilities, employing all the attributes and personal qualities you claim to have! The power and responsibility can be quite overwhelming and awesome! It will certainly reinforce your confidence, if you're successful. Mind you, since we are only in the outline planning stage, you've still got some time to adjust: will you be ready when the time comes?

Now the rewards, power, recognition, joys, remuneration are yours – well almost, because you have to earn them first – not just 'buy' them! You have to lead your whole team authoritatively and impartially – which of course they will expect you to – and you must respect the staff, and in turn earn their respect – and that of fellow partners or directors as appropriate. If you go about it the right way, you *will earn* their respect.

- People, including staff and customers, *will* look up to you.
- Suppliers will appreciate your buying power.
- Suppliers will recognize the influence you will have on *their* businesses.
- Your peers in other businesses and neighbours will respect you.

In the final analysis, there has to be an overall boss, manager, managing director, or chief executive. In addition, depending on the nature of the business, there also has to be someone:

- responsible for winning the business (the salesperson)
- handling the customer interface
- who is the 'technical' expert for the product or service
- in charge of production to whatever degree
- in charge of the money – the finance controller
- to enthuse and motivate the other staff.

Two very pointed questions: who will be responsible and accountable to customers, staff, the authorities, suppliers, shareholders (if any), and so on, for all these key functions in your venture? Who, in day-to-day practice, will actually carry out these duties and functions? The answer to both questions (and all parts of them), dependent on the size and scope of the business, is probably the same each time: *you*, the potential entrepreneur. There is no place to hide, nor should there be.

One characteristic of being the boss is that the buck stops here – right here and nowhere else: with *you*! It's a very isolated position at times (which anyone in such a position will confirm). This is one reason why it's useful to have the accountant's or bank manager's professional shoulder to lean on, and ear to listen to all your worries.

There may be respected colleagues, fellow directors or business partners with whom you can converse but ultimately all the responsibilities, liabilities and heartaches rest on *your* shoulders. Whether it's your personal job or whether tasks are delegated, the final responsibility and accountability remains with you for *everything* that happens in your business. This implies 'moral' responsibility and means legal accountability – backed by court rulings.

You now appreciate *why* you are without question the ultimate resource; your resourcefulness and ingenuity, like quick thinking on the feet, will need to come to the surface early in the planning and the operational stages. Don't waffle: don't dither. Don't attempt to pass any blame on to anyone else, especially in public (even if it *is* somebody else's misdemeanour, perhaps).

EXERCISE

Identify all the key jobs in relation to your own particular venture and assign responsibilities among any other key players.

EXERCISE

Write unambiguous answers to the following questions:

* ★ What will you *do*?
* ★ Why does the business need *you*, specifically?
* ★ What will be your positive, constructive and revenue-generating role in the business?
* ★ Is there a better or cheaper way of achieving these same answers – perhaps by buying in the skills or experience at a cheaper rate?

Simple, but obvious questions – yet frequently businesses attempt to start and pay out scarce money to people who are contributing very little or nothing at all. From a purely selfish and personal kudos point of view, it might be delightful to sit in the ivory tower, drawing fees, royalties or other money for doing very little: but, can the fledgling business really afford such luxuries? (The longer term is another matter.)

THE REAL BOSS

Now consider who's really the boss – the so-called boss, his or her staff or the customers? Ultimately it has to be customers, your role reverting to that of a facilitator – paving and resourcing the way for the staff and customers to make their contribution to the business, as easily as possible. So as far as staff and customers are concerned, look after them all; find and keep the best; and they'll look after the guy who thinks he or she is boss in the end!

SUCCESS YARDSTICKS

Success yardsticks were briefly mentioned in Chapter 2: in relation to personal objectives rather than those for the business, although they are interrelated in practice. Possible yardsticks for defining a thriving business on a personal basis were cited as:

- an ability to relinquish a full-time salaried position within a year or two – for example your spouse's or partner's
- an ability to become truly independent of a normal respectable salaried income
- allowing a particular monetary figure to be identified as a personal income target within a certain period of time – typically doubling and maintaining the relinquished daytime job salary within perhaps two, five or ten years, after taking account of inflationary factors
- having a particular lifestyle, cars, possessions or housing.

Whilst they will not be set in concrete (probably a satisfactory situation for the moment), they must at least be pencilled in; otherwise the business goals cannot be determined for keeping your business viable, profitable and on the straight and narrow.

EXERCISE

Write down the personal expectations (as yardsticks) for all the founder(s) in terms of achievement of something in your business.

Business Yardsticks

So this is now an appropriate point to consider the business side: after all a business without plans, goals, objectives and targets is ill-founded – like any organization. Fundamental to a well-planned business, yardsticks ultimately derive from the personal ones. These enable monetary annual turnover targets (compatible with the researched marketplace) to be nominated for the first few years, that the business can transcribe into:

- unit output per year
- annual profit figures
- number of clients gained
- working area
- number and total size of premises.

Business goals and *personal* objectives might touch on more emotional reasons:

- salary level
- fees
- lifestyle
- status
- power
- amount of freedom

- size of business
- return on investment
- value of business
- value and percentage of your stake holding
- elimination of all or certain competitors
- moving into better, larger or additional premises
- achievement of a specific number of branches
- achievement of certain take-over or expansion plans
- particular position in the marketplace league tables
- peer recognition or merely being given due recognition in the trade somehow
- ultimate withdrawal and lack of involvement in the day-to-day running of the business.

However they are expressed (and structured to be achieved within a specified period), they must be practical, capable of being attained, quantifiable and measurable.

They must be used regularly to continuously check the business performance. More will be said about this in Stage 4, Chapter 21; but for now, you must be prepared to plan carefully; and acknowledge that measurements and timely remedial actions must be undertaken in the future.

DECISION TIME

It is time to be bold: you should have picked up enough thought-provoking material with which to make a your rational choice, if it was not a fairly sewn-up case before picking up this book. Knowing the ground, there's no logical reason to put off making the decision. *The decision is yours*, as they say! Tick the boxes. You've:

- ☐ Got enough 'technical expertise' and know-how.
- ☐ Got some viable and marketable ideas, perhaps a suitable hobby.
- ☐ Examined how the business could operate.
- ☐ Considered your own suitability.
- ☐ Thought generally about resources, premises, finance.
- ☐ Identified the gaps and how they could be plugged.
- ☐ Thought about commitment, risk, family, and so on.
- ☐ Got some ideas about getting sales.

It's that hard critical decision-making time – your first management decision! Although you are being given full encouragement, you are equally advised to be brutally honest. Refer to Figure 4.

- ☐ No, not for me after all.
- ☐ Yes, but not yet – more courses and/or reading needed.
- ☐ Yes, but not yet – will get a job to learn the business, first.
- ☐ Yes, tell me how to go about it!

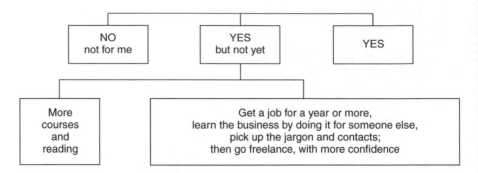

Fig. 4   Decision time.

Whatever your decision, you should continue reading the rest of this book in any case, to learn how to go about setting up the venture.

WHAT HAVE YOU LEARNT IN THIS CHAPTER?

★ Differentiate between key and non-key players in a business.
★ What is your role in a venture? How important are you, and why?
★ Who is the real boss of a business?
★ Why is it important to consider personal yardsticks and then set business targets?
★ List and consider the eight checkpoints possibly preventing you from starting your own venture.

8
Resourcing the Business

Broad decisions have now been taken about the nature of the proposed venture: initial thinking and soul-searching have been completed. This chapter starts to put the outline plans together (Stage 2), looking first at the main resources (after yourself) of premises, funding and core competencies.

PREMISES

All businesses need space in which to operate, even if it's only the kitchen table. Some need a lot of dedicated space. Property selection (area considerations, types of property and then particular properties) has an unquestionably dramatic effect on the fortunes of a business, but not one that can easily be predicted: hence time is needed to arrive at what appears to be the best practical decision.

Some businesses operate from a garage, home or spare room, depending on what the businesses are, and how they function in detail; and quite often while getting off the ground. Because this latter choice is usually low risk, it is a convenient way to begin, if it fits all the other constraints as well. Otherwise, many simultaneous parameters must be evaluated.

Area

- The prime consideration is that the premises should be appropriate to the business in terms of working space, image and presentation requirements (that is, for customers and priority revenue-earning areas) – and for the supporting infrastructure such as storage, offices, reception, kitchen. Many examples exist where this obvious statement appears to have been overlooked.
- Secondly, the customer base and other critical lines of communication, staff and supplies (even if the site turns out to be abroad) need to be carefully thought through.
- Thirdly, the premises must be located in the right country or geographical part of the city, town, village, or whatever, taking account of physical access for goods and the convenience of customers. This will have to include specific parking arrangements, nearby public carparks or simply the absence of double yellow lines and traffic wardens.
- Fourthly, pertinent questions need answers, backed with compelling arguments. The critical watershed is *need* or *prefer/want*.

Types of Property

- Does the business infer or specifically need old, new or purpose-built premises?
- Are 'permanent' premises preferable or mandatory?
- Could temporary premises be acceptable and suitable?
- Is the business best served in the town centre, High Street, secondary streets, edge of town, right out of town, shop-within-a-shop concept?
- Must the premises be used for *your* business alone?
- Could you be joint tenants with other concerns?

Other Considerations

- Most businesses need core working space; and access for customers, staff, various goods and services, and stock or raw materials.
- Even a private house like your home may need planning permission to run a business: so check first. Domestic rates (and house insurance for that matter) may be affected.
- You might be able to scrounge space from a friend, relative, another business or any organization that has temporary space to spare – even if it's not totally free (perhaps a favour of some sort, trading agreement, nominal rent).
- Some businesses could fit in virtually anywhere like a rural industry site, derelict farm, odd workshop, old garage premises or temporary office.
- Some need multiple addresses and/or multiple working sites.
- Some need prestigious accommodation addresses, because it is part and parcel of their image and at the core of their business operation.
- Some businesses naturally group together (like shoe shops in the High Street); on the other hand, is it necessarily a good idea to be close to a competitor?
- Some need modern industrial estates or business parks.
- There might be opportunities to have joint projects with universities, colleges, government departments and multinational businesses – depending on the nature of the enterprise. Close physical links might be highly beneficial to all parties.
- Central or local government offer positive incentives from time to time expressly to attract businesses. So enquire about and weigh up EEC, central government and local funding scheme and premises requirements, designated development areas, specially designated science and technology parks.
- Some local authorities offer limited office, phone, fax, computer, and other facilities to rent *by the hour*, which could be worth looking into, if only sparse facilities are needed.
- The wilds of some parts of the UK or continent may sound idyllic, but could be totally impractical – unless it is an appropriate business! With modern electronic communications, for example, it may be practical to work in remote parts, downloading (software, call-centre or other) information; and if all or most of the business is conducted 'over the wires'! Mainly or solely based

Internet businesses or certain non-electronic businesses (for example, agricultural, farming, tourist, artistic and craft businesses) come close to having these preconditions.

- A business needs to be suitably located from a Planning Authority point of view – or turned the other way round, certain local authority areas are designated for housing, commerce, industrial units, retail, and so on, and you will be obliged to fall in with these designations. This will involve research with the Authority and property business vendors, and letting agents.
- Some businesses virtually define the type of premises and where they are located. If consideration is being given to a village shop, pub, hotel, B&B, restaurant, petrol station, this might clarify the otherwise wide-open field, at a stroke – just as taking over another business may well do.
- Some sites (especially shops, hotels, and so on) offer domestic accommodation above the immediately usable area that may be of interest, either to live in (if the original house were sold to raise money for instance) or to rent out as a separate business.

Particular Properties
It is terribly important to take all the following points into account when selecting particular premises, relating primarily to proximity to people, facilities and access:

- locations of shopping centres, business, commerce and industrial estates
- locations of centres of population
- the availability of an appropriate labour pool
- where customers and staff live
- staff and customer car parking and transport arrangements
- how convenient is it for them to get to the premises
- problems associated with sites on a main thoroughfare, dual carriageway or clear-way
- convenience for trains, buses and airports, road networks and motorways, as applicable
- waiting restrictions
- where the venturer lives
- physical access (and not just people with a disability)
- convenient access to postal and carrier facilities
- access for supplies generally, or critical raw materials
- hazardous and non-hazardous deliveries and spillages
- deliveries out of the business
- suitability for communications with customers and suppliers, visits, demonstrations
- convenient banking facilities – either physically or certainly for advice
- a multitude of regulatory requirements perhaps (*see* Chapters 17 and 18)
- age and condition of the building
- why, exactly, it is on the market
- potential redevelopments

- planning restrictions
- cost of acquisition
- cost of work needed to adapt the premises to your needs
- fitting out costs
- time until premises are available and ready for your use
- cost of operation, rates and maintenance.

Summary

So, on the surface, there are endless possibilities, but in reality, bearing in mind all the constraints mentioned – including property availability when the premises are needed, cost compromises, lease lengths, and so on – the field gets rapidly restricted.

The most important thing is to get it right first time; and to be stable for a reasonable period – because a customer base and all other dependent services and supplies do not automatically follow a business round the country – if it has to move.

Drive Round Looking For Properties

Driving round urban and rural areas, looking at districts and locations in general and then specific properties is a good way to get the feel of an area.

- How busy and alive is it?
- Would it suit the image of the venture?
- How does it stack up with all the considerations listed above?

When the short-list of seemingly suitable sites, or even a single property, starts to emerge as a result of driving, contacting commercial estate agents, or scrutinizing advertisements, things have a habit of snowballing – probably for reasons of plain euphoria and of attempting to secure the 'ideal property'.

Nevertheless, make sure the homework has been done thoroughly (even discreetly) before making any commitment or even a loose indication to the vendor.

Cost of Premises

Cost of the premises is unquestionably a major issue; and whether the premises are purchased outright, bought with a mortgage, leased, rented, and so on. Property choice is closely tied up with funding because of the:

- amounts involved
- juggling that can be performed by the professionals in due course in connection with raising other funds
- taxation rules as defined at the specific time.

When the business viability is looked at in more depth in the latter part of Chapter 15, it will be seen that property acquisition, conversion, fitting-out, operation and maintenance costs can have a huge impact on the final answer. Sometimes a monthly outlay figure for rent, building management and servicing would be best; sometimes a lump sum (large or small) is called for; and sometimes both. Different ways of effectively paying for premises affect the cash flow calculations, contributing significantly to the viability question.

Finally, you should never commit to a particular property without taking professional advice – it could prevent a disaster at one extreme and save thousands of pounds at the other! Hence the professionals' fees are usually worth it, many times over.

There are many permutations. Whilst rent, lease or buy options exist, so too do possibilities to share the cost and share the facilities somehow with another business (there are many examples of this).

Another possibility is to take some or all of the initial business funding to buy a suitable property outright, and then to take a loan (with that property as security) for the money that will be needed for other business purposes, like stock, equipment and plant for example.

FINANCE

The next most-needed resource is funding. This is a subject which splits logically into two complementary topics:

- the various funding sources, their relative merits and drawbacks
- putting a proper business case together for the proposed lending authority to evaluate their risk and willingness to lend money.

Only Borrow If You Need To

Borrowing costs money, so only consider and ask for what is prudently needed – if any. Use your ingenuity and research to give you the most helpful and cheapest deal, with lowest risk. Interest rates can be arranged at the outset to be fixed, or alternatively they can be allowed to follow money market fluctuations. Even a small variation in interest rates can turn an otherwise healthy profit for one year into an embarrassing loss the next, when other trading conditions remain broadly the same. So don't budget too tightly, if the aim is to obviate this sort of problem.

When loans or other borrowings are granted, the lender always ensures that there are enough assets to cover the loan at least once over somewhere within the business or the family. Hence the phrase a *secured* loan. The risk is always with the business and/or the family, *not the lending authority.*

This thought gives rise to the cynical comment that loan money will usually be forthcoming when the business doesn't *desperately* need it. However, when the business really needs to borrow and wants more funding, the money won't be offered.

In other words, when it's sunny, you'll be lent an umbrella (just in case); but when it's teeming down, you will have no shelter!

The cynic will also observe (and probably astutely), that when you have your own business, which implies being the boss, you are still *not* the ultimate boss.

The bank manager, or his equivalent in the funding organization, is! So don't borrow if it's not really required, and certainly not more than is absolutely necessary allowing for safety margins. If you do, it will cost you interest – several percentage points above the banks' base rate set by the Bank of England currently.

The most obvious source of funding is from your own savings, an insurance policy payout, a 'windfall', a legacy or a lottery win! It's usually the cheapest way to get money, although if the business did not take the money, the money could be properly invested earning some interest in its own right. So effectively this loss of earnings is the cost of the business having the money.

Consider whether it would be beneficial to borrow independently for the business (if there is sufficient security in the immediate assets), and to invest your own money to get a higher return, if possible; the hunch is that you would be hard pushed to better the effective return from the business (and the 'reserve cash' is more accessible should the business suddenly need it) but there is a fairly high risk of losing some or all of it! There will be no instant access, guaranteed income or growth, or degree of security.

You are strongly reminded to distinguish between conventional investment ideas where maximum return, security and access are sought as the primary objectives on one hand; as opposed to investing in your own business (because it needs investment anyway) on the other, whereby the objectives of security and access revert to a secondary objective, even if there may be a good chance of a satisfactory return in the long run. But there are risks.

Why Do Most Businesses Need Funds?

All businesses need premises of some sort, and *most* need funding as well; but not all require *external* funding – it might be all *internal* from money put up by the founder(s), or reinvestment of profits (in due course).

Not all funding is quite the same. Money is borrowed for different timescales, for different purposes, reflecting different costs and risks to the lender, and consequently at different interest rates. The guiding principle is to attempt to match the source of funding to the purposes for which it will be used. In general, the funding for a particular asset should roughly match the expected lifespan of that asset as far as the business is concerned.

You would not finance a domestic car (unlike the house) over twenty-five years – simply because it is very unlikely to be kept for that length of time, or indeed to last for that period. You might *want* to change it during this period.

- Typically a building might be anything between a few years, if it is on a short lease, to ten, fifteen, twenty, or more years if it is purchased (similar to a domestic mortgage).
- Plant, vehicles, internal fittings and decoration may need replacement every two or three years.

There are *depreciation* yardsticks that the accountancy professions use, and tax authorities accept, for all these items – known as write-down periods over which the values are gradually written down in the 'books' of the business, reflecting their rough market values – usually a constant percentage, each fiscal year.

Distinguish between a *true need* to enable the business to get off the ground and flourish, and a *wish list*.

In the outline planning stage, quotations should be obtained for all the assets mentioned and the work listed below that might be involved with the business – together with a note of:

- the *practical* life span, or expected use or occupancy duration (whichever is the shortest),
- *when* they are needed (because not all will be needed right from the outset, and would be better phased in over a period of time, as the business confidence increases) – and *can be afforded.*

This is all part of the all-important task of minimizing risk and exposure!

Possible Funding Requirements – 'Assets'

- premises – whether by rent, lease or buy
- building work
- central heating
- air conditioning
- decorating
- shop fronts
- display cabinets
- fixtures and fittings
- furniture
- equipment
- plant
- vehicles
- stock
- raw materials.

In addition, there is a time gap between having to pay for such things as stock and raw material on the one hand, and getting paid for selling finished products on the other; during which time staff and the owner(s) will want to be paid, and other bills will need paying. So a temporary float covering these time gaps (usually referred to as *working capital* for financing the *work in progress* in a manufacturing context) is needed. This sum will fluctuate quite dramatically as business goes up and down through its normal cycle. It should all work out in the end, but the working capital (elbow room, if you prefer) needs to be managed somehow.

When talking to the professionals, they use empirical ratios of working capital to other parameters, depending on a particular business, which are quoted as guidelines. You should weigh up this valuable tradition-based advice in the context of your own business, and make a judgement accordingly.

WHERE TO BORROW?

Banks
The most likely sources of borrowing are the banks for *overdrafts* or sometimes what are termed *personal loans* to cover short-term working capital, and also for

other longer-term loans. These are the familiar *High Street Banks* (often the first port of call), but there are also *Merchant Banks* for the higher value advances and more ambitious schemes.

When talking to banks about the overall *facilities* the business requires, overdrafts will come up in connection with working capital, alongside the inevitable need for a current account (and, believe it or not, a deposit account for when there are temporary surplus funds in the business).

Banks and most other similar lenders don't publicly and deliberately take risks with their client investors' deposits; so they will almost certainly demand *security* in some form from the business assets, security from the founder(s) in the form of a personal indemnity, a first or second charge on their personal assets (like the family house if there is spare equity beyond any normal mortgage) – or combinations of these methods, simultaneously. Your house will have tended to increase in value anyway beyond the original purchase price: so it should have some spare equity against which loans can be made. Valuing the house professionally at current market rates for this purpose will cost money, as will lenders' arrangement fees.

Incidentally, don't forget that property prices can of course fall, leaving a real shortfall in security at one extreme, and resulting in an actual loss in monetary terms if the property were forced to be sold under these falling market conditions.

Generally, if a good business case is prepared and presented, and adequate security (as defined by the lending source, not the business) is offered, money will usually be advanced from some institution or other. If no institution wants to become associated with the proposed venture, it will almost certainly be because there is insufficient security or that the business is, or appears to be, too risky. Listen to this silent advice and revisit the drawing board – it may be prudent and timely once again.

If your business fails to honour its obligations for some reason or other, if and when it is called upon to do so, personal property, family property, home, lifestyle, and so on, are clearly at very serious risk as discussed in Chapter 4.

Agreements will need to be signed by all parties, and possibly with the spouses and partners as well. Hence the need to spell out the venture honestly in full detail at the commitment round-table discussions so that all participants (direct and indirect) fully understand exactly what's at stake, as well as the potential benefits.

However, if the risks are managed carefully, the arithmetic done accurately, the business run responsibly and carefully, and the business thrives, the risk to domestic and family security becomes much smaller and could eventually disappear altogether.

Other Possible Lenders
Alternative sources of finance are other finance and insurance companies, commercial mortgage lenders, solicitors investing on behalf of their clients, private individuals, friends and relatives – if the concept and risk appeal to them.

Financial Institutions
The financial institutions will behave in a similar way to the banks: but in all the

other cases mentioned above, funds might be advanced with or without calling for interest and capital repayments. The lenders might be content to take the long-term risk and reward, along with you and any other partners or shareholders (depending on the status of the business – *see* Chapter 17).

British and European Governments

Always investigate sources of funding from the EEC, local and central government for various grants and loans on offer from time to time, such as the Small Firms Loan Guarantee Scheme. In various guises there are development funds for entrepreneurs applicable to specific regions and schemes, particularly if it helps the development and employment prospects for a particular geographical region or group of people. Obviously, a grant (with no repayments) rather than a loan (even if with only minimum repayment terms) sounds a good idea in principle. Check the detail conditions of course.

Business Angels

There are people – probably unknown wealthy third parties at this stage – who have money to invest in a slightly risky or interesting-sounding adventure, known as Business Angels. Introductions are usually made by word of mouth via middle-men operating in this specialist field, advertisements, appropriate exhibitions or seminars. Watch the small print and take professional advice. Their interest is a good return on fairly well secured capital.

Venture Capitalists

Venture capitalists are a more traditional, and perhaps more respected, form of Angels. However, whilst the involvement could well be beneficial and certainly constructive, they will have a *strictly business and moneymaking* (rather than a philanthropic) interest, in order to be able to repeat their anticipated fortunes in the future. Again look out for their advertisements, and for their stands at seminars and exhibitions.

Speculative Investors

Beware those who demand a stake (small or otherwise) in the business, particularly voting rights or, worse still, a controlling interest! These various people could be, and probably are, pure speculative investors for relatively high risk and certainly high reward. They might also withdraw their money at some very inconvenient time in the future, leaving the business with a major problem that might well bring about its collapse, with significant personal losses!

Stock Markets

Although it is not usually for startup businesses, shares offered on the stock markets could be a source of funding. It is far more usual for the business to be well-established, and to be of an appropriate type, as far as potential investors are concerned, before a *prospectus* is issued and money from the stock market is attempted. The general public and institutional investors need to have real confidence in the business and its board of directors and management generally before they'll even consider it – and it takes time to build a track record.

This course is usually expensive, and needs professional advice and support. So discard this suggestion as a viable possibility at this stage, although it might be a possible option a few years downstream when the business has grown considerably and expansion is mooted. Several well-known business names have grown to a point where their shares are now traded on the stock exchange; and in many ways this is becoming considerably easier these days. Should you feel the need to raise additional capital through this route sometime, the accountant will be able to advise on the latest situation and conditions, and on how to proceed. A dilution of your shareholding, however it arises, will result in a corresponding dilution of your independence and decision-making ability.

Finance Houses
So far, relatively large sums of money have been considered to fund property and major expenditure (plant, equipment, stock, raw materials, general miscellaneous expenditure and working capital). But specific items like vehicles, shop fronts, tills, computers, furniture (in general terms tangible items that can move and will be replaced quite frequently) can be funded by mechanisms like credit agreements, hire-purchase agreements, rental agreements, through specialist finance houses generally. The finance arrangements are usually offered by the vendor of such items and are consequently not difficult to uncover and sign up to – and few questions are asked as well!

The interest rates tend to be higher as a consequence of the convenience and lenders' risk.

Take care on four main counts:

- Interest rates tend to be much higher than straightforward bank-type loans, as mentioned.
- They clearly are not flexible in that the money so advanced can only be used for the acquisition of the specified purchases.
- In total (along with all the other outgoings that might have been agreed), ensure they can really be afforded, even though they may not amount to much individually.
- The goods can generally be taken back, leaving the business exposed and vulnerable, if payments are not maintained – even monthly standing orders and the dreaded variable direct debits from the bank will be refused (with extra bank charges) if there are insufficient funds in the account.

Credit and Debit Cards
For day-to-day expenses, petty cash, credit and debit cards can be used; but these are usually very small sums of money for consumables like tea, coffee, stationery, and so on. Occasionally small capital or semi-capital items are acquired this way, like fax machines and computers.

Funding From the Business Suppliers

Finally, the cheapest source of funding is suppliers. Suppliers will eventually open a credit account for the new business when they feel they can trust the business sufficiently, or are prepared to take a reasonable and controlled risk. They might see it as a short-term opportunity to get a long-term potential customer off the ground. This is no more than *You scratch my back and I'll scratch yours*, of course.

They may supply some small quantity of raw materials or stock if the risk is perceived to be low and/or the value is low and/or if they very tightly control the payment terms. Many require three years' trading accounts or some other form of business or personal security before they trust the business, but clearly this is out of the question if it's a new venture. So sweet-talking the first one gives a first step, which with care can be used as a reference for the second, and so on. This is where knowledge of the particular trade, especially trade contacts from a previous situation, come in very handy. Eventually, suitable credit references and ratings will be built up.

Having obtained credit from a supplier for 30, 60 or even 90 days perhaps, a free source of money has effectively been uncovered: money that undoubtedly could be employed elsewhere! Although it is a form of revolving credit, it represents a lot of cash and hence 'free' interest. Keep it under strict control and be fair to the suppliers, otherwise they will cut off supplies, which could have critically disastrous effects on the business.

The point is, digressing for a moment, that your business is seeking supplier credit facilities, a good credit rating and full credibility (trust, honesty, integrity, ability to pay, and so on) from early on in the business in order to get this 'extended' cheap and rolling funding. So too, customers of your business will possibly expect similar reciprocal facilities, trust, and so on. This form of credit works both ways. Your customers could ask for such facilities from *your* business that could cost the business extra working capital – which neatly brings the funding sources topic back to the beginning.

EXERCISE

How will you fund your venture – in detail, and finance the monthly or quarterly repayments? How much will you be paying each time and at what interest rate will you be borrowing?

MAKING THE BUSINESS CASE

Stop and consider for a moment how you might react if you were to be stopped in the street, even by a friend, and asked to lend ten pounds.

Whether willing or not, and whether able to or not, you would almost certainly be somewhat curious and ask why. What other questions might be going round in your head, even if it was inaudible to the other party? So think how the professional financier might react to a similar question for a considerably higher sum (several thousand, several hundred thousands or several million pounds).

One of the main points of the so-called business plan (or business case) is to pre-empt questions like these – since the lender will want complete chapter and verse before any answer is forthcoming. It's not really unreasonable. The thought of a business plan might be daunting, but it's really straightforward and quite logical – as will be explained below.

It's worth reflecting on the possibility that the venturer might have some genuine difficulties compiling the business plan (even the draft version) – simply because there isn't really a good enough business case.

So perhaps this stumbling block itself might prove to be another example of a stitch in time – which really means, once more, taking another hard look at the whole project, to establish whether the problem is a major one (or merely a temporary hitch – in which case a solution needs to be found before a fresh attempt is made!). It could show that, in spite of your best efforts, you will still not be able to make, create, repair, move or do your 'thing' profitably enough to run your own business, after all overheads have been considered.

Preparation and Selling Skills

Asking for money will be another test of your skills at selling – so it's worth doing the proper research and homework for what is effectively a verbal presentation of the case. It will be followed by close questioning to ensure the proper groundwork has been done (both meetings in the form of a personal interview), and underpinned by a fairly comprehensive written document. Because of the interview, it is worth also looking smart and businesslike, even if it is not one's usual dress code! Remember, it's all about selling and knowing the proposed business; and image counts very highly!

In any case, no money will be promised or obtained without a solid business case; so let's look at the subject.

For the moment, your job is just to prepare the provisional draft case and sell it to the chosen professional accountant – and maybe other parties. The accountant puts it into words, phrases and terminology that the financial industry understands – and that's very important.

Making It Easy For the Lenders To Understand Your Business

Financiers generally are extremely knowledgeable and skilled in their subject, but not necessarily so in *your* field of expertise: there is an unquestionable language terminology barrier. They will not have your background and the case must be explained concisely, professionally and comprehensively, by or with a trusted middleman, like an accountant. Probably the financial world is completely different from yours, unfamiliar with your situation, although it likes the nature and concept of the business, the thinking and rationale, the personal and social implications, and so on.

The financier, whoever he or she is, may have to present the case to a higher manager, and so it is essential to leave him or her with a smartly produced and clear document, containing the full story – the business plan.

Don't worry, because the professionals will be in at this advanced stage:

- either preparing the case, with your inputs,
- or helping you to prepare the case,
- or jointly presenting it with you to the prospective funding institution.

BUSINESS PLAN

The business plan (first referenced in Chapter 1 as an interim objective) will particularly concentrate on the business as a whole. It will present some facts, figures and descriptive material that form important background information, to establish a level playing field on which all parties can build. Essentially, the plan will present the business case in the form of some fairly standardized thoughts. It will include matters that may not be familiar to you right now, although they are covered later; so don't be too concerned if the terminology is not yet fully understood and appears daunting.

Topics covered will include:

- a summary statement about the venture, identifying straightforwardly what is being sought
- the basic business idea
- the background to the situation
- the history of the enterprise
- an explanation of the motivation and precise timing
- personal profiles, including experience, expertise, knowledge, skills, aptitudes, attitudes, personality
- SWOT analyses for yourself, the other directors or partners and key figures
- short Curriculum Vitaes (CVs), for yourself, the other directors or partners and key figures
- roles, profiles, backgrounds of any other proposed business partners and key players
- business research, substantiated market research and marketing strategy, particularly advertising – effectively the abbreviated marketing plan
- realistic substantiated sales forecasts and sales plan in appropriate detail
- premises
- fitting out plans and costs
- equipment and plant
- vehicles
- total resources needed for the business
- a note of your own resources
- proposals as to how the gaps will be filled, especially the financial ones, of course
- the business status, shareholders and their equity (however it turns out to be set up legally)
- carefully thought-out cash flow projections (more about this in Chapter 15), setting-up costs, overheads, running costs generally, and a break-even analysis, including loan repayments!
- break-even point.

Break-Even Point

The break-even point is the particular time in the future when the accumulated business profits will have been able to repay the loans, and so on. Many businesses are interested to understand when they will start to make real money, after first paying back their loans. Before this point the business has an overall negative worth; thereafter the net worth is positive – so it's a significant point to want to anticipate.

EXERCISE

How long after commencing trading do you anticipate meeting your break-even point?

The business plan will continue with an explanation in detail of:

- why the money is needed, specifically
- how it will be spent, specifically (not on a world cruise, for example)
- how much money you and other own sources will be putting in
- how much is needed by way of external loans or whatever – and why
- the percentage share of all lenders (internal and external)
- what security is to be offered, from a personal and a business point of view
- any contributions to the business in kind, rather than just monetary
- successes to date, both in terms of pilot schemes and in winning other funding
- synopsis detailing the vital points about the finance package sought in what form is required
- a recapitulation of the reasons and security offered
- when it is needed and the repayment plan.

The short document should be:

- businesslike
- thorough
- complete
- covering all the salient facts
- concise – probably just three or four free-style pages, or it could take less
- professional
- possibly, in the prospective lenders' preferred standard format.

Lenders will give guidance as to the precise format for their business plans, although they do not vary very much.

Your contribution is to provide the raw information to the accountant; the more comprehensive the raw data, the easier and less costly will it be for the accountant

– and hence you. A very valuable by-product of this accountancy preparatory work, *not to be underestimated*, is the really thorough insight it provides first hand to you in understanding how your business works, even before the refinements applied by the professionals' cosmetic touch.

This will prove to be extremely valuable in running the business now, and also later when revised and updated business case information will be called for in the future, as it will be!

Not Just For Convincing Prospective Lenders

This is why it is such a valuable exercise to produce a business plan even if your business is not needing external finance. It will help convince the accountant, and hence you, that the philosophy behind the business is really sound, and could be a worthwhile enterprise. Such a plan might be needed downstream by someone anyway, sometime – and one is then readily available.

EXERCISE

Draw up a complete draft of the business plan for your venture – for real! One that's so exhaustive that it could be presented to potential funding authorities, although in practice it would be fine-tuned by the accountant first. Some of the topics will not be directly applicable or understood properly yet, but the underlying principles should be followed as closely as possible to make the document meaningful and valuable to its assessors. It can be completed as you read more in this book.

TECHNICAL RESOURCES

Whilst some additional *technical* knowledge to reinforce the other resources, will generally be very beneficial to the business, you might in fact need to learn the venture in the first place.

In order to pick up some (or some more) basic or more advanced trade knowledge and tricks of the trade, things like names, addresses and phone numbers of suppliers and trade associations, buzzwords, jargon, contacts, information about markets and customers, can all be acquired by:

- reading specialist books
- visiting competitors, discreetly
- visiting trade exhibitions, libraries and craft fairs
- networking
- keeping an ear to the ground – listening to the grapevine
- acquiring and reading books
- working on the Internet
- reading trade journals, newspapers, technical papers and publications like the Yellow Pages
- taking note of advertisements in various places and on delivery vehicles.

EXERCISE

What additional resources are needed for your venture (that is, those that you don't have personally)? Be as realistic as possible, indicating the approximate values, sizes, costs, and so on.

WHAT HAVE YOU LEARNT IN THIS CHAPTER?

★ What resources are needed for running a successful business, generally? Rank them in order of importance and priority, and place a 'tick' against those that *you* have right now, for your venture.
★ What are the main considerations when choosing business premises?
★ How do the location and nature of the premises affect the business?
★ List all (or most of) the considerations affecting choice of premises.
★ For what purposes is business funding usually sought?
★ Why might funding be needed for a business, precisely? Is all funding the same?
★ What are the funding options, and their relative pros and cons?
★ What are the solid advantages of producing a professional business plan if funding is being sought?
★ When no funding is sought, why is it helpful to produce a business plan?
★ Why do you need a wealth of 'technical' resources?
★ How can you supplement your existing knowledge?

9
Marketing the Business

The next few chapters fill in some essential background material. You should thoroughly understand this material on business development, finance and other matters before trying to establish and run your own business.

The business elements diagram (Figure 3 in Chapter 6) shows certain other skills that are needed, apart from the fundamental critical core skill. Expertise is needed in:

- Business development (marketing and sales) – Chapters 9, 10, 11 and 12.
- Finance and bookkeeping – Chapters 13, 14 and 15.
- Technology – Chapter 16.

Without such knowledge, your venture is probably going to fail, just as any other business would if it were operated obliviously of such valuable and vital information. So these next chapters should be regarded as merely a further level of necessary detail in formulating the whole plan.

You can think about these topics and embody this information (supporting the core business with vital peripheral operations) whilst continuing to perform outline, and later, the detailed, planning stages. Not all the topics have the same priority and relevance within any particular venture, and the information (if more should be needed) can be backed up with specialist textbooks, further courses and professional advice.

GETTING BUSINESS

These four chapters will help to confirm (if there was ever any doubt in the first place) that businesses need to win sales somehow. This explains the prominence and priority given to this subject.

Something that you may not have thought a great deal about in the past:

- If I started a small business, where would the business come from?
- How would potential customers know about my business in the first place?

To answer the second question first (because it is shorter) ... that's where *marketing* (specifically publicity and advertising) comes in: it will be elaborated on in this chapter. The first question could be answered by reference to the following nine groups of people.

General Public

It obviously depends on what the business is, but the general public at large (or a specific section of it) has to be a good starting point, if it's something they need or want (or could be persuaded about) and *if they knew the business existed* – which is where marketing comes to the fore again.

Personal Friends

Another source is one's personal friends, who might well get to know about your venture at an early stage – so they are also a strong possibility with appropriate handling. Whilst they will certainly publicize the venture, don't rely on them for too much business – as commented on before.

Former Business Contacts

What about your own business contacts, and the ex-employer's customers? Take care, in case it is deemed poaching and contrary to the contract of employment! It's not necessarily wrong, but check it out first. It's a good way to get customers, because they know and presumably trusted you from a past situation – particularly if an improved product or service for *them* is behind the new concern.

Other Businesses

Another source of customers is other businesses: and even big companies need supplies. If you refer to Figure 2 in Chapter 6, most businesses have an IN and produce an OUT. Consider the fundamental thought that your OUT is another business' vital IN. Their buyer needs supplies or services just as much as your business wants to sell. Their business must get them from somewhere simply in order to operate; your business wants to sell and the other business wants, indeed *needs*, to buy from somewhere otherwise they'll go out of business! Why not buy from *your* business, provided you've got what they want; and the terms (price, delivery, colour, size, and so on) are right for them and the businesses they are working for. They'll certainly need convincing (but that's what *selling* is all about).

Refer to the attributes again in Chapter 2; the other businesses will definitely need *persuading* to change suppliers, perhaps by offering special differentiators, positively distinguishing the products somehow. There must be real and identified *advantages to the buyer*, or some special introductory incentives, inducements or help accommodating the change.

OEMs

What about third party introductions, and what are known as OEMs, *other equipment manufacturers*? Suppose your business supplied or made piece parts that became widely respected and could be used in equipment or products made by other businesses?

For example, suppose your concern made or imported small electric motors; and other businesses needed suitable electric motors to incorporate in *their* products (such as food mixers, fans, vacuum cleaners and so on); tell them about your business, and *show them* specifically how it could help them; and how, by sourcing them from your business, they could benefit from overall 'better' products, terms, quality, reliability of products or continuity of supplies.

Cold Calling

Touting for business generally is a hard slog. It works if you or your representative on the ground (or phone, fax or Internet, amongst other methods) is a good salesperson and is persistent and polite. Be firm, insistent and very helpful, but diplomatic and professional. It is also illegal under certain circumstances: for example, if the business or individual has expressly told authorized government agencies, such as the Telephone Preference Service in the UK, that they do not wish to receive unsolicited sales calls.

Networking

Networking is a term used in many contexts but is primarily associated with spreading the word about your business – forming business connections and contacts through informal social meetings. It can become very significant if actively developed. *See also* Chapter 11 – Finding Customers – Getting Sales.

List, methodically *anyone* in your sphere of acquaintances who might in any way be interested (or who might know someone else who could be interested) in doing business with the venture – such as: family; friends; neighbours; work colleagues from previous employments; social circles; political colleagues; schools; churches; associations ; committees; golf clubs; dinner engagements.

It requires meticulous, but not overbearing, contact to be established and maintained with all your networking colleagues. Details about contacts should be kept up-to-date on a card index (or similar) and referred to periodically – name, address, contact numbers, e-mail address, age, domestic situation, hobbies, interests, occupation, employment and the like; their use in implicitly promoting your business, how you came to meet them, frequency of contact and so on; names and rough details about children, spouses, partners, interests, schools.

Contact them very subtly: they must not think they are being used. Gradually build a picture in *their* mind of *your* business and what it could do for them and their colleagues when they need similar products or services sometime. You never know the tremendous power of good and careful networking, but don't rely just on networking.

Intermediaries

Finally, however your business is derived, ensure that the methods work well – together, if relevant, with dealers, middlemen, contacts, branches, sales staff, call centres, the Internet and so on. Customers use many channels and mix them: for example they may do research via one channel and complete their dealings on another.

Internet

Most comments on electronic means of doing business and using the Internet for your business generally are reserved for Chapter 16; whereas the remaining chapters of this book concentrate on more traditional methodology. Having appreciated pre-electronic methods, you will be better placed to understand and appreciate Internet possibilities.

Summary

The *personal attributes* listed in Chapter 2 cited several high-profile outgoing qualities that would be useful if not virtually mandatory. Many of these characteristics are directly useful in *getting* business, however it is obtained, as opposed to simply running the other aspects of the business. Their contribution is greatest when getting sales for the business – keeping it alive and thriving. It is assumed that all other aspects of the business (technical, production, finance, and so on) are up to scratch.

Generating Sales

Notice the word *generating*. Sales do not usually arrive unannounced (although they may *appear* to sometimes – but this will usually be the result of some previous efforts). Sales, and hence the business prosperity, have to be proactively sought and constructively generated!

There are two interrelated parts to generating business. One relates to *sowing the seeds* (marketing) – covered in this and the next chapter, and the other *harvesting* (selling) – covered in the subsequent two chapters.

Marketing and selling are complementary: almost all businesses have the dual functions although they may not be differentiated as such. The two become confused in peoples' minds: certain areas overlap a little: they might even be carried out by the same individuals in smaller companies (or the sole person in the smallest category).

All businesses need marketing to help generate sales. Marketing functions tend to be less specific and generalized, whereas sales functions are seen to be tangible – and directly identifiable with the fortunes of the business. People who do not really understand sales and marketing, or who prefer to be cynical about them, pretend businesses don't need them – proposing that they could be reduced or eliminated (usually to save money!). As already stated, this thought is completely erroneous. All businesses need sales; marketing is simply the prerequisite ground preparation and seed-sowing phase prior to harvesting at sales time.

Two simple examples to illustrate the difference between marketing and selling.

- Think about the widespread publicity surrounding adult education courses including the college brochure, prior to actually booking yourself onto the course. You need to be informed about the existence of the course somehow, before you can enrol on it.

- Consider the publicity material and television or press advertising that draws you into a car showroom prior to buying a car.

In neither case are satisfactory levels of *sales* of courses or cars likely to be achieved without the *marketing* beforehand – planting seeds in the customer's mind.

Marketing is a generic term that embraces matters such as: publicity; image; public relations; advertising; promotion; presentation; market research; market testing; pricing and sales forecasting; publicity material and handouts, whose specific applicability and application to a particular business vary enormously.

Some of the above-listed words and phrases are frequently misused as industry 'synonyms' for marketing; whereas, in fact, the term 'marketing' embraces them all – and some others. The full applicability of some of the marketing principles and techniques will vary between businesses, because of their nature; but the rational thinking and theory is sound. The specific interpretation, degree and how it is applied will vary.

Sowing the Seeds

The softer the ground, the easier it is to dig; doing good preparatory work is half the battle – preparing the ground by advertising. As a new venture you must spread the word as widely, quickly and efficiently as possible within the target population.

Marketing can be commenced by word of mouth – simply telling 'everybody' about the business. Good targeted publicity simply tells the *right* people that your venture exists, showering them with all the exciting information about it:

- what the business does
- what it will do for its clients, customers, or *customers'* customers
- what is different about it
- why and how potential customers will benefit from your venture
- where it is
- contact numbers and names, and so on.

Advertising and Publicity

Meticulous, Eye-Catching and Clever Scriptwriting, Slogans and Logos
The secret of good advertising and publicity generally is to hit and saturate the marketplace with creative, memorable thoughts that *whatever* potential customers want, need or can be 'groomed' to need (in the chosen line of business) is not only readily available from your business, but the service the customers will receive is beyond reproach and will exceed their wildest expectation.

Create differentiators for the product: spell them out to make your business stand out from the run-of-the-mill competition. (The business will have to live up to this publicity and deliver the goods as promised – otherwise it will be a pointless, negative and costly exercise.)

Guidance is always available from the advertisement-carrying media and from specialist books – including codes of practice stating that all adverts must be legal, decent, honest and truthful.

The specific challenge is to demonstrate in the publicity and any downstream actions: *what your business can offer* to satisfy the potential customer's need and *why* that customer should even consider changing to your business – let alone actually doing business. It is not unreasonable, because you would regard other advertisements in exactly the same light, if the boot was on the other foot, and you were seeking particular products.

Drafting Publicity Material
The publicity should be attention-grabbing, slick, generally short and punchy. Ordinary advertisements (and Internet Web pages) have to catch the potential customers' attention, before they can continue to work. They must make the potential customers sit up and take note. It should be framed to put the potential purchaser's interests (and way of receiving the message) at the highest priority – as the best way of presenting the brief message. These sentiments should also be highlighted in the business plan, to give the lender added confidence.

Two other somewhat interrelated skills are very worthwhile mentioning here:

- the art of brilliant and catchy copy-writing for pinpointing the precise message
- writing interesting newsletters.

Good quality and impressive publicity material lasts a long time, but can be expensive: therefore only carry material that does not date quickly. Omit dated details (like prices, offers, personnel changes and latest orders), carrying *this* information in lower-costing newsletter type publications that are intended to have a shorter life.

Think where *you* would expect to find out if *you* were endeavouring to seek out a particular commodity or service, when undertaking any form of publicity (in the widest possible sense and employing any particular medium). The imaginative art is always to see the situation *from the customer's perspective (not the business owner's)*. This is quite difficult until you get used to it.

Keep an eye on the competitors' techniques as a good guide – but don't necessarily copy them!

Your Business Customers
There are in some views two broad types of customer – those who are merely end-users and those who have customers themselves to be satisfied (businesses of some sort). The former group have pride of ownership, a dire need or whatever, to satisfy as their motivation for purchase. More will be said in the next chapters on this motivational point.

Where other businesses are involved, it's always an excellent idea to think ahead anticipating the needs of the *customers'* customers; because, by doing so, you will create a small business to help *your* customers gain more business as well. Consequently, your venture benefits – all part of the 'can do' policy.

The analogy to seed sowing should now be apparent! Opening day (often referred to as Day 1) is too late; it must be started before launch, when the venture project is well advanced and certain to go public, and continued afterwards.

So, having grasped the principles and purposes of marketing your business:

- How do you go about it in real practical terms?
- What are the marketing tools and techniques?
- How do you spread the word?

All businesses certainly share common features and characteristics: but are utterly different. They are *unique* in fact, in that each one has different potential customers: geographical area, product or service, price band, social status and social grouping, and income group.

CHOOSING A BUSINESS NAME

The most important marketing influence is usually the business name coupled with a brief description of what it does. Think what other businesses have been called and the role the name has played.

The entire business could stand or fall; so it's worth thinking about the name and its presentation for a very long time, as it is often the primary means of recall in the public's mind. Names can be arbitrary handles, or they can carry some form of specific hint at what the business does – that should be helpful to a new venture. There could even be an 'official' name and a trading name, simultaneously. Business names can be grouped into five categories:

- Names can be purely variations on own personal names or surnames (like Marks and Spencer, Anne and John, and W H Smith, for example).
- Names can be totally artificial, although eventually memorable and meaningful – words or phases (like Tesco, TGI Friday and Virgin).
- Names can be sets of initials that were originally abbreviations for well-known, meaningful and descriptive phrases, although now established in their own right (like RAC, AA, ICI and IBM).
- Names can be virtually meaningless until they become known, which might be a slow process (like B&Q, or AJ Services – where two people collaborated in an unidentifiable and obscurely named business whose first names happened to be Alan and Jim).
- Finally, names can be purposefully explicit, identifying what the venture is all about (Office World, British Airways, Little Chef, Simply Flight Deals or Vauxhall Car Rental, for example).

Until the business becomes well known, something eye-catching, short, memorable, descriptive to some extent, possibly with a multiple meaning is favoured, because it hints strongly at what the business does, and is hopefully easy to remember. Consider the telephone answering equivalent – a nice easy and short name is better than longish phrases! The name might make a useful talking point in itself to reinforce the publicity!

Succinct and Memorable Message

It's really worth spending some time thinking about getting succinct messages across to the targeted marketplace, and ultimate aim of gaining business: it means making the market take note with the right image, memorability, and so on. Bounce ideas around other people to see how they react.

It is imperative for the memorability of the business and its image to choose the right name, logo, any slogan, gimmicks – and their combined presentation. Names have to conform to certain standards, rules and regulations. Chapter 17 says more on this subject; there is plenty of professional, positive and helpful advice available to guide you through the restrictions.

In connection with logos and house style ... lettering sizes, styles (fonts), print colour, background colour, the use of artwork and the lack of them (white space) are very important; this area demands equally constructive lateral thinking.

The same general comments go for choosing an additional name, for a *product*, *service* or *brand*, like [Ford] *Mondeo* or *Clover* ['butter'], if one is required. So much depends on the business – its planned catchment areas, projected image, typical customer profile and its proposed publicity machine.

WHERE TO ADVERTISE EFFECTIVELY

Spend Your Marketing Budget Wisely

Almost the first thing to be considered is the initial people you want to target (with future customers at least pencilled in). You must understand the particular market audience (marketplace), and aim directly at them. Advertising wastes money if it is not targeted closely – especially very general advertising.

Evaluate local versus wide publicity, and the likely constructive 'readership' or readers'/listeners'/viewers' genuine interests. Weigh up trade versus general public advertising. Assess colourful glossy magazine adverts as against the cheaper media. Consider the cost of the advertisement for the likely return. Be very careful, because the problem is that you don't usually know how effective it is (although there are ways of testing this to some extent).

Advertisements range from being fairly specific, promoting a particular offer or range of products, through to very low-key and subtle general adverts (as sometimes employed by large international chemical concerns like ICI, Shell and BP). You have only got to compare different style advertisements (and hence different messages). Some advertising can be very useful, especially for local geographical areas, in publications like the Yellow Pages and Thompson Directories.

Local and national advertising, as applicable to your catchment area, should be considered:

- on newspaper hoardings
- on buses
- on cinemas screens
- on radio and television
- on the Internet
- in shop windows

- in relevant specialist-interest magazines
- in trade journals
- in magazines
- in Sunday newspaper magazines or unsolicited shopping catalogues.

Advertising can be carried effectively on fundamental items, but it should only be employed if the business thinks it value for money (and appropriate to the image that it is attempting to create) such as:

- business cards
- envelopes
- postal franking machines
- notepaper
- compliment slips
- bags
- packaging
- labels
- pricing tags
- stickers

- signs on premises
- delivery vehicles
- brochures
- leaflets
- flyers
- mailshots
- telephone conversations
- fax messages
- e-mail correspondence.

Other Advertising Media
Stationery
Certain stationery will be needed in its own right, of course, regardless of any hard advertising messages.

Physical Presence
Depending on the products, image, and so on, the following valuable advertising locations are apposite (especially where there is something to feel and touch, something tangible to demonstrate, something to inspect or see, or something which is likely to be bought on impulse):

- craft fairs
- car boot sales
- exhibitions

- conferences
- seminars.

Internet
If you use Internet trading, very careful design is called for on worldwide web pages for maximum effectiveness and information currency. If you can do this yourself (either now or in the future) that's fine; but if you need professional help it's readily available through consultants, many books and courses. Techniques (and technology generally) are changing and improving continuously – which is why it is beyond the scope of this particular book. Get the latest ideas when you are ready.

Satisfied Customers

After a while, it will be realized how valuable satisfied customers are in spreading the word, by supporting and promoting the business. Be sure to look after your customers medium- and long-term, apart from any immediate business they bring! Use, to maximum advantage, any:

- contacts
- dealers
- retailers
- agents
- middlemen
- other shops
- any business connections
- networking colleagues.

Summary

It should be abundantly apparent that publicity is very necessary, albeit somewhat unpredictable in its precise worth – falling on fertile ground, as it were; closely matched to the prospective customer. Trial and error must be employed as there are no magic answers, even when the professionals (advertising and public relations, or PR, agencies) in this field are employed. It's usually big money, too; so be careful what you sign up to.

As part of the Stage 2 *Outline Planning*, the whole subject of marketing must be explored and tentatively planned, obtaining quotations against likely coverage: size of advertisement, quoted readership numbers, *actual readers* and length of time that the advert will be about, where relevant.

PUBLICITY AND YOU

Don't just operate between nine till five, as it were: but be around expressly when customers are around. Get involved giving technical papers, if appropriate, and get on to anything that will give positive publicity. If the products are appropriate, use the Internet, and give away photographs, videos, CDs and samples – either through the post or by hand.

Public image and market research are part of the general publicity machine – so are you. Think how often you will have seen public figures around when business initiatives are being launched – government ministers, politicians in general, business leaders like Richard Branson, Alan Sugar, Bernard Matthews and Clive Sinclair. Keep yourself in the public eye – preferably with positive deeds! Take every opportunity to publicize the business:

- be around
- be *seen* to be around in the community at large
- get on committees
- get on trade associations
- organize and sponsor events
- get editorial copy printed (with photographs) in local or specific newspapers, journals or periodicals
- get air-wave time (radio and TV interviews) somehow

- have a web page, since people expect it
- take the business out to the customers, at events, such as craft fairs, exhibitions, school parents' evenings.

Don't overlook anyone, who might then feel affronted if this happened (it can so easily happen, without realizing it), particularly remembering that one is *never* really off duty and out of the public eye – so no misdemeanours either.

It's worth recalling that the 'friend of a friend' syndrome and networking generally operate well: in other words, the person you speak to directly may not always be a potential customer but the real customer could be someone he or she knows and subsequently *communicates with*. So, however busy you might be:

- Always find time to meet and talk with customers and prospects.
- Always find time to meet and talk with all the network contacts that have been amassed.
- Do as much face-to-face talking as possible, although the phone, fax, e-mail and other communications media have their place.
- Actively support, mail and talk to all possible third parties – any middlemen, contractors, servicing people, agents, distributors, staff from other trades and businesses. Make sure they can positively and enthusiastically promote your business.
- Share knowledge with businesses and people who may be working alongside your business operations, and so on, under short-term teaming arrangements, or installations and servicing contracts.

You should ensure a fully supportive local impact by involving yourself and the venture in the community, local schools and businesses, as appropriate.

Another way is to get actively involved with the local Chambers of Trade or Commerce and Industry – with local trade missions, initiatives, adult education classes and exhibitions. Similarly with the local branches of the Institute of Directors or Forum of Small Businesses.

Beat customer expectations! Always give above-expectation service, speed, quality and convenience, and keep any promises that are made. Excel in the *can do* attitude.

Reputations take years to make, but seconds to lose! Yes, years and seconds, respectively. Quality of service in all its facets, customer satisfaction, marketing and all the other impressionable matters all serve to contribute to this long germination associated with reputation. Not only does it take a long time, but it's heavy on the budget as well; so don't waste it by one split second of carelessness!

In short, anybody who can influence the prosperity of the business (in any way whatsoever and by whatever means), must be kept fully up to date with the news: this aspect of the entrepreneur's workload is so important. It can, and will, over-spill beyond normal 'office' hours – including so-called social and 'off-duty' hours!

Market Research

Testing customer interest should be undertaken as part of the marketing process. Try somehow to test the market before going ahead at full steam – but without giving the game away prematurely. This can be done:

- with a semi-fictitious advertisement with a *home* phone number to give an indication of the demand
- by operating from low-cost premises and with second-hand equipment to begin with
- using a temporary shop-within-a-shop for a short while
- in the case of shop-style businesses, via small-scale trials or pilot schemes through car boot sales, craft fair stands and the like
- in subtle discussions with possible customers at your premises, trade seminars and exhibitions
- when networking
- using anonymous 'tasting' sessions – not necessarily physical tasting, as in food products
- new engineering prototypes within old or disguised outward styling
- 'free' customer trials in realistic usage environments
- using professional market research businesses.

Specialist organizations will handle these market research assignments for you, for a fee; but there are also the two valuable advantages of not encroaching on your business' own time and being 'anonymous' – which helps create more meaningful answers.

Contact and mail customers regularly:

- either to keep them informed generally of all the good news
- or specifically with surveys and questionnaires if these methods are deemed to be helpful and not too intrusive to the marketplace (and then analyse and use the data gathered to one's advantage).

Ask customers where and how they heard of the business; how and why they were attracted to it. Ask them what they expect from the business, what other products and services might appeal to them: listen to them, weigh up their responses. Do everything possible to stimulate need and if necessary to create a market by creating a need; but make sure it works to the sole advantage of you, and not to a competitor! A good existing market can always be increased or widened.

EXERCISE

What marketing options have you considered? What will they cost in total, and how much return will you see for each option?

COMPETITORS

Very few businesses have the field to themselves: there may be one or more existing organizations already in the proposed catchment area (that is, with sufficiently similar or identical businesses within the same street or town, possibly) that could be regarded as competitive elements.

Interestingly those other businesses probably regard *your* business as an equally potential reciprocal threat! That's worth remembering – even if you *are* the newcomer. Threats are often taken both ways, especially where there are unknown factors – even if the reality turns out to be different. At least there's some flattery in there somewhere, which should be worth an appreciative smile!

In some ways another flattering thought ... but you should also be permanently looking out for *another* new business starting up in due course that regards *your* venture as the existing competitor – the situation reversed. Forewarned is forearmed.

There is an argument (or backhanded compliment) that provides confirmation of your own analysis if there are already some businesses doing broadly the same thing, successfully. This could be assessed as positive proof that there was possibly a worthwhile market out there, on the doorstep as it were. Conversely, no competition *might* indicate that there is also no real business potential: just as it could signal a great opportunity!

Competition must be considered as a fact of business life – either now or later. It can be both good or bad news, which means competition wants weighing up carefully as part of the viability equation. If professional wartime spies succeeded in dangerous situations, you ought to be able to penetrate commercial competition somehow. Never get found out! Try to complete a SWOT analysis on competitors making appropriate inspired guesses where necessary.

Employ your basic survival instincts, cunning and disguise. Use discreet dummy customer visits and fictitious enquiries to establish competitors' product and price range, their pricing policy, skills, quality, product availability, terms and conditions, turnover, reputation, *your* reputation, and so on. Use trusted colleagues, network contacts, photographs, videos, exhibitions and market research organisations perhaps to solicit information and brochures. When talking to customers and suppliers, get their opinions discreetly about problems areas and experiences, along with brochures and other factual information.

Part of the Outline Planning work is to decide whether or not there is enough business (or extra business that could be tapped) without upsetting the viability calculations. An additional business, like yours, will have one of four effects:

- It could take some or all of the trade away from the existing concerns such that they have to curtail the businesses or even close down.
- The competitors might benefit indirectly from your business and publicity, and decide to sharpen their own operation to reap more sales.
- It might prove that there is not enough natural business to share. Your venture is simply not viable, without being able to create an *additional* market somehow.
- There might be an added attraction for the customers to have a group of similar businesses in one area, which could therefore be good for the venture – the concentration effect.

Respect and acknowledge the competitors, even work together at times, whilst at the same time looking after the interests of your own business.

There are many examples of the concentration effect – where several identical businesses are all more or less adjacent to each other and positively self-supporting. They have greater combined pulling power for the purchasing crowds (restaurants and shoe shops for example), than they would have individually. Another example is some small food shop groupings that really compete with each other, and yet have common customers, and a supply chain and national marketing umbrella for their corporate greater good (groceries and village shops).

There is honour among thieves (forgive the parallel). All similar businesses are liable to have commonality with your business suppliers, customers, staff mobility, trade associations, delivery arrangements and subcontractors: there will undoubtedly be a healthy grapevine. Thus any good or bad rumours, gossip and news will abound, and get back to all the businesses – and above all, the customers! It could severely bite or kill off your venture.

Competition is usually healthy, keeping everyone on their toes, if all parties play the game and don't unduly rock the boat. But if the boat does rock, any party might get tipped out – not necessarily the newcomer or the established business. Handling matters associated with competitive businesses is part of the remit for marketing activities.

Never knock competitors. Instead deal with them professionally; aim to be friendly, although the gesture may not be returned. Show the competitor that your venture is not a direct threat after all. Highlight the special features and positive differences relating to your own venture to the customers (*and to the competitor very carefully and selectively*):

- your discriminators
- customer care
- lower prices
- after-sales service

- shorter delivery time
- bigger range
- location
- friendly, knowledgeable staff.

If the people running the competitive businesses are reasonable folk:

- attempt to meet them
- be friendly

- stand tall
- know the business arena backwards

- be politely resolute
- be superbly confident
- attempt to allay their fears.

Maybe, you should attempt to work *together* to your mutual advantage, outwardly supporting each other in complementary ways, such as possibly servicing different segments of the same market (different product ranges, different groups of customers, and so on).

EXERCISE

Who would your competitors be – either by name or by category?

EXERCISE

How will you analyse the competition? Produce a SWOT analysis for each competitor.

EXERCISE

Indicate the strength of your competitive sources. Could they be a significant problem?

EXERCISE

How would you deal with them, or live with them, so that your venture thrives?

SHOP WINDOW DISPLAYS

Anyone who has studied window displays as a customer will quickly realize that this is demonstrably a form of marketing. Don't forget to make the most of your own business window displays if it's a shop-style business; or even if it isn't for that matter – provided there are product display cabinets for customers to see, touch, handle the products and become excited about them. There is a huge power in a brilliant display of the stock!

NICHE MARKETING

Finally, this is an area that is definitely worth contemplating: it's a simple concept. It relates to a very narrow range of goods or services that will appeal to an equally very narrow range of customers. It means looking for, and exploiting, a niche in the wider market: implying differentiators to align with customer choices and demands. It could lead to dominance in the market – becoming the standard setter, a leading authority and one of the few suppliers or manufacturers: even the only one, perhaps. It's a bit like a top-of-the-range car market (Rolls-Royce for example, rather than Ford) – and not all venturers will want or be able to get into this market.

The theory is that if you specialize in a very tight range as opposed to a wider range of products (and market your business accordingly – perhaps over the

Internet), the venture will attract a realistic number of correspondingly highly specialist customers. They are often very highly demanding but they expect, and are prepared to pay for, the best. They will come from far and wide; so the business will attract a large catchment area – even mail-order and export. For the real expert in his or her field, there can be minimal competition if the service quality, product quality and so on are absolutely top rate. But it needs strong belief, courage and accurate research.

If the reader's hunch is correct, customers will find it rewarding; and your business will be very welcome in the market place – making it very profitable, if tackled the right way. The risk will be higher, initially.

WHAT HAVE YOU LEARNT IN THIS CHAPTER?

★ What are the nine very broad sources of getting business?
★ How do you make a thriving business enterprise?
★ Differentiate between the marketing and sales functions.
★ List the various constituent parts that comprise a marketing function.
★ How do you spread the word about your business? What media do you use?
★ What message should you get across? Who do you tell, and why?
★ Where do you place your name, addresses, phone/fax numbers and basic message?
★ What are the main options to consider when choosing a name for the venture?
★ Where and how should businesses consider advertising?
★ Where does the owner personally figure in marketing the business?
★ What are the four possible effects that competitors might have on the scene?
★ What are the benefits and responsibilities of niche marketing?
★ How would you use the Internet?

10
Pricing and Sales Forecasting

Part of the marketing function, although not in the same mould of seed-sowing ideas, is the consideration of prices and pricing strategy. From marketing information (and good sales intelligence) stems the concept of predicting a sales forecast – the two topics for this chapter.

How do you establish your selling prices in your own venture?

PRICES VS. COSTS

Prices should not be confused with *costs*. All the various elements associated with the design and production of the core product or service (in general terms, creating, doing, repairing, moving or making it) must be included. *Costs* represents the total end-to-end money that the product or service has effectively cost the business, and include:

- materials
- all labour (salaries and wages)
- warranty
- delivery
- installation charges (if applicable)
- costs associated with distribution, selling and marketing
- any miscellaneous items
- apportioned overheads of the business generally.

The selling price could be the same, higher or lower. If that item is sold for less than the amount it actually costs, a loss would obviously be incurred that, if repeated over the entire output of a business, would mean a loss for the business as a whole: obviously not good news and a suicidal course of action! Unless there is a deliberate policy of undercutting the costs of some lines, as loss leaders (as bait to get customers into the shop or showroom or whatever), selling prices should always be fixed above cost calculations.

The individual selling price *on average* should always be more than the cost to make or acquire the goods; and the positive difference is the profit margin. The sum, in monetary terms, of all the profit margins represents the profit for the business. (More later in Chapter 15.)

Price is not directly related to cost, contrary to common belief. Price is governed by what the seller believes the marketplace will stand – what the customers think is an acceptable price. It's rather like the secondhand price of antiques, cars or houses: from the seller's point of view it's the maximum that it will fetch at auction or on the open market, and from the buyer's point of view it's the lowest you can negotiate to pay. *There is simply no fixed answer* – which may come as a surprise to some readers!

However, for simplicity and hoped-for uniformity across the marketplace, some selling prices are virtually fixed, strongly suggested or recommended by manufacturers in the case of shop, showroom and warehouse stock, although discounts might influence matters.

Selling price = cost figure + mark-up (say 50 per cent of cost figure)

or

Selling price – margin (say, one-third of selling price) = cost figure

In other words, a mark-up of 50 per cent on the *cost* figure (if that were to be the base reference) is the same monetary value as a margin of one-third on the *selling* price. Prices can generally be modified up or down at the owner's discretion, within the guidelines and comments presented later. However, selling prices are in practice determined by things like:

- specification
- quality standards
- colour
- size
- quantity
- presentation
- packaging

- delivery
- installation
- after-sales service and support
- warranty
- discounts for purchasing in bulk, quantity, for 'cash' – or for a variety of reasons.

These objective or quantifiable parameters (reflecting tangible costs) are further influenced by subjective factors, such as:

- scarcity
- *customers'* perception of rarity
- competition
- perceived value for money
- *customers'* perception of the worth of convenience or alternative options (use of his or her own transport or public transport).

Having established a selling price using these and other factors as well, VAT must then be added (if applicable) – *see* Chapter 14. For the moment, ignore VAT in the comments on pricing.

The following thoughts on the subject of prices will demonstrate how fickle prices can be:

- Some people will always pay the asking price without question.
- Some will always haggle – on principle.
- Some will only pay the lowest price they can – on principle.
- Some will only deal where credit facilities are available, or credit cards are taken without surcharges being imposed.
- Some will only buy if a large discount is quoted. This implies that not all discounts are *real*, even though the 'discounts' might be emblazoned all over the products and services! (Think of advertising in connection with out-of-town furniture outlets for example. Be very pedantic: what was the true baseline *before* the discount was applied; and how meaningful was it?)
- Some customers buy a much larger quantity to maximize an alleged saving (even if it means actually spending more money). A good example is *Buy one and get one at half price* or *three for the price of two.*
- Others are inspired by so-called 'free' offers, 'free' gifts, bonus points and other similar incentives.

Others will buy almost regardless of price – but against *tangible* physical 'facts' like:

- a notional or firm description or specification
- model numbers
- colour
- dimensions
- weight
- free delivery
- warranty terms
- no-quibble guarantees
- availability on the Internet.

Some will buy almost regardless of price on *less tangible* concepts like:

- personal service
- friendly understanding staff
- attractive merchandise
- attractive staff
- quality
- after-sales service
- loyalty cards
- preference for dealing with certain personalities, shops, suppliers, businesses, warehouses
- promises made by the salesman, such as pledges relating to delivery time, model arrival times at showroom, prices being held, new housing releases being made, the classic one of projected future rates of return on investments and insurance policies, and so on.

The psychology behind customers' reasons for finally accepting (or rejecting) a particular offer is quite fascinating – emotional and *often totally irrational.* Their situation is often driven by time availability for making the purchase, car parking time expiry, parking on double yellow lines, having an imminent meeting, other matters on their mind, children and so on; and maybe frustration for whatever reason, like unhelpful assistants, rude staff and having to queue!

First Example of Irrationality

Irrationality is typically based on a deal being discussed over an extended period for an expensive item like a household appliance – a cooker or a washing machine. The customers are baffled or overwhelmed by the multitude of apparent pros and cons between the models.

Because of the difficulty in making up their minds between the two short-listed models, the salesman 'throws in' a final offer of a short extension to the warranty (which probably costs the dealer nothing in practice) *at no extra cost* to the customers – specially wheeled in at this late stage of the deal on *just one* of the models, to help the customer make up his or her mind.

The customer, just as the salesman planned, makes an instant irrational decision – the quick reaction based almost entirely on this minute glib offer. A moment's thought would show that the true value of the 'offer' is insignificant within the *total* context of the deal. If the product was as reliable as suggested by its superb specification and appropriate price (reflecting good quality merchandise), it probably would never go wrong anyway; and the *true worth to the purchaser* of the small extended warranty would in fact be proved to be zero!

Second Example of Irrationality

Choosing between two expensive, but similar, cars on the basis that only one has a cigar lighter – especially when the purchaser doesn't smoke anyway! In reality, the comparisons should have been made on important matters like the basic construction and reliability of the vehicles (performance, mileage, engine, bodywork, style, tyres, wheels, braking system, safety, convenience, running costs, and so on).

PERCEIVED VALUE FOR MONEY

Observations over a very long period have convinced the author that price is unquestionably important to many customers; but so too, especially for the really careful and thinking customer, is the *overall perceived value for money* (taking into account all the factors mentioned above and a few more besides), and subsequent 'hand-holding' if he or she has any problem downstream.

In the end, customers collectively influence marketplace selling prices: the so-called *market forces*.

The Florist

So in the case of a florist business, for example, the prices you might charge are governed primarily and practically by many factors (roughly in this order of precedence), such as:

*   social category of clients
*   affluence of marketplace

- the particular catchment area (practical distance for attracting and servicing customers)
- quality of service
- customer care factors
- attractiveness of the individual flower arrangements (perceived by the customer)
- the additional features at whatever 'premium' (worthwhile added value as perceived by the customer – wrapping or phone ordering for example)
- flower availability and costs – time of year and weather factors
- the specific range of services offered *in relation to other similar businesses* in the catchment area
- trading conditions generally (amount of business about)
- trade conventions and guidelines
- competitive local trading environment.

There are no quick reliable answers; but plenty of trial and error, and competitive comparisons. All the factors above will have a bearing on the prices charged, implicitly or otherwise. From the customer's angle, perceived value for money by him or her will prevail.

The medium- and long-term continuation of the business is governed by how the charges are viewed by the marketplace – perceived value for money individually, or (taken as a whole) market forces once again influencing matters. Prices must be kept constantly under review because factors and circumstances change frequently.

COMPARATIVE PRICES

Another way to fix prices, using some or all of the above sentiments as well, is to ask what the *alternative* would cost the customer, and base the price on that as well (not just competitive prices for the same thing).

Airport Taxis
For example, a taxi firm wants to fix a price for taking clients fifty miles each way to the airport for the fortnight's annual holiday.

If the client took his or her own car and parked it for two weeks:

- it would cost in wear and tear
- it would be subject to running costs
- vehicle and contents security could be a consideration
- there would be a fortnight's convenient but expensive airport parking
- there could be added time penalties and luggage-carrying inconvenience, however, for less expensive off-airport parking
- there would be some subjective factors, like stress and hassle for the holiday-maker to accept.

These items would cost the client a finite and sizeable amount of money (although the *customer* may have chosen to ignore all the real costs): so the taxi could fix its rate at about three-quarters of the total bill for the airport alternative and still offer genuine door-to-door service – a considerable saving of clients' time and money, without any tiring driving or courtesy coach hassle. Quite an attractive proposition for the client, and one calculated to gain business for the taxi firm.

Both the client and the taxi firm should be happy with the deal, with the added proviso (applicable to all selling situations) that the benefits and their real implications are made crystal clear to the client! That's vital. Note that this price is established regardless of *what it actually costs* the taxi firm – but review the earlier comments at the beginning of this chapter when costs and selling prices were discussed.

Bridges, Tunnels and Ferries

Another similar example concerns newly constructed bridges and tunnels, or newly instituted ferry services. Again consider the alternative – a long, time-consuming drive that suddenly has disappeared! What's the sum of all the motoring costs (including depreciation, wear and tear, running costs and so on) and time and frustration that could be saved? Relate the scale of charges to the alternative cost so that both parties are in a win–win situation!

Careful Research

These examples illustrate the factors that businesses should use to assess selling prices; but be prepared to experiment *carefully* if necessary. Remember it's considerably easier to lower prices, than to raise them – and 'instantaneous' discounts should always be justified to the customer, without appearing to simply give them away irrationally.

The subtleties of pricing policies and all other marketing parameters arise out of basic market research – asking direct and indirect questions of the marketplace and customers:

- listening carefully
- gauging reactions
- gleaning comments and observations obliquely
- simply asking customers carefully and directly
- reading between the lines
- sending or giving out carefully worded questionnaires to customers and potential customers.

Information on products, specifications, product range, selling prices and business image can be gathered and weighed up with any other relevant factors (to be embodied in subsequent designs, modifications or retrospective changes). This process plays an important part in setting up the venture in the first place.

EXERCISE

Create the pricing structure for your own venture.

SALES FORECASTING

Assuming that your marketing works satisfactorily, you now have to make a sales forecast. Many people get cold feet at this point! This is understandable, but unnecessary. Be realistic: you should be assured that the orders *will* arrive if the spadework has been meticulously carried out. So have faith!

Customers will arrive and phones *will* ring bringing enquiries to your business, whatever it is. Deal with them and respond promptly (*see* Chapters 11 and 12), even if only to acknowledge; but phone them back and respond constructively and professionally. Try to arrange visits, produce quotations, and turn every enquiry into can-do business. Be ready to process and fulfil the orders whenever and however they arrive – by:

- person
- post
- phone
- fax orders
- mail-order
- e-mail

- agents
- dealers
- Internet
- middlemen
- distributors
- shops.

With these positive thoughts in mind, think of the total venture in a different light. Think of it for a moment as merely a *group of mini* ventures, each representing a smaller category of your entire range of products and services that will be offered within the first year, at least.

(Until you get used to it, the sales forecasting seems a lot of work, but it isn't really if it becomes second nature. It can be done manually or by computer spreadsheets.) The following seven steps will prove valuable:

- List the individual smaller categories down the left-hand column of a sheet of paper.
- Consider how many items in each category will be sold in the first week of trading: add the numbers to the list.
- Repeat the exercise for all subsequent weeks covering the next twelve months to produce an annual estimate of the number of units (and value) for the first year's turnover for your business.
- If it were appropriate to your particular type of business you could express even more confidence in these mini forecasts by attributing specific names to specific orders – assuming you handled the individual sales correctly.
- Repeat the exercise for every one of the individual categories, adding them up to represent the business as a whole once again. Translate the numbers of sales into monetary terms – value of sales – for the first day and week.
- This information, usually presented on a sheet of paper in tabular form, comprises a number of rectangles in the grid that should be completed with the number of unit sales for that category of product, or their value, or both somehow, in a particular month.

- A final row and a final column can be added for totals, and the bottom right-hand rectangle so formed, would show the annual total figure for the whole business that reflects your reasoned intuition, and should be viewed against other criteria for safety.

The above individual figures aggregate to produce *annual* estimates, based on realistic statements that *average* sales for each category of product each week that you claim will probably be achieved. They have been worked from the *bottom up* which should give you every confidence, and are based on the realistic assumption that the marketing and sales strategy has been properly devised and undertaken, bringing forth timely fruit.

Don't forget to include, when planning ahead, that as word gets about, there should be a natural increase in sales; and also that most businesses have seasonal or weather-related influences on their trading pattern. In mathematical terms, the sales are not linear, but neither are expenses – as will be seen later.

Projected Annual Sales

You will now have arrived at a *crude estimate* of the annual sales turnover for the first year of the operation. You will need to rework the first set of figures several times for consistency and refinement as other thoughts emerge, but that's the norm!

Sales Forecasts

Figures 5 and 6 show two example pairs of sales forecasts – for each of two different businesses – one a shop and the other a central heating installations concern. Notice specifically, for these examples, that the entire product range has been *crudely* consolidated into just four price bands or *approximate* prices. It is unwieldy to consider every individual price, so in practice, they are grouped to represent *average* price values or categories of business. The entire shop stock has been considered in the four categories; and, in the other business – central heating – the four values might represent:

- contracts for complete central heating systems at an average notional figure (the highest)
- smaller jobs – perhaps extension radiators (the second highest)
- a 'bread and butter' line that averages out evenly during the year (the third highest)
- some small accessories trade (the lowest band).

Monthly predictions have been made for the number of items sold (unit sales) within each price band, in each business.

The unit figures have been *rounded* as necessary to produce monthly *estimates* of sales, by value.

Notice, in the manufacturing business example in particular, that exact multiples of the unit sales expectations are not necessarily translated into corresponding

Sales forecast by numbers of units for each product

Item	Unit value	Jan	Feb	Mar	Apr	May	Jun	Jul	Aug	Sept	Oct	Nov	Dec	Total
Product 1	20	100	175	250	300	350	400	425	325	475	500	550	700	4550
Product 2	5	200	350	500	600	700	800	850	650	950	1000	1100	1400	9100
Product 3	2.5	400	500	600	600	800	1000	1100	700	1200	1200	1400	1600	11100
Product 4	1		500	1000	1500	1500	1500	1500	1500	1750	2000	2000	3000	17750
Total forecast		700	1525	2350	3000	3350	3700	3875	3175	4375	4700	5050	6700	42500

Equivalent sales forecast by value for each product

Item	Jan	Feb	Mar	Apr	May	Jun	Jul	Aug	Sept	Oct	Nov	Dec	Total
Product 1	2000	3500	5000	6000	7000	8000	8500	6500	9500	10000	11000	14000	91000
Product 2	1000	1750	2500	3000	3500	4000	4250	3250	4750	5000	5500	7000	45500
Product 3	1000	1250	1500	1500	2000	2500	2750	1750	3000	3000	3500	4000	27750
Product 4		500	1000	1500	1500	1500	1500	1500	1750	2000	2000	3000	17750
Total forecast	4000	7000	10000	12000	14000	16000	17000	13000	19000	20000	22000	28000	182000

Fig. 5 Typical shop sales forecast.

Sales forecast by numbers of units for each product

Item	Unit value	Jan	Feb	Mar	Apr	May	Jun	Jul	Aug	Sept	Oct	Nov	Dec	Total
Product 1	2000	1	2	3	3	4	5	5	4	4	4	5	5	45
Product 2	200		9	113	20	23	25	26	21	24	25	27	35	248
Product 3	100	10	10	10	10	10	10	10	10	10	10	10	10	120
Product 4	20		112	137	100	150	225	225	135	85	150	150	110	1579
Total forecast		11	133	163	133	187	265	266	170	123	189	192	160	1992

Equivalent sales forecast by by value for each product

Item	Jan	Feb	Mar	Apr	May	Jun	Jul	Aug	Sept	Oct	Nov	Dec	Total
Product 1	1000	5000	6250	7000	8500	10500	10750	8000	7500	9000	9500	10250	93250
Product 2		1750	2500	4000	4500	5000	5250	4250	4750	5000	5500	7000	49500
Product 3	1000	1000	1000	1000	1000	1000	1000	1000	1000	1000	1000	1000	12000
Product 4		2250	2750	2000	3000	4500	4500	2750	1750	3000	3000	2250	31750
Total forecast	2000	10000	12500	14000	17000	21000	21500	16000	15000	18000	19000	20500	186500

Fig. 6   Typical manufacturing sales forecast.

values of sales: this is because the *unit* value does not always hold up precisely in practice. There can be specific orders targeted that don't automatically correlate with neat unit values. So think of the notional unit sales having been *derived* from the values (that is, calculated in reverse order) and then rounded rather than fractionalized. The important bottom right-hand value figure is valid, and still prevails for forecasting purposes.

EXERCISE

Produce a sales forecast, by quantity and value, for each month.

EXERCISE

What annual turnover value do you put on *your* business? As a top-level indication only, how does this align with the crude calculations indicated in Chapter 4, allowing for realistic approximate profit levels?

RATIFICATION OF THE SALES FORECAST

The sales forecast must be produced as realistically as you possibly can, since the entire prospects for the future of your venture are critically dependent on it. Nevertheless, it is only an estimate, because it is fundamentally only inspired crystal-ball gazing.

If, in panic, you say that *there might not be any sales* and that the forecast is unreal, there can of course be no venture either! Fortunately, this pessimistic view is not realistic if the research groundwork, and subsequent marketing and pre-sales work have been rigorously and carefully undertaken. There *will* be sales!

The figures should also be analysed, again and again. They should be compared with those derived from all your other research findings carried out in the *concept* stage; and gross figures for this country and the entire global marketplace, in the chosen field. Useful comparisons can be obtained in confidential discussions with your accountant, trade contacts, exhibitors and the like; or from published statistics, publications, journals, magazines, books or whatever. Write down these findings whilst they are fresh in your mind, crosschecking them, *keeping them as up-to-date as possible*, and monitoring any special trends.

All information gleaned should be amalgamated with specific local knowledge to estimate your share of that total market, allowing for competitor's bites of course. The more the figures are analysed and checked against any available sources (and adjusted if necessary), the more confidence you (and ultimately your advisors) will have.

They should be further refined in the *detailed planning stage* – sometime later. Once the business has completed its first year, you will have established a track record. The first year *actual* sales figures (omitting any special one-off sales) form a good starting point for the second year's *forecast* – and so on.

Part of the process is to make a rough forecast of the sales volume for the subsequent year, and also for shorter periods as well sometimes. So that's why it's such an important part of the spadework to estimate the potential business prospects.

Having produced the best possible annual sales forecast, and probably planned certain expenditures against its achievement, the business must endeavour to meet and exceed its sales forecast.

To endeavour to meet the annual sales forecast (which may appear very formidable with hindsight and especially at the beginning of the year), break down the seemingly enormous task again into much smaller weekly or daily elements – practical expectations and mini-targets – by identifying specific product groups or categories. Assign mini-targets to individuals, and the final goal will seem easier to control and thus achieve.

MARKETING PLAN

Finally, you should consider your business, its desired image and objectives; and then draw up a so-called marketing plan ready for implementation. It should take account of all the factors mentioned in these last two chapters in particular, including overall marketing strategy, marketing messages, advertising media, detailed ways of making it happen, responsibilities, pricing policy, export policy if applicable, what is expected to be achieved, and so on. It needs an appropriate budget to reflect the potential business turnover and the financial, personnel, time and other resources available.

EXERCISE

Draw up your own marketing strategy and plan.

WHAT HAVE YOU LEARNT IN THIS CHAPTER?

★ Differentiate between costs and selling prices?
★ How, in principle, are selling prices determined?
★ What factors should be taken into account when estimating product costs?
★ What is the predominant single factor that influences selling prices?
★ List some of the main underlying considerations that influence selling prices?
★ How is cost related to price?
★ What is market research for? What should you do with the data?
★ Why should you produce a sales forecast?
★ How do you go about it to give you the maximum confidence?
★ How and why do you ratify a sales forecast?
★ If the forecast shows a desperately low annual figure, what should you do next?

11
Finding Customers –
Getting Sales

The previous two chapters presented *seed-sowing* or marketing techniques, laying the foundations for getting sales (and hence revenue) for your business. The next two will help make the forecast become a reality and to *reap* a good harvest! Chapter 11 helps to identify customers; it explains how to seek them out, how to deal with them and how your attitude will influence the outcome.

The word *customer* is used for generic convenience, but it really refers to someone who *might be about to buy* or who *has bought*. During the earlier stages of having a look round, preliminary discussions, and so on, the terms *prospective customer* or *prospect* are nearer the true definitions. Nevertheless, for simplicity the word *customer* will be stretched to include people in the early stages of the process as well: so be aware of the difference and don't ever presume a true customer or sale prematurely. Just because a prospect has entered the premises, you can't assume he or she is going to be a customer, as such. Don't count your chickens ... !

All businesses can help themselves by being proactive in seeking customers – merely by advertising, responding promptly to all enquiries, and also by adopting certain techniques to identify and nurture customers who might not otherwise be introduced to the venture.

ATTRACTING CUSTOMERS

Customer Groupings
Eleven categories of customers are identified.

Previous Contacts
You may have relinquished an employed situation to set up the business, in a similar line. A huge implicit database of names in the form of clients, previous customers, satisfied customers and other contacts (for previously mentioned contractual reasons, preferably remembered and not written down) will come in extremely useful, as will business and personal networks, card index names and general trade lists. This very long 'list' represents a whole raft of potential customers: one by one, they must be contacted. The contacts and/or their bosses (hopefully *decision-makers*) should be told personally about the new business, how it came about, and sent leaflets, brochures and samples. This is a rich source of customers.

- Send them an invitation to the launch of the business whenever it takes place, and make it worth their while with suitable refreshments, possibly some good entertainment and a famous personality from the particular trade, or even show business (if appropriate to the business and its image).
- Get an appointment with each one individually to tell them more about the venture *personally* (either just before or soon after launch). Tell them what the business can probably do for them, get them interested and excited. Obviously be positive but don't *outwardly presume* that your business knows exactly how it can help them.
- Talk constructively about something your business could really get its teeth into – however far off, embryonic and remote their project is at the moment. Show samples.
- Find out (from them directly, the grapevine, their brochures or whatever) how your venture might be able to help them. Do not, under any circumstances, actually tell them before you have had their problem explained to you. Just be patient and diplomatic before jumping in with both feet: you might put them off for good.
- Get them *to your new premises* to have a look round (if helpful and appropriate, and obviously if there's something relevant and *worthwhile from their point of view* to see).
- Get them to really *want* to do business with you. In a face-to-face meeting tell them all the *whys* and *wherefores*; and above all, explain *how* your new venture could help them, if only they would allow an opportunity for the project to be mutually explored.

Acquire or Purchase a Database of Customers

It is possible to acquire part or all of someone else's entire business (if it proves to be worthwhile for you at the agreed price), complete with its existing customer base. These previous customers will almost certainly want accessories for, an upgrade to or a replacement of, their present purchases. Think of buying a list of customers from a car dealer or computer provider. Thus it is possible to *buy* an entire business or effectively a customer list in one swoop.

It is also possible to take over and continue with another business' contacts – its after-sales service list (for example, washing machines, televisions, cars or central heating systems), not just the list of potential sales prospects. This will effectively constitute a list of longer-term potential customers.

Business mergers and inter-business agreements to service a particular market also produce lists that represent prospective customers (like those providing warranty service only, on behalf of national retail chains, like Currys and Dixons).

Sometimes copies of customer lists, relating to previous sales of non-related products, are sold and bought for profit. It is also possible to purchase customer lists from organizations set up explicitly to compile such databases extracted from questionnaires distributed to customers. Think of all the unsolicited mail or phone calls you get at home and business, and of 'customer survey' phone calls.

Cold Calling

Get into cold calling on other businesses, if yours is likely to be totally unfamiliar to them (it probably will be initially, if not later on as well). Use foot-slogging, although this method is hard work and somewhat unrewarding (depending on the business); *you must get to talk to the decision-maker – or else it's a waste of time and effort.* It can certainly be useful for instant decision type of transactions like house-to-house calling. As mentioned before, it is also illegal under certain circumstances. A low hit rate is the norm, so be prepared, thick skinned and forewarned. It really isn't for the faint-hearted.

Use controlled, reliable and up-to-date lists for advertising and cold calling through telesales, e-mail, phone, fax and web sites. Fax machines are available that will automatically dial a series of pre-stored fax numbers sequentially, and consequently send a regularly produced news-sheet to a large number of targeted customers. But be aware of the legal constraints.

Third Party Selling

A frequently encountered way to get business (depending on what the business is) is to appoint commission-only agents, other freelancers, dealers, distributors. These ways to promote the business are generally known as third party selling arrangements and save considerably on the direct sales costs.

They will need proper contractual arrangements to protect you and them – another area for the professional; and they will need *good training* in your *entire range* of products and competencies. The dangers that might adversely affect your business, in this modus operandi, are that the persons concerned:

- are insufficiently rewarded
- might be insufficiently trained by you
- might not be sufficiently aware of your venture's capabilities
- might carry *competitors'* catalogues
- might change their allegiance in the future.

Agents, wholesalers, dealers and distributors can be selected and appointed through trade advertisements, exhibitions, newspapers and recommendations from other businesses; they advertise their availability and range of contacts through these media. Often they operate on commission-only agreements and can sell your products (at relatively little extra cost to them) to their established customers that have been created from related or completely unrelated lines.

Turnkey Arrangements

Another way of doing business is through *turnkey* operators, in which a group of usually related products (but not necessarily so) are sold by so-called turnkey or linked arrangements. Typically these might include land acquisition linked to the client's own design of dwelling and then coupled to house-building deals, and even to finance, furnishers and removal firms – one purchase contact is dependent on the previous, piggybacking right back to the root. They are not popular with customers because it limits their choice, and the deals have bordered on restrictive practices in the past.

Networking
See Chapter 9 for details of how this should operate. It's very valuable in all sorts of situations.

Your Own Publicity and Personal Availability
On the principle that nobody has such a vested interest in your business, and therefore will not enthuse about it more than you, you should:

- Be seen.
- Be around when anyone needs you.
- Find out prospects' possible needs, problems, wants.
- Promise and supply help (personally or from the business) when they need it.
- Train yourself to recall all the relevant personal or business details about each contact: it shows lasting interest in them and their situation.
- Categorize all contacts into different timescales and priorities.
- Contact them regularly: do not neglect them – as relevant to their situation.
- Don't make a nuisance of yourself.
- Don't attract any notoriety.
- Invest evening and free time.
- Publicize your business' differentiators.
- Give talks to local societies: be prepared to talk publicly about the venture: you never know who's listening!

A good way to get publicity for yourself and your business, mentioned earlier, is to take space at:

- exhibitions
- craft fairs
- school parent evenings
- seminars
- local events

Government Tenders
Depending on the nature of the business:

- Get your business' name and interests on local/central government tenderers' lists.
- Seek out and respond to tenders in the field of your expertise.
- Propose unsolicited tender responses.

This is valuable, but competitive, business (needing careful screening) with complex tender documents to read and respond *to* and *with*! It is exceptionally time-consuming, but worthwhile if successful.

Job Advertisements
Respond to job adverts, offering an *immediate* solution to a client's publicly declared needs (even if it only *starts off* as a quick temporary measure, whilst their recruitment and interviews supposedly take place).

Internet and E-Commerce
Modern businesses should seriously consider the e-commerce option for advertising and getting sales either as a substitute for all or some of the above methods, or as a supplementary process. *See* Chapter 16.

Previous Customers
Many customers, once hooked and satisfied, will return. As sales begin to build, they can become reference sales for getting further business. But only quote genuine reference accounts that represent well-satisfied customers and prestigious sales, *and with their permission if appropriate.*

Often, satisfied customers are very pleased to tell other people about their choice of product, service or supplier, if it's not overdone. It confirms their good taste! The easiest way by far to acquire a customer base, as it were, is to keep the one that has been built up already. Keeping existing and satisfied customers, rather than losing customers that have to be perpetually replaced, has to be the best policy!

EXERCISE

Draw up a provisional list of your customers – at least in groups, if not individually.

EXERCISE

Draw up a detailed action plan to contact known networking contacts.

Conclusion
The broad principles of handling all customers is essentially the same; but the mechanical details will be far from identical. Customers can be categorized into those who:

- Predominantly have an appointment arrangement (loosely referred to in this book as a *non-shop* situation).
- Are virtually free to walk in (like a *shop*). This concept of customer accessibility to the business is fundamental to the way business is obtained and the venture thrives.

Non-Shop Customers

Firstly, if your proposed business is not of the open-shop style, it is more than possible that your OUT is just the desperate IN someone else has been searching for – think back to an earlier chapter and think positively.

Shop Customers

Secondly, on the other hand, if the business is a shop, store, showroom, garage, guest-house, hotel, restaurant or pub, and some open-attitude manufacturing businesses, amongst others, it is deemed to be a *shop-style* operation in the practical sense that customers take the initiative and are entirely free to approach the business, merely entering the premises via open, or at least unlocked, doors.

This type of business still has crucial work to do in order to grow and maintain its position. It will take all the techniques and observations mentioned in this and the next chapter to turn the visits into real business opportunities; but there should really be no problem attracting and keeping customers, although slightly different techniques need to be applied from those applicable to non-shop situations. However:

- An ability to successfully advertise the presence and capabilities of the business somehow is assumed.
- A choice of a good site (with parking) that is basically accessible to most people in the chosen catchment area is assumed, and where there should be some passing trade.
- The customers, once inside the business premises, like what they see, are assumed to be dealt with courteously and helpfully, and then make their purchases. They will return for more, spreading the word for your business in the meantime.

In other words, provided the owners do their bit responsibly in response to those customers who *do* find their way there, no difficulties should arise.

DEALING WITH CUSTOMERS

Identifying and getting customers to the premises is essential, but only one part of the process. The mechanics of actually dealing with them once they've arrived is another. It is beneficial still to consider them in the order of non-shop and then shop customers, as will become clear later.

Non-Shop Customers

Your customers do not generally arrive unannounced. You know they are coming, and have cleared diary and physical space, if necessary, to accommodate them. You will have told reception (if applicable) so that that person can do the proper welcoming thing and be a good host or hostess. This particular topic is covered toward the end of the next chapter – it's all part of the image-building!

Here is a detailed ten-step broad agenda that should be roughly the same for any non-shop customer, although it should be adapted to suit the specific situation. Above all, it should feel natural and unpressured. The process of establishing the customer's needs should be discreetly objective and not appear as a tireless inquisition!

Preparing Very Thoroughly
As with any other meeting:

• prepare thoroughly
• sort out the meeting objectives
• decide what it is hoped will be achieved, *before* it begins
• resolve not to talk about money matters until things get 'hot', otherwise they can be brought up too early, and before the entire project or whatever can be properly assimilated
• know the services, products and capabilities of the venture thoroughly – and where they might fit in and satisfy the customer's needs
• be patient, keep wide awake and alert.

Setting the Scene
The golden rule is that the customer always needs to be treated courteously and acknowledged, in *any* selling situation! He or she then need to be respectfully and *sincerely* greeted, and relaxed. You must do your best in this direction even if the circumstances are far from perfect. Don't keep the customer waiting! Some businesses offer a seat, light refreshments and smalltalk to break the ice.

Incidentally, the true story is told of a narrow-minded cost-conscious multimillion pound international company with a turnover of over £200 million who discovered that £6,000 a year was spent in total on light refreshments and that by not serving tea, coffee, or biscuits this sum could be added to the profits. As a result, customers felt shunned, and sales started to drop by well over this amount of course; secretaries went out covertly and bought from petty cash the various ingredients (but the effective cost in lost time, travel to the shops, preplanning *and* the refreshments was far in excess of the £6,000) although the sales began to rise again. Mistakenly, the finance people did the same thing on sales staff travel and taxi fares, ignoring staff goodwill and the greater picture once again! Don't get caught yourself.

If the customer wants to see the boss, a particular individual (or an acceptable substitute) and he or she is not available, not much buying and selling is likely to occur; therefore there must always be someone available to see and *make time* for customers. There is nobody, in the business context, more important than a customer: therefore no job more pressing than trying to make a sale, however imperative or urgent other jobs might seem to be!

Again it varies according to the business, the personalities and the surroundings, but the principles are nevertheless valid and serve as a guide.

- Know *precisely* who you are dealing with: always find out who the customer is *exactly*.
- Always help the customer by thinking ahead through to the customer's customer and possibly beyond – think back to the chained or sequenced INs and OUTs of a business in Chapter 6.
- There might be a far better alternative solution if the matter were considered as an entity right through to the ultimate user (end-to-end as it were, without an artificial intermediate point) that could save all parties time, money and delivery problems.
- Meet the customer's expectations: try to exceed them – that's what gets business.

Building Mutual Confidence
Having got the customer in a communicative frame of mind ...

- Find a location where each has the undivided attention of the other – no interruptions from other people or phones – including mobile phones and pagers!
- Go through the personal introductions (names, positions, areas of responsibility and exchange business cards).
- Establish whether there are any constraints, like time pressures, and so on.
- 'Sell' the *personalities* (the business representatives) as likable, friendly and professional businesslike people. Use some credibility and confidence-building stories, at the earliest stage of the introductions.
- Then 'sell' *the business*, and its broad range of products generally.
- Then 'sell' any *particular products* (covering much the same approach as the advertising and other publicity as far as the broad message is concerned), using similar confidence-building examples of what the business has to offer.
- Make absolutely certain that everything mentioned can be substantiated and delivered where it relates to the future 'promises'.

The real point of the introduction is that *personal* credibility and other supporting qualities have to be firmly in place, in the mind of the customer, as non-negotiable prerequisites for spelling out the capabilities, competencies and credentials of the *business*.

The aim is to give the customer sufficient trust and confidence for him or her to impart details of their project quite freely – which could of course be highly confidential. A mutual feeling of trust has to be created before going any further – and it must not be undermined during the remaining stages of discussion and negotiation! Make the customer feel great and important; but equally stay in control of the meeting.

Eliminating Time Wasters
You must establish fairly early on in the meeting (but very discreetly, of course) how sincere and serious the customer is about the project under discussion, because (bluntly) your business cannot afford to waste time and money on non-starters. This may sound harsh and unnecessary (but it often happens). Check

whether the customer or client is convinced that the project *needs* to be under-taken, or whether it is just an idle time-wasting exercise!

- Is the customer really serious about it?
- Has the customer already spent any other time, effort and money on the project?
- Why is it needed – to fulfil one of *their* orders maybe?
- Does he or she have the capability, perhaps, to do it in-house anyway?
- Are they merely seeking some technical know-how, getting a benchmark costing or competitive quotes, or other ulterior motive like competitor espionage?
- Is the project backed by other more senior customer staff (if any), a budget and the means to pay eventually?
- Equally as importantly, you must establish whether or not the customer really believes your business has the capability to handle the project.

If the customer does not appear to be very serious, use diplomacy to bring the meeting to an end, keeping the door open for possible future enquiries. Remain on good terms by saying something like, *Thank you for telling us a little about your project, but I don't think it's quite our territory.*

Asking Pertinent Questions

Questions serve to determine the real underlying reasoning, thinking and pur-poses: to understand the maximum about the customer, project context and project. Customer questioning must not be forced, but must flow naturally. Questions should be well-focused, well-thought-out and *open* to encourage longer meaningful answers, rather than *closed* ones that only invite a blunt *yes* or *no*. In practice both types will be used.

Open questions are framed to begin with a word (or phrase) that investigates, like:

- How ...?
- Why ...?
- Who ...?
- When ...?

- Where ...?
- Which ...?
- What ...?
- What if ...?

Finding Out the Problem

Use these discreet questioning techniques and other conversational methods to:

- Get the customer talking about his or her want, need, project, problem require-ments.
- Get them to reconfirm their sincerity and budget.
- Get the customer to explain any specific background, such that the business can get to work on it meaningfully and constructively.
- Exchange information.

Employ any documents, sketches, drawings, scale models and brochures from both sides that might be helpful, and also 'white boards', flip charts or notepads – depending on the subject matter and context. Even video conferencing might be appropriate.

Listening, or more accurately really, very careful and constructive listening, is the paramount requirement. Sometimes in complex situations a team of two or three people is appropriate, each taking a particular interest in his or her own field, but listening (and being able to recall later) as part of a team to get the correct interpretation and nuance.

This technique shows understanding, technical competence, careful consideration, thought, confidence and professionalism – boosting customer confidence.

- Translate the received messages into your own business' way of working, specifically identifying with, and solving, the customer's problem.
- Always steer the customer in the direction of your venture and its capabilities, asking more questions if necessary with the aim of getting complete satisfaction and agreement.

Your meeting should remain as relaxed and natural as possible, to extract the greatest understanding of the project (together with any constraints) and to explore ideas and suggestions drawn from the whole of your accumulated knowledge and experience. Its purpose is to exchange information and examine possible solutions, acceptable to both parties: from the customer's point of view, the eventual solution must build on and enhance, the customer's reputation as well as his or her original scheme (to bring it to life, if applicable).

Reinforcing Your Understanding and Constructing a Tentative Solution In Your Mind

- Always prepare the story thoroughly (rehearsing it and playing 'devil's advocate' with colleagues in private beforehand).
- It must be customized to the recipient, even if it isn't really novel and has been broadly used many times before.
- It must sound honest, plausible, fresh and unique.
- Anticipate, prepare and ask pertinent and probing questions (building on the paragraphs, above).
- Try different angles of discussion and questioning to ensure consistency of the customer's story and the clear understanding of the listeners.
- Double-check material points with different questions that are really asking the same thing.

Endeavour to lead the customer (gently in the business' direction, of course), so that there can only be one possible conclusion; but let the customer think he or she has made the choice – and that's very important. It's all about giving the customer the satisfaction that it's his or her choice, whereas in reality it's from both parties, especially the business owner(s).

- When you thoroughly understand the problem, think about and prepare your costings carefully to agree a selling price, taking into account the sentiments expressed in Chapter 10. Take sufficient time and, if necessary, get back to the customer later.
- Always discuss and give estimates and quotations, if applicable.
- Show the customer *how* the real underlying problem will be solved to impart confidence. Further discussion may be needed to achieve common ground until enough of the important points are met, if they cannot all be met first time round.
- Demonstrate that the business has a viable solution that meets every, or at least most of, the important needs. Be realistic and consider whether you are expected to struggle to meet the rest of his or her points, where the customer requirements present a *genuine problem* to you.
- Offer excellent demonstrations *on the customer's premises*, if appropriate.

Explaining Fully the Features, Benefits and Implications

- As each product or service feature is brought out, point out the benefit that it brings: but even more important show the customer *why* this feature and benefit are valuable, and what it will actually mean for him or her.
- Clearly deal with one point or feature at a time and make sure the consequential *what this means for the customer* is well driven home, appreciated and accepted!
- The feature, benefit, and so on, has to be important in the *context of the customer* and his or her proposed purchase: if it isn't, don't mention it; or if it is likely to be counter-productive, certainly don't mention it!
- It is so important to really understand the detailed points of the customer's project, especially the aspects that are of great concern – often referred to as the *customer's hot buttons*. The more that can be matched and answered constructively (*with acknowledged features and benefits*), the more the customer will warm towards doing business with you.
- Ask if all requirements have been met, or even exceeded. Go through part or all of the process again if they haven't.
- The aim is to get as many brownie points for your business as possible, because each one gets a subconscious tick of whatever magnitude in the eyes of the customer and subsequently attracts a positive value in relation to the price and gradually begins to win the customer over.

Giving Customers More Confidence

- Make a point of showing them the business, small factory, design studio or whatever to impart confidence that the business can be trusted to handle their work; tell them about relevant contracts to give extra confidence. In any case, even if this particular enquiry leads to nothing, it's all good publicity that may help this customer or another (to whom this one talks), in the future.

• Show them the latest designs and models, perhaps future ideas, and ask for *and listen* to their views.

This is the subtle application of market research and, at the same time, elevates the customers by choosing them (so they believe) specifically to solicit their views.

Concluding the Business Meeting

Your business has to carry out the work to the customer's wishes and instructions; and must feel both competent and comfortable with the work, and the eventual physical acceptance. The reputation of both parties must be boosted in their respective fields.

It is very important to explain carefully to customers *how* your business responds to their problem, and the benefits of dealing with your business. It will give added confidence.

Having reached a mutually acceptable deal, comment on the fact (if it doesn't happen naturally) that *that seems to be all agreed* or words to that effect. Then explicitly ask for an order *at the right time* to close the deal; and timing is very important – not prematurely.

Confirm it all in a written format, in keeping with the value and complexity of the deal. The exact nature of the business and the way the venture is set up will, with the aid of the professional advisors (at the right point in the detailed planning), establish the best format for the written confirmation – whether it is a formal contract, Letter of Intent, or merely only a carbon copied handwritten page from a commercially available duplicate book.

Whatever arrangement is concluded, it should bring some immediate money and potential profit into the business, and (with a well-satisfied customer) the possibility of repeat business or an ongoing contract.

If closing a deal proves elusive, several different closing techniques are mentioned towards the end of the next chapter.

Having obtained the order, it is always courteous to express sincere thanks, with the promise (to be meticulously honoured of course) that it will be initiated straightaway, will give a good solution (or whatever), will be delivered on time, and will undoubtedly give pleasure for a long time in the future – or similar appropriate sentiments. It is obviously prudent to choose the right words for the specific situation so as to be genuine.

Don't forget to promise *and give* excellent after-sales service, if and where relevant.

When all has been agreed and the parties are even more relaxed (possibly over a drink or a meal) *don't* go over the ground again – and don't let anyone else, either – because the customer might start to rethink and have doubts about his decision. They may be completely ill-founded doubts, but you will have to take time to more or less start all over again!

Shop Customers

Compare this *three* point notional agenda for shop customers with the non-shop customer handling routine – which is why the non-shop customers were considered first. Essentially the general scheme is the same because the same understanding has to be reached by a similar process. It has of necessity been shortened, because time may inevitably be severely against a shopkeeper and his/her staff, and it would be too clumsy in any case.

Establishing the Same Courteous Contact

A shop's customers usually arrive unannounced, although some phone first.

* The first challenge is to decide whether he or she is a prospective customer, and not another type of visitor, a competitor 'spy' or sales representative from another company.
* The second is to make an *instant assessment* of the genuine customer as regards how they expect to be received and treated. Don't be put off guard by superficial appearances. It could well be some top executive in a major company, dressed in casual or scruffy clothing whilst out shopping! Equally, it could be a little old lady, who happens to want to spend several hundred pounds, right now!
* Greet them appropriately, recalling and recognizing them if you know them.

Obviously, it is not normally appropriate to sit them down and give them refreshments, subsequently show them into a meeting room – although such things do happen in certain types of shops or showrooms. Set your own stall out as seems most appropriate.

In a shop situation, the earlier-mentioned initial pleasantries would be unnecessarily over-the-top, embarrassing and impractical. Nevertheless, you should strive to isolate the customer as best you can, and give undivided attention, whilst still leaving the shop manned (which can be very difficult at times, without enough high-calibre staff).

Establishing How Much Time the Customer Has

* All customers, especially shop customers might be short of time and/or might need to make decisions with their partners and spouses – so assess this matter on its merits and adjust the selling occasion to suit.
* It could be that there isn't enough time for the customer to become sufficiently informed about the venture and its products, – or maybe there's some other unsatisfactory situation.
* Be pragmatic and, where absolutely necessary (that is, there really appears to be no other alternative compromise), suggest and fix another more convenient meeting, although there is a risk of losing the sale altogether.
* Filter out, carefully, the time wasters or those sheltering from the weather.

Helping the Customer Explain and Decide What He Or She Is Looking For
Fundamentally, the staff in contact with the customer have a major responsibility to adopt the right attitudes, dress carefully and behave professionally. They should use all skills (and they will usually improve with practice) and diplomacy at their disposal to help understand the customer's needs and problems. Remember the customer may be far from clear and explicit in his or her mind, so much probing will be needed – probing without in any way harassing or upsetting the customer of course. Be genuinely helpful and positive.

- Always approach from the front (never from behind), to eliminate the awkward embarrassing surprise element.
- Go through broadly the same routine and questioning process very gently and subtly as with a non-shop business (scaled and adjusted to suit the occasion and situation), covering some limited form of introduction.
- Find out what the customer thinks he or she wants or needs, or what seemingly unconnected problem is being tackled, and so on.
- Obtain a fairly precise understanding of what to offer the customer.
- Be professional, business-like and sincere.
- Lead the questioning carefully and naturally towards just one logical conclusion in favour of your venture.
- Suggest and steer the customer towards something that fits in with the business, that is, something in stock if possible.
- As soon as the moment seems right, propose something.
- Take the product off the shelf (metaphorically or actually). Let him or her handle it, or try it out – that way the customer will stand the best chance of *convincing themselves* that that is what they want or 'need'.
- Create a chance for the customer to appreciate the relevant features and benefits *applicable to his or her situation* (first-hand and in their own time).
- Do encourage the customer to get a hands-on feel for the product to convince him- or herself about the features, benefits and *ultimately what the product, service or project solution will do for him or her*, their image, reputation, and so on.
- Give a convincing but simple demonstration. The important point to watch is that the salesperson does not upstage the customer by a brilliant performance on the 'product' – otherwise the customer will be turned off fast; because he or she will know or think that they cannot do the same!
- Always give customers confidence and beat their expectations.
- Close the sale as soon as possible by *leading* the customer to the till and dealing with it personally – *but* at the right time (not prematurely, because you may not get a second chance).
- The post-decision steps might be a contract, or Letter of Intent, but more likely actual payments (cash, cheque, credit card, debit card, credit terms, and so on – *see* Chapter 13). Make sure you are familiar with till routines and your lack of knowledge doesn't expose you. 'Delivery' (wrapping and/or just handing over the goods) will usually happen simultaneously, of course.
- Be appreciative of the customer's business.

There may be several options to bring to their attention, but it is best if they are constrained to one, two or possibly three, at the most. Too many and they *will have to think about it* and go away. The sale will also have disappeared! More about this under *closing techniques* in the next chapter.

You are reminded of the hardware shop customer in Chapter 3. In the first scenario, no questioning took place; whereas in the second, the sales assistant diplomatically searched every avenue until the complete background was understood: then, and only then, did she interpret the customer's real needs and achieved a win-win situation.

YOUR OWN SERVICE EXPECTATIONS

Recollect what is regarded as best practice in your particular business field. Compare modern shopping experiences with these levels of service: and you will discover huge deficiencies that cause frustration and irritation! In the majority of present-day cases, standards of service generally are falling in the familiar, yet oft frequented, shops, stores and out-of-town shopping complexes, which in turn causes a dramatic loss of sales.

So formulate a business strategy embodying your ideals: deliberately throw out all the bad ideas. The stark and sad reality is that you don't have to 'improve' much on the customer treatment standards of today's retailing scene (and some other businesses as well), to make a dramatic step forward. Any small improvement should start the business off in the right direction, although several simultaneous steps should be taken to have the maximum benefit. Visualize new and fresh concepts that might give a novel and appealing twist. Then establish *your* standard of service: it cannot help but provide a better service.

Give the customer freedom and time to weigh the matter up with a spouse, partner, friend or colleague:

- Give them 'space', but be there to hold their hand when they need it again.
- Offer a seat, peace and quiet, light refreshment if it helps – and it probably will.
- You must remain in control by continuously observing the situation *discreetly* so that you can act or be available when the customer expressly asks or shows it with body language.
- Your critical judgement is to be available and on hand, without being obtrusive.
- Don't pester or 'pounce' on the customer.

MISCELLANEOUS POINTS

- Be ready to spot your own business' shortcomings – before the customers do!
- Show a positive friendly attitude above all else.
- The starting point for adopting good selling attitudes – whether a *shop* or *non-shop* environment, or in *any* other selling situation for that matter – is to put yourself (amongst other things) into the right mental attitude for meeting and influencing a customer or whoever. This must happen even at obscure times of

the day and evening, early in the morning, even on off-days, when there are problems at home, and on occasions when someone or something else has caused annoyance.

- Practice working out quickly who people are – without asking leading questions. Be courteous, sincere, polite and obviously customer-friendly. Smile, approach and greet the customer (and any work colleagues, family and friends), opening and closing any doors for customers as you go about this pleasurable *duty*.

- Everything relevant to the business has to be taught to, and practised as second nature by, all the staff in the venture. Ensure that they maintain the customer-visible stock and premises in clean, well-dusted, working and tip-top condition.

- The staff must be thoroughly familiar with the products and know how to use and demonstrate them. The true story was experienced of a shop assistant in a well-known High Street name, selling watches and other high technology products, who could not show the customer how to adjust the watch hands – is there anything more basic in this scenario?

- The yardstick is simply what standards you and the customers expect, because these should be the absolute minimum standards that you should *strive to beat* each time.

- Every time a personal knowledge gap is uncovered (and it *will* be occasionally), get it sorted out immediately, so that it can never happen again. If you get to a point where answers to customers' questions are not known, be honest and admit it (don't fudge or flannel, because it will be spotted, tarnishing your reputation); and then off-line, establish the answer, remember it for another occasion when it crops up and if appropriate relay the answer to the customer.

- It's worth repeating the crucial maxim to treat all customers carefully, respectfully and sincerely because they ultimately pay the wages. Don't under any circumstances deliberately or otherwise provoke or upset them: but if this does happen, apologize immediately and try to retrieve the situation.

- If they leave your premises happy, believing they have got a good deal or a 'bargain', they'll come back again, and again; and recommend you to other prospective customers.

- Be courteous towards all *groups* of customers, their relatives, friends, colleagues and staff (not just the present 'leader'): because, apart from influencing things right now, they might be promoted to be the next decision makers in years to come! They'll remember the good service, honesty, trustworthiness, and so on – and come back to you.

- You should be able to create equivalent impressions for running a restaurant, pub, guest-house or hotel, or whatever business you are thinking of, without any difficulty. The broad principles are the same, although the details will vary. Try not to behave as a Basil Fawlty.

- During the outline planning and concept stages of your chosen venture, compulsory but discreet visits and investigations of other such businesses should be arranged – compare notes to check out the operation from a customer's point of view. This can only be done before the venture starts, like any 'spying' – or else you may be recognized!

Summary

Whether a formal or informal meeting, or a best possible shop floor meeting with the customer, give him or her, and the matter in hand, the fullest attention.

- Adopt the right mental attitude – right from the outset.
- Always behave impeccably, and in a business-like and organized manner.
- Be punctual, especially if the meeting is on the customer's premises.
- Be alert, shrewd, enthusiastic, positive, tenacious and determined (but not aggressively or so that it is noticeable, but subtly and diplomatically).
- Maintain natural eye-contact; don't look down (to try and hide as it were) but equally don't stare either.
- Present a warm personality, but don't overdo it.
- *Always* talk to, and *listen* very carefully to, customers.
- Listen carefully and constructively with an approximate ratio of 60 per cent listening to 40 per cent talking, taking in everything that's offered.
- Get as quickly as possible to the precise reason for their visit.
- Double-check statements using interesting interrogation techniques, employing open questions.
- It's important to understand precisely what customers are saying and equally important to appreciate what they are *omitting* to say. Are they withholding something? Why?
- Read between their lines as to what they really might be thinking about your business.
- Always be willing to oblige, but stay firmly in control of the situation.
- Demonstrate your own and your business' technical competence.
- Back up the discussions with clean samples, new leaflets, polished and dust-free stock, as appropriate.
- Use the occasion to find out any trade or competitive snippets; and for market research.
- This could be the first of many such meetings down the ages.

Customers Make Your Business

Remember five crucial things:

1. Mutual respect, image and professionalism are the essence of the relation-building.

2. Your business is on the line.
3. Your business reputation is on the line.
4. Your personal reputation is on the line.
5. *It's your remuneration, family and lifestyle* that are on the line – and your investments!

EXERCISE

How would you go about getting business for your own venture – no generalizations?

EXERCISE

In relation to your own particular venture, document your marketing and sales strategy.

WHAT HAVE YOU LEARNT IN THIS CHAPTER?

★ What are the consequences of not getting business?
★ How do businesses go about getting sales, in practical terms? List the ways of finding customers.
★ Distinguish between attracting customers and dealing with them.
★ How do shop and non-shop style customers differ?
★ What are the common principles in dealing with customers in non-shop and shop situations?
★ List the ten steps for handling non-shop customers, and the three equivalent, but condensed, steps for shop customers.
★ What constitutes the best attitudes for dealing with customers?
★ What are the five crucial points resulting from how you treat customers?

12
Customer Psychology

This last chapter on business development (marketing and sales) covers some basic psychology associated with customers and selling to them so that you will understand to some extent *why* people buy; and how your business, through training and teamwork, can turn this knowledge to its advantage.

Customers, being complex emotional people, need to take seemingly complicated and unwelcome decisions sometimes. Also, they have to be treated carefully, because they are directly responsible for making all businesses thrive or crash; they also very directly pay wages of course!

As customers yourselves on many occasions, you have made very many purchases, for a whole variety of reasons. You may have gained experience of business purchasing. You should think back and add your own experiences to the comments below, and then mix them with the comments so as to best serve your own venture.

In modern convenience stores (supermarkets, and so on), customers help themselves or select goods themselves from catalogues (known as self-service or self-selection); and then pay somehow. Nowhere is any member of staff involved in actually trying to *persuade* a customer to buy (or very rarely anyway). The best service the customer can expect is for some mild advice from an assistant, who has effectively read the catalogue product details before and *may* have had a brief chance to undo the packaging and see (or even experiment with) the product.

However, in the case of the car showroom, for example, the customer is often pestered while a salesperson tries too hard to make a sale – often to the point of being a nuisance and *irritating* the customer.

This chapter reviews where some genuine and constructive *selling* or *persuading* has to take place, before the customer buys – whether a personal customer, a small business, or a business with large buying chains.

Some interesting questions are raised when customers are involved:

- Who *exactly* are the customers, anyway? This may seem obvious, but read on.
- How are they identified and what turns them on?
- What motivates them?
- What makes them want to buy?
- Why from any particular organization?
- How do they make their decisions?

As a result of marketing the business, people hear about it, start to become curious in the new phenomena, and interested in:

- how the business might be able to help them
- what the business can do for them, their family, friends or *their* businesses
- how your business might be able to solve a particular need or problem.

Strictly as customers, they are not in the least bit interested in the well-being of your business – only what it can do for *them*! They have a continuing vested interest if it *continues to help them* as long as they need it, of course.

Although there might be an element of curiosity in your new business, their interest is basically narrow (not quite always), and they are understandably selfish in how their needs, passions, problems, and so on can be helped. Generally they are not interested in giving your business money for its own sake, but in exchanging money for something in return – something which *they* need or want primarily, something that solves a problem for them, first and foremost – but happens to cost them precious money! Hence their hesitation and diffidence sometimes in agreeing or deciding to part with money.

CUSTOMER MOTIVATION

Man or woman has a hierarchy of needs (as proposed by Abraham Maslow in 1954) starting with things like oxygen, water, warmth, shelter, clothing and food and widening to pure luxuries. These needs exhibit levels of 'priority', depending on previous satisfaction of more fundamental needs. There is an essential difference between *wanting* something for its own sake, and really *needing* it to survive, as it were. There is a huge difference in buying motivation between anyone who is really desperate for food and warm clothing (because they are miserably cold and hungry) on the one hand, and the luxury goods purchaser on the other. Maslow segregated them into five groups:

- physiological
- safety
- love
- esteem
- self-actualization.

Some commodities are really essential for supporting life, health and physical security: others only support our lifestyle. The good news for your business is that this statement demonstrates that your business has as good a chance of success as any (as sooner or later we all have inevitable needs to be satisfied), if your business addresses and solves his or her problems, needs or wants, and customers are handled by the business the right way.

If you understand a little about the art and psychology of selling, you (not your competitor) will capture customers, and their spending power. Since everyone has this series of basic wants or needs to be satisfied, the tussle for customers is not *whether* to spend: as often as not it is *which business* to patronize, since the need or want must be satisfied somehow!

You should be really encouraged by these thoughts. Your unequivocal objective is clearly to persuade them to purchase from *you*, as opposed to a competitor's business. That at least should reduce the complexity of your objectives for the task in hand, and get your mind properly prioritized.

This notion gives rise to two further thoughts: the customers' reasons for buying in the first place, and the main decision platforms supporting the primary purchase decision.

BASIC BUYING REASONS

Usually the purpose for the purchase, its value, its size, the complexity of the product, the ease of making the purchase (and also the committee or individual behind the decision) all come into the equation, in varying degrees.

The first distinction to observe is between customers that are buying on behalf of their business (with customers to satisfy themselves) and those that are buying purely for their personal use.

A range of highly emotional and very rational factors drives customers, extending from the spur-of-the-moment decisions (impulse buying, as in the conveniently situated handbag and cosmetics departments in many big stores) to very carefully considered and well-thought-out decision-making processes by managers or teams of decision-making committees.

Business Buying Reasons

Reasons behind business purchases are effectively predetermined. They sort themselves out to a large extent in that businesses have to satisfy *their* customers. Consequently, materials and stock are essential to maintaining their business' existence. These primary drivers quickly and easily determine the choice and location of reliable suppliers, with key terms of business (such as price, availability, quantity, quality and delivery times) being paramount – as they radically affect the profitability, turnover and customers' satisfaction.

These business-driven necessities take away the sense of special occasion that would otherwise be present if it were a personal purchase, of course. Bluntly and simply, it's up to you to persuade these customers that they should come to you instead of a competitor, maybe even their traditional supplier.

Personal Buying Reasons

However, in the case of *individual people*, it is surprisingly sometimes more complex! This is because of our emotions that get in the way of straightforward rational, logical decision-making. Also these customers do not usually have the continuous and incessant pressures that a business generates. An individual's motivation for buying very much depends:

- on the products
- how essential the needs are
- where they fit in the hierarchy
- their mood, time and instantaneous spare money
- their disposable income.

Firstly, momentary pressure and the degree of desperation determine how much these customers really want or need the commodity; and consequently how much they are prepared to pay. Secondly, the initial decision to even *consider* being able to buy will rely on cash or credit availability, or other payment method. Thirdly, in some circumstances their degree of desperation is often influenced by factors like novelty value, new model availability, exclusivity, and so on.

Collectively, and elaborating on buying motivations, some of the reasons behind personal purchases are an amplified catalogue from Maslow's list; but you will recognize the familiar deadly sins buried in them:

• sheer necessity	• gluttony
• fear	• sloth
• jealousy	• pleasure
• anger	• personal image
• shame	• status
• lust	• prestige
• envy	• ownership for ownership's sake
• covetousness	• pride.

Customers Do Not Always Know What They Want

Finding out what customers *really* want or need can be difficult – even impossible! Consider these instances:

- Some customers, whilst generally aware of their needs and problems, can't see or think of a solution – for example, the hardware shop customer in Chapter 3, who had a fundamental interest in putting up a kitchen shelf, but didn't appreciate (or think about) what it entailed precisely.
- Alternatively they are genuinely browsing and looking for ideas – for example, presents for someone.
- Other customers often know what they want: but can't seem to get the right match for their 'specification' – for example, they just know that they want some sort of a roasting joint for Sunday lunch, some fresh fruit or other goods; but can't decide what to buy.
- Often customers know *exactly* what they want – for example, half a kilogram of fresh, unpackaged, washed, English Granny Smith apples.
- Equally, there are also gradations in the thinking and genuine open minds about their purchases when they enter your premises.
- Customers may think they know, but they may not have thought their situation through well enough, they may have come to a wrong conclusion or they might have changed their mind during your gentle interrogation. Also, their minds might be on other matters.

As a business, you have to seek out precisely what the customer is looking for.

This means extracting his or her *customer's specification* (what they are intuitively working to) by tactful interrogation – matters like:

- colour
- size
- quantity
- quality
- weight
- characteristics
- features

- benefits
- why they want it
- what it will do or achieve for them (an ego satisfier, perhaps?)
- price band
- the end user (if not themselves), and so on.

This constructive communication between the customer and your business is clearly important, and conducive to business – otherwise no meeting of minds will ever transpire! Diplomatic questioning, the technique first mentioned in the previous chapter is the vehicle for subtly teasing out the factual and subjective backgrounds to their 'problems'. So some more persistent questioning, talking round the subject subtly and discreetly, or 'nudging' may be necessary, leading to a possible solution – and even to a solution that may not have been considered by the customer previously (and for which the customer might be very grateful in the end).

Questioning may not succeed if the customer is completely uncertain, is deliberately setting out to thwart your actions, or really doesn't know – or if he or she is naïve, shy or silent; or is genuinely looking for ideas. They might not have stable ideas or goalposts.

Which Means That
As you home in on clarifying the customer's thoughts, the essential selling point is to mention, and fully develop, the features of any products that might be of particular interest to them during the selling exercise. These features will have particular benefits and *this means that* ... phrases associated with them *must be spelled out* and acknowledged.

There are several mini-stages deriving from each feature to remember, for you to get off pat. It is exceptionally important to complete driving home the point tactfully by showing the customer precisely why and how this particular feature is useful, applicable or vital to him or her in their own situation.

For example, you could point out that a particular electric hand drill has a variable speed control and forward and reverse rotation ability. *So what?* You should point out that these features enable the user to gradually start to drill holes slowly and with more precision – leading to better accuracy, more professional drilling, less unsightly false starts and is, therefore, quicker in the end. Also you can put screws in and take them out using the drill – again very convenient, slick, much quicker and certainly takes less effort! These are all customer advantages that individually support a notional increment towards the total price, when the time comes to consider it. Although features (including their derivative benefits and applicability comments) have an implicit matching price for the *customer*, it is very important to specifically show that the total package of the benefits appear *larger* than the selling price – not the other way round.

One-To-One

Normally, sales situations are best handled on a one-to-one arrangement as far as the seller is concerned – otherwise the customer can split the seller's arguments and won't hear a consistent story; it will create doubts and lack of confidence.

However, there are times when a *double act* can help; so use it occasionally.

- Sometimes whilst making a relatively complex and important selling point (that the customer has obviously not latched on to), the 'stooge' can play dumb, sensitively interrupting the lead seller and, on behalf of the customer (ostensibly), create an opening for the point to be remade, and perhaps more emphatically.
- Personality or chemistry problems can arise quite naturally between customers and individual persons from your business (even the venturer personally). Accept that such situations may occur (don't worry about them); merely try to match the customer with the most suitable person from the business – horses for courses.

EXERCISE

In the case of your business and its products, what are the relative discriminators and benefits; and what do they actually mean to the customer? Think them out carefully for real. Are customers going to be able to take advantage of these features?

CUSTOMER HESITATION

Never prolong the selling exercise more than necessary: close the sale (whether it is a shop or non-shop situation) as quickly as possible.

Nevertheless, customers frequently have difficulty coming to a decision, and will often hesitate and declare that they want time to think about it. Sometimes this is all in order, and must be respected (*see* Chapter 11, *Your own service expectations*). However, very often they are just plain shy, frightened off and want to put off making a public declaration; they want to avoid the evil day when decisions have to be made. In these cases, help can be offered and it usually works. It's a technique that acknowledges human weakness and makes it much easier for the customer (in this case) to conclude the business he or she really wants – and what he or she came in to do, of course!

Step by step, the business discussions and negotiations have been moving towards a narrowed short-list of remaining points; and one by one, even the so-called objections have been negated through continued talking; and yet there is still hedging and an unwillingness for the customers to commit themselves. This is where closing techniques are brought in, and if well and subtly done, the *customer himself* or *herself* concludes the deal – and buys.

CLOSING TECHNIQUES

Carefully lead the questioning as close as possible towards a unique conclusion. If customer body language indicates his or her thoughts (for example, asking whether credit cards are acceptable or merely taking out a wallet or purse), this is a positive sign. Otherwise, you can use a direct closed question asking whether he or she will take the goods; but it doesn't always work ... simply because it invites a rebuff, either because the question is not appropriate, is ill-judged or is not best timed.

So sometimes a particular *closing technique* can be employed that narrows the options to be made and makes the customer feel more comfortable and less threatened as it were. These techniques, applied well and with practice, will get you a long way – whatever the style of business or category of customer.

There are no simple rules for these seven closing techniques, but their use and timing must be judged carefully. They can be brought in at various points in the meeting or selling situation and be used in combination. The trick is to bring in appropriate ones diplomatically and naturally when it is hoped they will be most effective to close the sale quickly. They can be used to discuss quantities, delivery schedule, prices, terms, and so on; or you can make use of genuine deadlines and special deal opportunities.

Alternative Close

Give the customer *just two alternative* (no more) options, virtually as closed questions (minimal possible answers); *Do you want a large or a small packet? Do you prefer the red one or the blue? Is it size 12 or 14?* perhaps at the same time passing the appropriate packet, colour or size. Questions (from the list under *customer's specifications* above) could pose similar choices in model, engine size, style, delivery, quantity, and so on.

By saying *Yes* to one of the alternatives, it avoids a head-on possible clash that sometimes follows from asking the direct question *Will you take it?* or *Is that OK then?* (what do you do if the answer was given as *No*?).

As soon as *either* alternative favourable answer is given, assume he or she has come to a positive conclusion, and take the merchandise and the customer to the till.

A familiar old favourite, *Your place or mine?* supplies an automatic answer to another implicit question.

Secondary Question Close

Another technique that avoids posing the main question, is asking another secondary one. The answer to this one hopefully then gives a green light for the main implied question – somewhat as before.

For example, if a travel agency is trying to conclude a booking and the customer is dithering, they might try *How many passengers will be travelling?* – which of course presupposes that *somebody* is contemplating travelling and wants a flight booked.

When we deliver the shed, will the concrete base already be down? is another example, where the customer wants something (in this case a garden shed), but won't or can't bring themselves to commit to the final act.

Or another one, *Would you like it wrapped?*

Or in a technical business arena, the following might be applicable *We could combine all three units on a single base, would that be better for you?*

In all these cases, maybe further closing questions will be needed first; the aim being to draw a positive answer from the unasked direct question, and take the customer to the till as before – or whatever.

Assumptive or Conditional Close

The third scenario hinges on an assumption concerning a lesser topic (only part of the main issue), and shows an undecided customer buying something large in a shop. *If we could arrange delivery for when you get home from work ...* Hopefully the answer to the immediate question is positive (if not try another, after a few moments), and the main question is also implicitly answered. These questions have an *if* in them, somewhere.

If our delivery van is back early this afternoon, we could bring it round straightaway, if you like.

If we can get a green one for Monday [when the sale will have ended], *we can let you have it at the sale price. And you said you would particularly like a green one, didn't you?*

If the boss and I can agree to a price reduction, will you take it?

Emotional Close

Emotions, referred to several times already, play a very significant part in helping customers to make up their minds, particularly prestige, pride, personal image, status, pleasure, fear, anger, sheer necessity, jealousy, shame, lust, envy, covetousness, gluttony, sloth, ownership for ownership's sake.

I suppose you'll then be the first one in your road to have double glazing or a new-registration car?

At least you'll feel a lot safer at home tonight with these new locks fitted.

You're the second person to get one today – one of your neighbours bought one this morning and she rang to say how pleased she was with it [her new microwave, for example].

Summary Close

Another of the closing techniques has already been tried on you in this book probably without your realizing it – *see* the end of Chapter 7.

After the selling conversations seem to have covered all the relevant points and answered the customer's questions and hesitations satisfactorily, the salesman or woman would have tried to bring the matter to a close – but unsuccessfully. The next move should then be to go through the subject again, briefly, either verbally or on a piece of paper, summarizing the main points of the discussions.

The end portion of Chapter 7 is reproduced below:

You have been equipped with the ground rules for reasoned argument, and there's no logical reason to put off making the decision. *The decision is yours*, as they say! Tick the boxes. You've:

- ☐ got enough 'technical expertise' and know-how
- ☐ got some viable and marketable ideas, perhaps a suitable hobby
- ☐ examined how the business could operate
- ☐ considered your own suitability
- ☐ thought generally about resources, premises, finance
- ☐ identified the gaps and how they could be plugged
- ☐ thought about commitment, risk, family, and so on
- ☐ got some ideas about getting sales.

At this point, you were asked to make the decision, on the valid assumption that you had physically or mentally ticked all the mini-boxes. So all you had to do (and there was really little room for manoeuvre, without losing face) was to tick the larger box, as it were.

This is a typical summary close, whereby every point should have already been covered and implicitly agreed. The final tick (*Yes* to the overall implication) must be assumed and the overall deal agreed to.

Pros and Cons Close

Not dissimilar from the last in some respects is the Pros and Cons closing technique. After lengthy discussions, usually, a sort of balance sheet can be drawn up on a sheet of paper, flip chart or white board. It lists all the advantages of, and good points about, your solution, product or service on the left hand column. And lists the disadvantages and bad points (as far as the customer is concerned) on the right-hand column. Both parties compile the two lists together and conclusions drawn at the end. The lists clearly identify the Pros and Cons of the proposed deal.

The Pros side can be dealt with by you (racking your brain hard, of course), assisting the customer as much as possible. Unfortunately, on the other column (Cons side) most of the work is left to the customer alone, with only trivial ones supplied by you (who otherwise has a complete mental block!). Hence, the Pros should win and the customer draws the obvious conclusion!

Puppy Dog Close

Finally, particularly in non-shop situations, where all else failed and the order is lost or about to be lost you can apply a sorrowful about-to-cry *Puppy dog* sort of face and say, *Mr Brown, of course we respect your decision and are naturally disappointed to lose the contract, but that is your privilege. We do understand. For our internal analysis* [or whatever] *would you mind telling me the reasons for not going ahead* [or *for going to the competitor*].

At this point the seller effectively follows a similar process to the closing technique above, and itemizes all the aspects of the product that *apparently* didn't appeal to the customer – so that they can be addressed internally on the face of it.

The point is that the seller now has an *agreed* list of the perceived problem areas (real or imaginary – because they may be cited just as excuses), and is uniquely and cleverly in a position to understand them better, and hence to attempt to rectify them. It's possible that this list turns out to be smaller than originally thought, or that the so-called problems didn't really exist at all!

With suitable words like, *I'm sorry, I didn't really understand how important that point was for your project, I think we can do something about that*, knock them down, one by one, very carefully; and after all the extra interest and attention that has been shown, well you never know the customer might change his or her mind, reinstating the business after all!

If All Else Fails

Finally, on the subject of closing orders, there will be a few situations in which you will not succeed in spite of all the effort that has been put in. In these situations, possibly introduce a colleague or the boss to see what they can do: a new face and a new angle or approach might help if it doesn't antagonize the customer, of course. Otherwise, simply thank the customer for his or her time, but let them leave on amicable terms and invite them to give your venture an opportunity to get involved again in the future sometime. Keep sending Newsletters and Christmas cards!

TOO MANY SIMULTANEOUS CUSTOMERS

Problems arise when there are too many prospects or customers needing attention at the same time (a busy time in a shop for example). If this should be the case, there are ways to deal with them, and ease matters.

- First and foremost, don't panic; but maintain the business-like attitude and professionalism, *concentrating hard on the immediate customer* – the one being handled, because there's usually only one chance! Give this customer virtually 100 per cent of the attention, momentarily forgetting the last one and also similarly forgetting the next one. However, you should still noticeably acknowledge all of them.
- Don't ever ignore customers completely: acknowledge them and explain you will be with them as soon as possible and/or ask another competent staff member to help or hold the fort, if anyone is available. If people see the staff are really trying to handle the situation, are working hard and not idly chatting and ignoring them, they are usually happy to wait for a short time. This is where team working comes into play. A cup of tea or coffee, or cold drink, biscuits and a seat work wonders in the meanwhile!
- Even so, sometimes customers may genuinely have time constraints; in which case someone should responsibly and briefly apologize to, and *tactfully* interrupt the present customer with the minimum of fuss, so that the seller can offer

to get back to the waiting customer at the earliest opportunity, somehow. This promise must be kept. A real balancing act!

- As soon as you are able to deal with the customer, apologize once (sincerely of course) and get down to business straightaway. Maybe apologize briefly again when the customer leaves.

HOME VISITS

Instead of the prospective customer visiting your premises, certain businesses or trades visit the customer's home – like cleaners, domestic helps, plumbers, gardeners, decorators and builders.

The customer-handling principles still apply rigorously of course, but additional points arise. As a general rule, the customer's property, house, family, friends, visitors, animals, cars, general belongings and possessions must be meticulously respected, and not over-commented on except as a conversation icebreaker in the opening rounds or unless the customer brings them up. Neither must they be damaged or moved (without deliberately replacing them), picked up or handled, unless it proves to be necessary whilst taking measurements – but extreme care is advised at all times.

Don't open cupboard doors, drawers, or attempt to chat up anybody in the house – unless of course the customer instigates these points – and even then, keep matters at arm's length and a professional stance maintained.

None of these common courtesy points should give rise to any surprises.

Always On Duty
In dealings with customers, whether at home, the shop, showroom, in meetings in non-shop environments, in the street or socially, customer-handling is exceptionally important, and critical to all stages of the business. You must be able to anticipate and deal with all these situations nonchalantly and quite naturally: many people *are* quite capable of handling and *subtly influencing* other people in any of these potentially off-guard situations. Be professional and business-like all the time and don't relax the alertness. Every customer is important to the business.

IDEAL AND NON-IDEAL CUSTOMERS

Another observation on customers: Your attitudes (as boss of the own venture) and that of your staff, if any, go a long way in influencing which of a further two categories customers fit in: those that help the business, and those who definitely don't.

Ideal Customer
An ideal customer is one who considers the service or product to have exceeded expectations. Not only had the perceived value for money been exceeded, but he or she certainly comes back for more and also recommends the business to friends. The customer is friendly, cooperative and helpful; and makes constructive suggestions, backing them with actions. Continuously satisfied customers will

grow the business for you – look after them, nurture them, make them feel important. Treat them as you would a direct financial investment.

Bad Customer

On the other hand, a typical bad profile describes a customer who is never (if ever) publicly satisfied with product or service. He or she claims that the goods or levels of service often, or always, fail to meet even the minimum level of satisfaction. The product is certainly not perceived as value for money. He or she is definitely not friendly and is often grumbling.

The customer grudgingly (or never) comes back for more, often makes complaints or threatens legal action; and certainly advises all his or her other friends not to patronize your venture – which obviously helps kill the business. Whether it's the customer's fault or personality, or whatever, or whether it is the owner's is almost irrelevant, because the damage is done. Ultimately it is the owner's problem to sort out. Bad customers will help destroy the business.

Moral

Encourage customers to be in the 'ideal' mould: convert the maximum number of bad ones to good or ideal ones – which is not always easy. If they can't be converted with whatever it reasonably takes, you have to gracefully put them out of your mind, and get on with the business – and without making matters worse of course.

Even in this day and age (let alone that of previous generations), the customer is still always right, and must be seen to be right – *even when he or she is wrong*!

Quite frequently, what starts off as a complaint, if well handled, can turn out to be a sales opportunity after all. So complaints could even be welcomed in some circumstances!

When the pressure is on to get many different jobs done – particularly less important administration and background jobs – the cynic has been heard to say *if it wasn't for the customers we could get on with our work*! Recall the written-in-blood maxim that customers make the business and they pay the wages! A lost customer, for whatever reason, is lost profit and possible lost reputation. And reputations, although lost in seconds, take years to gain.

STAFF TRAINING

A word about you and your staff … You frequently hear that *you can't get the staff these days* or similar observations. Don't judge too hastily. Three relevant questions need to be asked:

• Can your recruitment screening be improved?
• Are you paying enough money to get and retain the right quality people?
• Are you training them thoroughly when you have [freely] chosen them?

Maybe it's the business owner at fault, not the staff alone, if at all?

Ensure that everybody concerned in the venture, including all staff, have enough to do, so that they are not standing around doing nothing, getting bored and hence chattering amongst themselves. This looks terrible, is bad for customer image, is discourteous and rude, and costs the owner money and reputation ultimately. Motivate them and encourage them to be positive about your business. There are always background jobs to be done which is where your management skills come to the fore. When customers are around, merely use body language to ask the staff to do certain things, rather than tactlessly giving verbal instructions or what amounts to dressing-downs in public.

Training staff (if you intend to have any staff) is emphasized here as a matter of very high priority. Train everybody to work as a team, reacting and doing things automatically. This all helps with the public image. Management and sales staff need thorough training in:

- the entire capability of the business
- products and services
- competitive knowledge
- dealing with customers (*see* Chapter 11)
- presentation, speaking and sales skills
- appropriate attitudes and dress code
- operation of equipment, computers, software and facilities
- areas that shadow the entrepreneur, in general (apart from those concerned with business ownership and directors)
- the various procedures and routines for use in customer-related matters, like till drill
- where things are kept, including all major stationery and office equipment
- the stock and how to use it
- thinking for themselves
- fire and safety procedures (staff and customers).

Concentrating on training sales staff is not the end of the matter. All the so-called support staff have a vital role: people (if your business has them) like receptionists, switchboard and telephone answering staff generally are the first voices, attitudes and impressions of the business that a prospective customer receives. If the customer is not suitably impressed, it may also be the only one and the last chance! If they get irritated, there is unlikely to be another – and customers are all very precious and essential to the business. So train these people to understand and execute their very important responsibilities to the full.

The business depends critically on the initial contact with the prospective customer! Train all your staff to know who 'customers' are, ideally to recognize them, and to fully uphold the business image in their presence – and dress and behave appropriately. Don't forget that customers can be strongly influenced by what is said and done by servicing and delivery staff. These people are also your 'sales' staff, flying the flag for your business, and needing appropriate training, encouragement and reward.

Telephone Answering

You should put yourselves in the enquirer's place – endeavouring to answer and speak in the best and most helpful way. Answer promptly, and don't keep the caller hanging on whilst various recorded messages are played, allegedly ensuring the *best possible service*. It definitely isn't. Also customers clearly prefer free or plain conventional national phone numbers: not premium rate numbers!

Greet the customer courteously and politely; say as little as possible initially, satisfying the customer that the correct phone connection or extension has been made, and then get on with the business he or she wants to talk about. Anything else will be seen to be completely unnecessary and a waste of time – and increase the phone bill – unless *the customer* asks for more details of course.

Give the name of the organization (shortened to a manageable word or group of words if necessary), or however it becomes generally and popularly known; and *possibly* the name of an individual – the potential irritating point being that a customer may be in a hurry, wanting to get on with whatever is on his or her mind without listening ritually to what is perceived to be a load of unnecessary, time-wasting and irrelevant rubbish!

Be sure to grasp quickly, and really understand, what is being asked. Put the customer through to people who can competently handle their enquiry, if it is beyond the immediate person's knowledge – and explain what is going to happen. Monitor the call to ensure the extension has answered, and if not take a name and number so that the business can (*and will*) ring the customer back. *We are not allowed to take messages* is not what either the customer or the boss should be hearing!

Finally

Getting business is crucial and fundamental, which explains why these last four chapters have dwelt upon the subject. If these chapters bring forth fruit, then the business as a whole is almost bound to as well!

Another small point concerns eating and drinking. Don't do either in front of customers, nor leave dirty cups, mugs and other crockery around – whether finished with or not. There should be some private area for this purpose (*see* Chapter 19). The obvious exception is enjoying a meal or drink with a customer, perhaps, after concluding a successful sale.

It's a somewhat overworked phrase, and more reminiscent of dog shows and the like, but it's a good memorable maxim: as far as the business venture is concerned, aim to be the *best in class* in the eyes of the public, customers or marketplace. In the light of the observations made in the previous chapter, even a modest improvement over many contemporary businesses will make a considerable difference to the fortunes of the venture. Nevertheless, aim to be the best by a large margin – the standard by which you and your competitors will be judged. Your customers will be the final arbiters!

Brilliant marketing (seed sowing) is the precursor to getting sales (harvesting); brilliant sales forecasting is not an end in itself – but it's a propitious target to achieve and beat! Businesses need targets (derived away from the immediate heat as it were) in order to have an 'independent' yardstick to aim for.

EXERCISE

Anticipate the likely staff, their roles and their training needs for your venture.

EXERCISE

If you have no staff, how will you manage sickness, holidays, and so on?

EXERCISE

How can the business afford them and how will you find them?

SALES PLAN

Finally, as with the complementary marketing plan in Chapter 10, you should again consider the totality of your business and its objectives; and then draw up a *sales* plan ready for implementation. It should take account of all the factors mentioned in these last four chapters in particular, especially the last two, including overall marketing strategy, sales strategy, detailed ways of making it happen, who are the prospective customers exactly, how they will be targeted, responsibilities, what is expected to be achieved. The document will probably be more figure-based than the marketing plan, although both will explain the detail in words. The sales plan will also need an appropriate budget to reflect the potential business turnover and the financial, personnel, time and other resources available.

EXERCISE

Draw up your own sales strategy and plan.

WHAT HAVE YOU LEARNT IN THIS CHAPTER?

★ Why should you take comfort from the concept of the hierarchy of needs?
★ What are the essential differences between business and personal purchasers?
★ Mention some of the personal buying reasons.
★ Name some of the customer specification points.
★ List the seven closing techniques. Why, how and where are they used?
★ What are the characteristics of good and bad customers?
★ What is their impact on the business?
★ Discuss the statement that *if it wasn't for customers, the business could get on with its work*.
★ Why is staff training so important, including that for the support staff? Who gives the first impression of your business?

13
Getting Paid

Getting sales is an exceptionally important aspect (crucial in fact) in any successful business: but getting paid for those sales is even more appealing. This chapter looks at this imperative topic.

Getting paid is not always easy and certainly not automatic. It is viewed from both sides of the fence because of the parallel between your business wanting to receive payment for *its* sales, and the business' suppliers equally wanting payment for *their* sales – the subject of the business debtors (relating to sales) and that of the business creditors (relating to purchases). Credit control is touched on.

Methods of getting paid in shop situations are applicable to all types of business, so it will be examined first. Non-shop situations attract other forms of payment as well.

The possible forms of payment can be summarized as:

- cash
- cheques
- electronic transfer
- cash on delivery
- prepayments

- plastic cards
- sale or return
- extended credit
- invoices.

FORMS OF PAYMENT

Cash
The most obvious method, standing the test of time, is good old-fashioned cash – coins and notes of course. Most British notes emanate from the Bank of England but some are issued by the banks in Scotland, Northern Ireland and the Channel Islands: the banks should accept all of them.

Airports, aircraft, ports, ships, international trains, travel agents, banks, bureaux de change, overseas countries and the like, would deal both in English and foreign currencies at agreed exchange rates – fixed high enough to cover normal bank currency rates as well as handling charges. Some businesses work in multiple currencies, including the Euro, keeping separate and complex accounts for each currency, that finally have to be converted to a single currency for business accounting purposes and comparisons.

Cheques
Cheques should be backed, preferably, by £100 or £50 guarantee cards issued by the respective banks. This card number must be inspected personally and written

on the reverse side of the cheque *by the business staff*; not anyone else and certainly not the customer. Signatures and other details must match. There are also various forms of British and foreign currency-based travellers cheques that should be treated as advised by your bank.

Collectively the coins, notes and normal clearing bank cheques (and many travellers cheques) are regarded as cash sale transactions for the business, handed over by the customer who should then be given a receipt in exchange and be free to take the goods (cash and carry operations). Alternatively, the business will probably arrange for them to be delivered if they are bulky.

These forms of payment represent 'cash' when banked, although any cheques may require a few days to be deemed clear, before they can in turn be drawn against. As much business as possible should be transacted by 'cash' – for all types of business – because it is *safe* money, and represents the quickest and easiest way to get money into the bank.

The word *safe* indicates that the money has been handed over, the deal is completed; and is not the subject of short or extended payment terms.

Electronic Transfer

Another way to get money into the bank account fairly quickly is to get it transferred electronically – by direct transfer via the banks' BACS (or similar) clearing mechanism. In this case, the [distant] customer pays money directly from his or her account (or over the counter in person; and by phone, fax, e-mail, Internet, and so on, with appropriate safeguards and authorization). It appears in your business' account at your own bank and branch, but might take a few days to happen. Domestic bills are paid and salaries are received this way – you may have encountered them.

Cash On Delivery Or Completion Of Contract

Sometimes goods are delivered against some form of agreed, postponed payment at the delivery point, although this is not so common these days. The carrier (even the postman) expects to receive payment in exchange for the goods, and gives receipts accordingly – known as COD (cash-on-delivery) transactions. Drawn-out contracts (building work and made-to-measure clothing, for example) would not expect the final payment until the job had been satisfactorily completed.

Prepayments

There is a closely related type of payment arrangement with which you might get involved, where money is paid up-front (a tangible sign of good faith, supporting an order), the balance being due on completion. Examples come from the car industry, central heating suppliers, and others when deposits are taken against *customer orders* for things that are not actually in stock.

Sometimes with project type of work, plant engineering, builders, and so on (which can represent large or very large monetary sums), cash in advance, royalty advances, advance payments or stage payments are frequently encountered. Advance payments and deposits help mitigate the need for as much working capital, and are effectively used as such; so are very welcome. Much of the tourist and travel business expects complete payments in advance.

Prepayments generally get real money into the business, minimizing potential outstanding debtor situations – *see below*. There is usually a contract or agreement alongside these payments that sets out the terms and conditions for the project, and obligations of all parties.

Credit and Debit Cards – 'Plastic'

Shops and businesses usually accept conventional 'plastic' or credit cards – VISA or Mastercard predominantly, but also charge cards such as Diners and American Express (Amex). As far as a business is concerned they operate in similar ways. For the customer, charge cards do not allow extended repayments, whereas credit cards do. Retailers and Mail Order businesses (again with safeguards) will encounter many different types of card, with associated electronic readers, automatic dialling facilities for central authorization codes, and so on. There are customer-inserted PINs being used these days.

There can be a significant set-up charge relating to the supply of the service generally, and the equipment and telephone lines to support it. But this must be viewed positively against the extra business and profits it will probably generate (and included in the cash-flow forecasts and costs of setting up the business). However, the traditional 'manual' or old-fashioned slide machines will pay dividends, as a last resort, although it takes a lot longer to process the dockets; these little machines are particularly useful where craft show and other off-site transactions occur, or when the mains power fails!

Electronic facilities behind credit card transactions clock up entries on accounts for you, by means of which a periodic settlement will be made by the card companies (monthly or weekly if requested), at the same time debiting the customers' accounts accordingly.

With the electronic facilities behind debit cards, like Switch and Delta, the retailer builds up credits and settlements as before; but the customers' accounts are, or can be, debited almost immediately. That's primarily why cash-back facilities are often attached to *debit* card arrangements but not *credit* cards.

Sale Or Return

In both shop and non-shop environments, goods on *sale or return* (SOR) will be encountered, at the discretion of the legal owner or sender of the goods. No real invoices, only SOR ones, are raised as it is a good idea to keep track and accountability of the goods somehow.

A growing number of shops (especially selling clothes and books), whilst looking indistinguishable from any others, operate on the basis that virtually all their stock is supplied on SOR terms from some central warehouse or other source. The advantage from the owners' point of view is that any stock held in the wrong sizes, wrong colours, too large a quantity, is slow-moving or is unpopular, at one outlet can be moved on to another. This is a form of SOR operating as an indigenous policy (with appropriate administrative schemes in place to support it) within the group.

It contrasts with that relating to the individual supplier, acting on his or her own to provide limited SOR stock. For a novice-venturer, it's a brilliant way of getting the shop, showroom or display area filled for very little outlay. The legal title remains with the true owner of the goods (they are supplied for nothing, as it were) and only paid for when they are sold. All the time the goods are lying on shelves in a non-public warehouse, they will never sell; so if the manufacturer or wholesaler ships them to a [free of cost] showroom, there is a far better chance of converting them to money for both parties – so there's good method in the apparent generosity after all.

In a similar stocking connection, phased purchases and deliveries are a possibility, against deferred cheques and legal documents known as Bills of Exchange (legally enforceable IOUs!); there must be funds to meet them at the appropriate time – or else!

Another (informal perhaps) way of both getting paid and paying for higher price items is to be handed, or to give, a series of postdated cheques dated at, say, monthly intervals. This practice is somewhat dubious – the cheques could be lost, they might not be honoured, the account on which they are drawn might be closed, they are not so neat and legally enforceable as Bills of Exchange, and so on – but they are cheaper and convenient.

Extended Credit – Pay By Instalments
Also on the shop side in particular, but not confined to them, are Finance House credit arrangements – credit finance for customers of businesses who sell larger items like cars, furniture and shop fitting. They are broadly subdivided into Credit Sale Agreements, Hire Purchase Agreements, Rental Agreements and Leasing Agreements, depending on the fine legal print reflecting the legal situations.

The appropriate pros and cons for these schemes are complex; but there are people who specialize in this whole field.

If you intend to stock these products, offer such credit facilities, give advice on these matters or generally tell customers about finance schemes to help sell your products, you are required by law to obtain a Financial Services Licence. The chosen finance house will advise you on procedures.

Credit By Invoice
Finally, the predominant method of payment for non-shop environments is the invoice – with written terms and conditions (the so-called small print) often on the back! Certain shop-style venture customers (like schools, other businesses, local authorities, honoured private individuals) use them. No cash is generated at the time of sale, but a month or so later, it should be. The vast majority of businesses have to offer credit terms of some sort – especially if they are not organized as a shop concept.

Contractually, the debtor customer is within his or her rights not to pay up until the end of the credit period, if periods of 30, 60, 90, 120, 150, 180 or more days (nominally up to 6 months or more) of credit have been agreed. The creditor might deliberately exceed those periods to gain more interest-free finance for the business, or because of forgetfulness, or, most likely, because the business is short of cash – which is a euphemism for funds of all sorts!

If your venture becomes a bit tight on funds as a result of slow paying customers, it could offer special short-term cash deals to otherwise conventional invoice customers for a special discount: it's not often used but it's worth having up your sleeve. There are many similar examples of this sort of situation – with comments in the press like, *To take advantage of these offers you must book and pay by a certain date*. The ultimate object is to get money in as fast as possible. Even profitability takes a back seat sometimes, and this is all to do with cash flow (*see* Chapter 15).

Your own venture can, and possibly will, at some stage get into similar straits for some periods, because of real problems or just because sales and revenue tend to fluctuate seasonally. You can appreciate why debtors exceed their payment terms: equally, you will certainly not wish to upset customers. A mini dilemma.

GIVING CREDIT

As any salesperson who is paid commission on sales will tell you, meeting and exceeding targets means money. It may mean money to the *salesperson*, but not necessarily to the business *until the debtor actually pays up*.

Credit (to customers) must be kept under scrutiny and control; it is a phrase that comes to mind in this context, although the subject was previously touched on in Chapter 8 when dealing with financial resources. If your business offers credit, someone in your venture must be responsible for this important topic – you possibly! The objectives for the credit controller and the salesperson can be directly opposed of course. One clearly is cautious about the customer's ability to pay whilst the other desperately wants the business!

Your Credit Control
Just think carefully about the following questions, in relation to (a) your business and (b) a specific customer:

- Should your business give free credit?
- *Why* are you prepared to give him or her credit?
- Will the business survive and grow if the credit facility is denied?
- Can your business afford to give its customers any free credit?
- Where's the funding coming from, and how much will it cost your business?
- How creditworthy is the customer?
- How is the customer's trust and *creditworthiness* to be assessed?
- *How much* credit is your business able to give to any particular customer?
- Can you trust the potential customer, who will probably not pay for several weeks?
- Will the individual, authority, school or the business pay in the end?

- Can they afford to pay and will they pay, without a legal fight?
- Do other people get paid satisfactorily by them?
- How much credit should be given?

Clearly a delicate matter, that could unquestionably apply both ways. It's all a *quid pro quo* situation and a certain amount of trust and faith is needed – especially when one or both businesses is new. Often it's a case of no credit, no customer – and hence no venture. So not much choice in practice.

Limited Credit Initially

The short answer is to give limited leeway initially. As a pattern of good satisfactory payments starts to show, allow more credit in exchange for some extra business. (Use the 'favour' to ask for more business in return.) Most similar situations work out all right in the end, and there are remedies if they don't.

You can better understand the reverse situation when your venture is trying to get credit from its suppliers – and the questions that will have been going through their mind. Same problem, the other way round. Refer to Chapter 8 on financing your venture.

Debtors and Creditors

Turning to so-called business *debtors* (that is, people or businesses who owe money to your business, for goods and services your business has supplied to its customers) – on *credit* as opposed to 'cash' sales.

When your business owes money to third parties, those persons or organizations are considered *creditors* of the business, and your business correspondingly is deemed to be a *debtor* of the other parties.

These are very confusing terms, but they will become clearer as your business develops. You do not have to be an expert in these terms, as accountants have to know about these matters. You know what to do or what sort of books to read.

SLOW PAYERS

Some debtors of the business (individuals or other businesses) will delay paying their invoices until the last minute, as their norm. So be prepared. Any reticent payers should be smartly chased by phone and then by letter. Be fairly firm in bringing them into line before matters get any worse, refusing to supply further raw materials or stock until they pay up. This strategy is so critical to their survival that it normally works.

Further similar action a month later should take place if nothing has happened or no explanations received. He who shouts loudest is more likely to get paid first!

These financial matters are usually discussed by money-type persons talking to similar money-type persons, who understand each other's situations; so it should not hurt the generally good business arrangements; but make sure it doesn't, as that could be counterproductive in the end.

Remedies

In theory, *overdue* payments can warrant additional interest payments! But is it worth the hassle for small percentages, loss of goodwill and loss of future business?

In the later stages, you can threaten and/or take legal action, through solicitors and the courts – take care because it will really kill the customer as far as future business is concerned. Equally *threaten* bankruptcy or liquidation – but again take care, because if the errant or broke business *is* liquidated, it will be *years* before any money comes through, and even then it will probably be only a very small percentage, if anything, of the original figure.

There are also debt collection agencies who will retrieve the money for a fee (usually a percentage of the total debts that they have 'bought'), without you lifting too many fingers; and there are factoring organizations who effectively buy the business debtors list, and are then free to chase the debts however they prefer. Whilst these routes can be helpful, the price may be considered too high and the basic principle may not be acceptable. Factoring organizations (as they are called) have little regard for your customers – and that's not good for customer goodwill, loyalty and future business. Debt collection agencies and factoring organizations both relieve you of hassle, freeing your business to pursue its ordinary business and providing immediate cash – which are useful benefits.

THE MORAL: KEEP ON TOP OF EVERY SITUATION

Don't let matters get out of hand in the first place. Get paid as soon as possible, only pressurizing debtors carefully where you have to; because these same customers will also bring future business. Get as many straightforward cash sales as possible.

Inevitably, any business is liable to incur a bad debt occasionally. Don't lose an unnecessary amount of sleep over it once it has happened, because what is done is done! Learn from the situation, avoiding it happening again. Raise the prices slightly next time to compensate, by including a percentage for this sort of risk, if possible.

Never rely too heavily on one customer in the first place: spread the business as far as possible. However much we all like to receive a very large prestigious order, it must be firmly remembered not to put virtually all one's eggs in one basket. This way, if a debt goes bad, it will not have an *utterly* disastrous effect on the future liquidity and viability of your venture.

Corresponding Sales Strategy

A large number of smaller customers is a very much safer policy than two or three more major customers or ongoing contracts, even if it takes a lot more effort, and results in much more work.

At the time of getting the original sale, some very obvious discreet checks can be made to mitigate problems at a later stage and, equally importantly, time wasting in the prospect stage. In the course of questioning the prospective customer (particularly one who will be invoiced), establish the degree of commitment, whether the money has been allowed for in their budget, and whether they are in a position to pay. This might take some tact, of course, but it may save problems later on.

EXERCISE

Consider how you will operate payment methods, credit control and minimize monies due from your debtors.

SAUCE FOR THE GOOSE ...

Concerning payments from you to others, there is obviously a parallel situation whereby the suppliers might turn the tables on your venture as described above as far as remedial actions are concerned. Your venture must also pay its creditors (suppliers) on time, having first discussed and negotiated the best possible terms; or else they will hold up future deliveries that are needed to generate future sales, revenue and profit. However, it can be a cheap source of borrowing if kept firmly under control – certainly not a source of finance to be ignored.

WHAT HAVE YOU LEARNT IN THIS CHAPTER?

★ What are the various ways of getting paid, and what is the advantage of getting 'cash' payments?
★ After 'cash', what is the most frequently encountered payment method, especially in non-shop situations?
★ In what circumstances would certain forms of payment be more appropriate or likely?
★ Why is it necessary for you to use credit facilities and to give such facilities to customers? What precautions would be prudent?
★ How is the cost of giving credit determined?
★ What are the risks of not offering credit facilities?

14
Understanding Business Finances

Half the battle with running businesses is to understand financially what is going on. This chapter looks at business expenditure, bookkeeping and management information. It provides some fundamental knowledge of business finance.

If you are not skilled in these topics, not really interested yet or do not want to get your hands dirty as it were, there is no need to take an active part in *compiling* the figurework. As stated elsewhere, finance is important but it is not the only consideration in running a business. There are outside experts who deal with these matters as their bread and butter and are pleased to do so, whilst the venturer carries on doing what he or she is best at – probably the technical matters.

You must understand broadly what items are entered in the *books*, and why. You must understand from a financial point of view what is going on, and aid diagnosis of any business problems. So understanding principles is important; doing the nitty-gritty is not. Understanding the meaning of the final figures is also important, but this knowledge will come naturally as the business progresses and as the accountant sits with you to interpret the first few sets of figures.

BUSINESS EXPENDITURE

Successful businesses take in money as a result of sales. In the core activity itself and its supporting infrastructure, they consume or expend money. Some of the costs are relatively small, whilst others are quite significant. Expenditure is conveniently thought of in two main categories by accountants and the tax authorities; and the time-honoured accounting conventions treat each category differently.

- The normal everyday *operating* or *running* costs (or revenue items) which include those directly attributable to the primary core function, supporting administrative functions and cost of *selling* the products or services.
- Expenditures associated with *capital* items, which are fewer but generally more costly.

RUNNING COSTS

The subdivisions overlap to some extent and are not quite as clear cut in practice, as indicated below; they are subject to variations depending on the precise nature of the business, and hence the accountant's interpretations of expenditure items in the light of conventions and tax law.

Labour

Costs for labour (whether permanent or temporary) often account for the largest bills. They embrace the directors' fees, wages, salaries, owner's drawings, pensions, Permanent Health Insurance, PAYE and National Insurance contributions.

So when cost savings have to be contemplated, labour costs are often the first to be scrutinized, although they also have a major impact on the head count and hence directly on the productivity of the business.

Stock and Raw Materials

The cost of stock and raw materials is usually the next largest expense, although the exact ranking of these costs and labour costs is dictated by the nature and size of the business.

Stock *management* or stock control is closely related to the immediate subject of the cost of physical stock:

- treading a very fine line between overstocking and premature deliveries on the one hand
- being able to meet sales and/or production demands on the other.

One of the management arts is to keep this physical stock, and hence its value, as low as possible – especially when it represents getting unnecessary supplies before they are really needed (commensurate with being able to fulfil all the orders on time and, equally importantly, not losing sales because of stock shortages, and so on).

Storage of stock (space rental or its equivalent, together with possible limited shelf life of damaged or out-of-date stock) costs money, and shows up in working capital or possible overdraft requirements. This in turn attracts additional interest burdens.

There are sophisticated computer programmes to assist in this area of the business, with semi-automatic ordering programmes based on restoring stock to pre-determined stock levels – this can link with sales tills.

Vehicles

Another large bill is represented by transport costs for company cars, vans, delivery vehicles and fork lift trucks (whether for running costs, fuel or acquisition). It is another subject that calls for very careful budgeting and shopping around, together with a gradual build-up policy as the business grows.

Premises-Related Costs

The choice of premises will in part be influenced by how much work needs to be done before the business can start to earn revenue, and how this work will be phased.

Premises have to be prepared by decorating, fitting out, adding a shop front perhaps, and equipping areas for design, 'production', customers and administration. These activities cost money initially, as well as periodically thereafter for repairs, maintenance and cleaning. The premises possibly need heating, lighting and air-conditioning. There could be costs associated with water, gas, oil, electricity, various cleaning and production chemicals, water, sewerage and waste disposal. Refresh your thoughts by turning back to Chapter 8.

Travelling Expenses

All employees and the owners have to travel in the course of their duties occasionally – to visit suppliers, subcontractors, customers (not when sales related as such), finance institutions, other professional people and customers (when in buying mode). Other reasons for travel might include service calls, other business visits, exhibitions, conferences and seminars. To support this necessary activity, businesses have to fund travel and living (away from the main place of work) like hotels, travel, meals, snacks, tips and certain customer entertainment.

Administration

Basic administrative expenditure will be incurred for many miscellaneous items, including printing of business stationery, business cards, compliment slips, order acknowledgements, invoices, remittance advices, labels, pricing tags, hospitality, and non-sales-related communications (postal, courier, phones and fax services).

Professional Fees and Miscellaneous Costs

Businesses incur professional fees for solicitors, accountants, auditors, and so on. There will be various trade and other subscriptions. There will be items like rent, rates, recruitment costs, bank interest, other interest and even charity donations.

Selling and Marketing Costs

The costs of *selling and marketing* can be quite high in comparison, and seemingly out of proportion, which is why they have been specifically highlighted. They are absolutely essential, since without sales there would not be a business. *No sales and marketing investment – no business!* (Of course the same general comment can also be made about *any* key aspect of the business; without a core, there would equally be no business, for example.)

Face-to-face selling time in front of serious customers is *productive*: hosting customer visits and attending exhibitions, seminars, trade shows is less efficient. Attendance at business meetings, and outside committee meetings, meetings with an indirect marketing and selling aim are just as necessary, but even more inefficient: they still cost time and money. However, all these activities are in the ultimate name of trying to promote the business and its products.

One way to minimize them is to plan your routes and time to the best advantage, but in the end, it's the overriding prospects and customers that must govern everything. After all, customers do contribute to sales revenue where the deal is successful.

Unfortunately, waiting for colleagues, sitting around in reception areas, waiting around for appointments and out-of-pocket living costs (accommodation, meals and snacks whilst on the move), and travel (whether by car, bus, aircraft, train or whatever) are all *unproductive* selling costs – although businesses won't get far without them.

Advertising costs money in itself, as do all communications in the broadest sense. These are pure marketing costs (even lower efficiency) including postage, phone, fax, letters and e-commerce costs. Other marketing costs are the design and production of PR material, leaflets, brochures, web pages, printing, photographs and videos.

Taxation

Taxes themselves (including Value Added Tax) are not a business expense. From an accounting and taxation point of view, all legitimate business expenses have to be *wholly and necessarily incurred* in the running of the business. They are included here for completeness. Corresponding budgets have to be carefully established and monitored.

VAT

The turnover limit relating to business annual turnover (excluding VAT) for compulsory registration and therefore being obliged to charge VAT varies. Equally, if your business is registered, VAT can be beneficially reclaimed on most items of expenditure. If the turnover falls too much, the business has to de-register. A very convenient way to remember this threshold figure at the moment is to relate it to average weekly turnover (excluding VAT) of about £1,000, but VAT regulations (rules and precise thresholds) tend to change with Budgets. Not all products and services attract VAT. If you are charging VAT to someone else, or if you are having to pay it on their invoices, the nine digit VAT number, assigned by the Customs and Excise authorities must be shown on any invoices and relevant paperwork.

In business accounting, it is almost universally accepted that all the figures are considered exclusive of VAT for internal purposes. VAT is only taken into account when reporting figures to, or paying over to and reclaiming from, the Customs and Excise Authorities. It is isolated into a separate column in the accounting 'books'. As with most other business-related taxes, the cost of collecting the money falls on the business.

For most businesses (basically those that sell to concerns that *are* registered for VAT and can reclaim it), selling prices are quoted on goods *excluding any VAT*; those customers realize that it will first have to be added to their bill and paid before *they* can show it in their own books and reclaim it – cf. sales tax in the USA and elsewhere.

Conversely, in shops, hotels, restaurants and the like where VAT is generally not able to be reclaimed, the conventions are that the displayed prices reflect the incorporation of VAT on applicable products and services. Receipts given to customers show the VAT element, where applicable, so that it can still be isolated for accounting purposes, and reclaimed where appropriate.

CAPITAL COSTS

Capital items, and interest charged thereon, are treated differently from *revenue or operating* expenses as far as accounting and taxation are concerned. The precise nature of the business, with agreement from the tax authorities, will determine which items are deemed capital. Items like computer software, office furniture, fitting out, building work, licences, intellectual property rights, and so on, could be treated in different ways depending on how they are regarded. Some businesses will require the minimum of 'equipment and tools'.

Capital costs cover the acquisition of items like property, cars, vans, lorries, trailers, plant, equipment, computers, signs, shop fronts, tools, jigs, tool-making equipment, workshop equipment, working platforms, heavy or light production equipment, special equipment for moving items around like hoists, trolleys, lifting equipment, ground-based cranes and overhead cranes.

In many cases, the purchase value as such is not an allowable expense for tax purposes. Instead, a *percentage* of the purchase price called *depreciation* is allowable over several successive years – a sort of running cost analogy. The actual percentage is liable to fluctuate with each government budget.

The amount of capital expenditure depends to a very large extent on four factors:

- whether the items are purchased outright, as opposed to leasing or renting
- the nature of the business as mentioned above
- the availability of tools, plant, equipment, furniture and fittings on the second-hand market, which should not be overlooked
- the fundamental question of priorities (what is absolutely essential, what makes life better and what is relative luxury).

A typical cumulative budget (not just *monthly* figures) for the business expenditure is shown in Figure 7. Each month the *cumulative* amount for the period covered by the budget is shown: so that it can be directly compared with the running totals produced by the bookkeeping. The figures are generally straightforward, with each amount of expenditure shown for each month corresponding with the items of anticipated total spend to date; the employer's allowance (of say 15 per cent) is crudely based on the salary and wage totals, for you and the staff, paid out in the *previous* month, and primarily represents deducted payments of tax and NIC to the authorities one month in arrears, for PAYE owners and employees. No bank loans are assumed (apart from overdraft): therefore, no provision is made for regular repayments.

	Jan	Feb	Mar	Apr	May	Jun	Jul	Aug	Sept	Oct	Nov	Dec
REVENUE												
Sales	2000	4000	6500	9000	11500	14500	16000	17000	19000	21000	23000	25550
Invoices	0	9000	19000	30500	45000	63000	83000	98000	111000	127000	144000	162000
TOTAL INCOME	2000	13000	25500	39500	56500	77500	99000	115000	130000	148000	167000	187500
PAYMENTS												
Suppliers	4000	7500	9500	13500	17500	20000	23000	26500	30500	33500	36800	39200
Cash purchases	100	120	155	195	220	240	265	300	310	335	365	395
Salaries	500	1500	2500	3700	5100	6700	8300	10100	11900	13900	15900	17900
Wages	4000	9000	14000	19000	24000	29000	34000	39000	44500	50000	55550	61000
Other drawings	0	0	0	0	0	0	200	200	200	200	200	200
Employer	0	675	1575	2475	3405	4365	5355	6345	7365	8460	9585	10710
Rent	1250	2500	3750	5000	6250	7500	8750	10000	11250	12500	13750	15000
Rates	525	1050	1575	2150	2725	3300	3875	4450	5025	5600	6175	6750
Publicity	1000	1500	2000	2300	2500	2700	2900	3100	3300	3500	3700	3900
Oil/gas	0	0	400	400	400	700	700	700	900	900	900	1200
Electricity	0	150	150	150	310	310	310	450	450	450	600	600
Telephones	0	95	190	285	380	475	570	665	760	855	950	1045
Vehicle running	60	120	180	240	300	360	420	480	540	600	660	720
Fees	0	0	0	0	0	2500	2500	2500	2500	2500	2500	4000
Stationery, post printing	500	700	800	900	1000	1100	1200	1300	1400	1500	1600	1700
Bank charges, interest	200	200	200	260	260	260	325	325	325	395	395	395
TOTAL PAYMENTS	12135	25110	36975	50555	64350	79510	92670	106415	121225	135195	149580	164715

Fig. 7 Typical cumulative budget.

BOOKKEEPING

The subject of business expenses leads conveniently to bookkeeping, which may sound an uninteresting side effect of running a business because it detracts from the main interest – unless of course the core of the business is bookkeeping as the chosen business venture.

- It is very important, and is *not optional.*
- It's a distinct job that can be done by outside help.
- If you can do part of it (enough to let you thoroughly understand what is going on in the business), that's a good objective in itself.
- If it is a pain, or if you do not feel sufficiently competent, you don't have to do it *personally*, but it must be done responsibly by someone.

You will gradually begin to take a constructive interest in the figures, as a way of providing insight into what's happening. This is where the attributes of astuteness and an ability for figurework, mentioned in Chapter 2, come in handy. It also helps in situations like suspected *fiddling of the books* or potential fraud.

Accounts and accounts

Departing for a moment, by way of trying to minimise some point of possible confusion over terminology.

In the conventions adopted down the ages by the accountancy profession, there is a global interpretation of the term *Accounts*, meaning the summation of all the accounting and bookkeeping information, over the period in question (usually a year); but there is another interpretation that relates to keeping track of moneys owed to and by individual persons, suppliers and other organizations, whereby each separate person, business or other organization has a separate *account*, page, or sometimes folio, in the *ledgers* of the business venture.

One term tends to attract a capital letter, the other doesn't.

Why Keep Records?

It's reasonable to ask, *Why keep records, anyway?* The answers, to be referenced later, lie in:

- outside credibility – with the authorities, shareholders and creditors

- outside visibility to bankers and financiers
- comfort factors for suppliers and others
- business management tools
- understanding how the business is working
- understanding where the money is coming from and going to
- the law requiring books and records to be kept – for employment purposes
- the laws behind the Companies Acts (if applicable), business taxation, VAT (if applicable) and PAYE
- ad-hoc tax inspections.

Accountants will keep the bookkeeping records up-to-date on a daily, weekly or monthly basis (if required), make up the Annual Accounts and prepare all the legally required information and taxation returns (see later). Auditors (who are often accountants anyway) have a legal role to produce an acceptable independent assessment of certain business accounts.

These are very positive and constructive reasons why the 'books' need to be kept fully up-to-date and accurate. Bookkeeping must be carried out responsibly, accurately and in a professional manner. Your own bookkeeping will probably not be your core activity, but it runs alongside it to lubricate the business. Without good bookkeeping, the business will eventually grind to a halt.

- Bookkeeping saves time, money and patience, in the end.
- It is simply good practice to support a policy of neat housekeeping to encourage the business.
- It provides essential management information to enable the owner(s) to ensure that budgets are being adhered to, and forecasts for sales and other very important parameters are met.
- Bookkeeping provides visibility for monitoring and controlling the business, an audit trail, along with all the consolidated data for the mandatory Annual Accounts package to the authorities and outsiders.
- In short, it enables the owners to see how the business is performing, which can generate policy changes before disaster strikes.

Everything, regardless of category, must be noted down and *categorized* under specific headings or columns, and different *accounts* so as to give a total comprehensive picture. The various categories of sales and expenditure (reflecting all activities) should be set up to be directly relevant and meaningful to everyday activities. You should discuss with the chosen accountant what columns and methods should be adopted beforehand; as the accountant has to do the follow-on work. Anything that helps this smooth transition and extraction of the relevant figures must be a good thing since it will be easier and much more convenient for the professional and *therefore cheaper for your business*.

Whereas much of the income and expenditure will be as a result of the normal trading or everyday running of the business, as shown at the beginning of this chapter, income and expenditure derived from other sources (if any) has also to be tracked and accounted for – such as:

- borrowing
- capital injections
- loans to the business
- investments from shareholders
- incoming dividends
- disposal of assets
- sale of investments

- purchase of assets
- investments
- payments of dividends
- repayments
- instalments
- interest
- taxation.

Bookkeeping in Practice

For accuracy and financial safety reasons (and the fact that it represents best practice in the profession for a variety of solid reasons), *double entry* methods must be used if a manual system is employed, as a self-checking discipline to reduce clerical errors.

The so-called books of Accounts can be kept as computer records (this will probably depend on the size and complexity of the business, and the accountant's preference). Computer software looks after this 'double entry' discipline automatically, as it were. There are follow-through software packages that enable accountants to produce the downstream consolidated Accounts and taxation returns.

Your Bookkeeper
He or she:

- should have a meticulous, accurate and enquiring mind to track every single expenditure item
- should create and keep good quality reliable records with proven software packages on computerised systems, or purpose-designed rulings in specially designed Accounts books
- must log all primary entries *daily*, even if derivative actions are less frequent
- be intelligent enough to question certain transactions and be alert to fraud situations
- should be competent to work unaided up to 'trial balance' – *see below* – when the accountant often takes over
- may be involved with daily banking.

Notice that payroll and VAT are not mentioned, although an ability in this direction could be very useful.

Every individual primary document (incoming cheques, outgoing cheques, current balances, direct debits, banking details, petty cash vouchers, cash and card transactions, till audit rolls, accounts paid, accounts received, receipts, invoices, payroll transactions, tax, VAT and NI details) should be itemized, monitored and reconciled. Ledger accounts showing all incoming invoices and corresponding payments, and all outgoing invoices and corresponding payments, should be kept.

Management Data

Figures should be produced to *trial balance* level, which any book on account-ancy will explain in more detail. Essentially, it consists of listing and adding together into one summary document all the balances of the *individual* accounts (whether credit or debit as *at any particular date*) assigned to every individual person, supplier and other organization. It will be produced at least annually, but more probably, monthly.

The final pair of figures shows how much is owed to, and how much is owed by, your business, in total. The owner(s) must appreciate how these figures change from one trial balance to the next, and the figures will contribute to good internal accounting practices.

- Accounts are not merely produced to keep accountants in work (although they certainly appreciate the thought and the fees, no doubt).
- They play their part in assessing and evaluating a business, and its progress.
- Business Accounts and management information serve the same function in your business as personal health checks and vehicle MOT annual testing.

BOOKKEEPING LEADS TO THE ANNUAL ACCOUNTS

Bookkeeping culminates in a concentrated source of data that the owner(s) and their accountant advisors can study and use to make inspired decisions. Whether or not the figures are determined manually or by computer software is immaterial pro-vided they turn out to be accurate and a fair reflection on the business activities.

- Potential suppliers, trade creditors and money lending institutions all want reas-surances that their money is safe and will be repaid when requested. They want to see that the business is healthy.
- Taxation records and calculations are necessary by law for the Inland Revenue to agree what taxes have to be paid.
- Management and/or directors can assess historic progress and trends, the ongo-ing viability and the potential of the business.
- Formal Accounts are required by law for limited liability companies, and simi-lar legal entities, as prescribed by the Companies Acts – but more about this topic later when business trading status is discussed.

Other Services From the Accountant

When it comes to working out net pay for the directors or any employees (and VAT calculations, if applicable), your bookkeeper may deal competently with these matters but there are experts who will do it for you – again it could be some-one who does this for many clients within the accountant's office who also deals with all the personal taxation forms and returns in relation to the employees and any of their *perks*.

It's a big and responsible job (depending how many staff there are, including the owners – assuming salary or wages payments are paid to them explicitly) and one that must be done. A system, open for inspection by the tax authorities, must be established for someone to handle these aspects of the business on your behalf.

On the subject of bookkeeping and employee payrolls, there are many specialist courses and books available if you want to do it; but it takes time that could be better used exploiting your own expertise to the full – in other words, it could cost profits. You should do what you are personally best at, and outsource the rest.

WHAT HAVE YOU LEARNT IN THIS CHAPTER?

★ What is the owner's role in the financial affairs of the business?
★ What are the main costs associated with business?
★ What are the two main categories of business expenditure?
★ Broadly, what are the differences between revenue and capital expenses?
★ List categories of expenditure for businesses generally.
★ What are the current approximate criteria for VAT registration, the advantages and disadvantages?
★ What records does a business need to keep, and why?
★ Why undertake bookkeeping anyway?
★ What are the benefits of good bookkeeping, and who should do it?
★ Why is a cumulative budget useful?
★ Why do you need an accurate management information package?

15
Creating Business Management Information

The complete package of management information includes the Annual Accounts, determined from bookkeeping, but it can also embody forecast material of any relevant parameters, like sales, deliveries, revenue and cash flow.

Several slightly different versions may be produced from the master Accounts to suit differing needs, so that they can be used by the tax authorities, the accountant, creditors, and (if appropriate) by the directors, shareholders, Companies House and hence the general public at large.

TRADING ACCOUNT

In any business, you clearly need to look to the future but you also need to know what has happened retrospectively. Every year the business must produce a summary of its trading operations – the so-called Trading Account that could look similar to Figure 8 – what actually happened (as opposed to what was expected and forecast). It merely summarizes:

- The total expenditure and where the money has been spent.
- The total income and where it has been derived.
- The difference between the two summary figures, being the business' net profit (or quite possibly, a loss!) for that year.

Each year the Trading Account simply tells the story of how well or otherwise the business has performed during that year. It's similar to seeing a nostalgic video of the last holiday (that can't be changed of course), and the events are strictly blinkered so as to see nothing outside that particular year.

Trading Accounts represent spot assessments of what has happened in the business during the last year. One year's Trading Account can thus be readily compared with another's to help understand any changes, or to view a trend in a series of changes over several years – which is very important information. In practice, consecutive yearly figures are often printed side by side, aligned for comparison purposes to highlight trends.

The individual annual profit and loss figure will be copied across into a

Item	Total	
Revenue		
Cash sales	24975	
Invoices	158752	
Total income		183727
Payments		
Suppliers	37261	
Cash purchases	458	
Salaries	17530	
Wages	59840	
Other drawings	200	
Employer's contributions	10058	
Rent	15000	
Rates	6600	
Publicity	3900	
Oil/gas	1286	
Electricity	752	
Telephones	837	
Vehicle running	856	
Fees	3150	
Bank charges, interest	315	
Total payments		158043
Net profit		25684

Fig. 8   Typical trading account.

so-called *profit and loss account* (like all the other individual *accounts*) for the business, that will show cumulatively and by a series of single figures how the business has performed over successive years.

Prepayments and Deposits

For the purpose of creating the Trading Account, any money paid to the business in advance, like deposits or advance payments against long-term contracts, and money paid by the business in advance to others, like annual insurance premiums and subscriptions, represent complete or partial prepayments for products, services and projects not yet completed (by definition), and hence they represent pro rata debtor and creditor entries against the books of the company until the obligations are fulfilled both ways. The Accounts take note of these adjustments.

Single Universal Cutoff Date

They take account of all incoming and outgoing invoices, instantaneous trial balance figures, any transactions paid to the bank up to the date in question, any cheques actually written (although still in the post perhaps) and the bank statement – in other words, there must be a single effective cutoff date that is applied universally throughout the Accounts which will be the last day of the accounting period.

BALANCE SHEET

Also at the end of every trading year, coinciding with the production of the Trading Account, is a 'statement' showing the present state of the business, compiled under the same conventions as the previous paragraph with the same universal cutoff date, such as:

- its assets and liabilities generally – the state of the 'union' as it were
- what it is owed
- what it owes by way of both shorter-term and long-term creditors
- its state of liquidity – how readily the business could produce 'cash' if it had to
- its working capital
- its borrowings
- what it has done with its accumulated trading profit or loss
- the owner's and other contributors' various cumulative stakes in the business, shareholding
- estimated values of any intangibles like intellectual property, patents, goodwill and so on.

This document, also produced annually by the accountant, is known as the Balance Sheet, and typically shown condensed as in Figure 9 overleaf. Balance Sheets represent an updated annual snapshot, as it were, of the health of the business . They, too, are often printed in adjacent columns for ease of comparison, which should be made between successive annual versions.

RETROSPECTIVE VIEW

The Trading Account and Balance Sheet can only report retrospectively, and in themselves do not predict the future.

However, like tea leaves, they can be read and interpreted singly or together to highlight and comment on individual figures, comparisons and *trends*. Together with any forecast information and any other general intelligence that could affect the business either way, they can anticipate both good and bad news, or even indicate a preliminary estimate of the next set of annual figures.

Diagramatically, as the business progresses from Day 1, the interrelationship of these two types of document is shown in Figure 10 on page 167.

Each year's trading activities, as summarized in the Trading Account, modifies the previous year's Balance Sheet to form the next Balance Sheet. The apparent and nominal present worth of the business at any point in time is represented by the latest Balance Sheet, as modified later by any succeeding [complete or partial] trading activities and forecast information.

Fixed assets		
Premises	65,271	
Vehicles	10,548	
Equipment	45,376	
		121,195
Current assets		
Stock	35,845	
Trade debtors	6,592	
Prepayments	2,683	
Cash at bank/in-hand	1,769	
	46,889	
Current liabilities		
Trade creditors	9,547	
Prepayments	1,073	
Corporation or other business	2,854	
Other creditors	1,967	15,441
Net current assets		31,448
Total assets less current liabilities		152,643
Longer-term creditors		32,000
		120,643
Capital and reserves		
Capital investments		80,000
Reserves broadly, cumulative profits		40,643
Goodwill very difficult to evaluate		?
		120,643

Fig. 9   Typical balance sheet.

This integrated information package allows business navigational decisions to be made. The documents must be studied and interpreted: heads in sand are simply not allowed. The decisions could range from:

- broadly more of the same (that is, no major policy or strategy changes)
- implementation go-ahead for expansion plans
- major pruning and cutbacks.

Further constructive decisions along with their incumbent risk assessments as to what the consequences might bring may have to be made. There could in fact be a

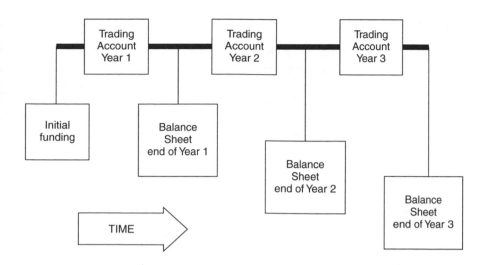

Fig. 10   Interrelationships of financial reports.

large number of diverse combinations, permutations and conflicting priorities to be evaluated before important resolutions can be finally established – but that, unfortunately, is life.

Buying Another Business
Reference was made in Chapter 6 to the possibilities of buying another business as a way of starting off (or indeed of expanding) the venture. Recent Trading Accounts and Balance Sheets for that business are a good starting point, but certainly not the only documents or factors that need to be considered. The way the figures are interpreted or presented is very subjective – thus making the whole business difficult to value accurately. Some figures are fairly factual, tangible and straightforward; but others are much less so (and very difficult to assess – and all this in spite of hopefully meticulous bookkeeping).

You can see how complex it can be to assess the worth of the business, let alone its *practical worth to the prospective purchaser.* It's your own money at stake. Just imagine a situation in which the bookkeeping had been deliberately or carelessly neglected; or, worse still, deliberately falsified for some obscure reason – without the innocent prospective purchaser realizing. The consequences would be potentially disastrous.

Several years back, a headline-hitting example occurred whereby the Accounts had been falsified in one of the big multinationals. They were fraudulently prepared: or, constructively presented and economical with the truth. Supposed experts had examined the books prior to purchase, and were 'successfully' fooled – with millions of pounds of shareholders' money at stake. False claims had been made about the prospects for the company – and the purchase of the company went ahead without anyone realizing – until it was too late.

167

PROFIT AND LOSS

The unquestionable motive behind the vast majority of businesses (not *all* curiously) is to make a handsome profit.

Contrary to uninformed opinion, controlled profit exists for a specific purpose: it is certainly not a dirty word. Indeed, it is a sign of a thriving business and a necessity for a healthy business. Clearly if the expected profit were to be a loss, it could cause alarms and short-term problems, like preventing dividend payments, and future investments – for expansion, new developments or new products. If comparisons show that the annual results were getting worse year on year, that would be a very serious problem that would need investigating and rectifying.

If the effect of one year's trading were a loss:

- In itself, this would not be disastrously bad news: stop and consider that shortly after Day 1, a snapshot would probably reveal a huge investment and probably a trading loss since launch – simply because the business had not been operating very long, and had not had a fair chance to build up a head of steam.
- On a longer-term timescale, an individual loss must also be viewed constructively against all the snapshot figures, comparisons and trends in the management information before you really become downhearted.
- It must also be considered against any special circumstances (expansions, investments, acquisitions, and so on) that might have triggered it, contributed to it or caused it.
- Some businesses purposely plan to have losses for all sorts of reasons, including these three: a deliberate policy of buying into the market with low prices, possible pending closure or tax avoidance.
- The advice from your accountant will be extremely valuable, and surprisingly perhaps, *not necessarily* gloomy.
- Accountants and other experienced businessmen and women are able to take a dispassionate view, basing their decisions on their long-term hunches and intuition, and not just the short-term instantaneous reactions.

Gross and Net Profit

There are several other adjectives associated with the word *profit*, of which two are most frequently encountered. Accounting conventions dictate that after the sales figures, from which are deducted the cost of sales (stock, and so on), the Trading Account highlights a figure for *gross* profit. This gross profit figure is used to pay the various trading expenses, listed in the previous chapter, leaving a figure for *net* profit. Net profit is used to pay a variety of things like dividends, taxes, research and development for new products (commonly known as R&D), and future investment generally.

However, whilst businesses should not normally aim to make a loss (certainly not a prolonged cumulative loss), there are some, as mentioned above, who actively only set out to break even, that is to make zero net profit, deliberately – perhaps because of their constitution or charitable status, because, in general, charities are not allowed to make a net profit.

In order to circumnavigate this constraint, brought about primarily by the strict interpretation of accounting conventions, they transfer the expenditure items that are normally taken below the net profit line to a point above it instead – thus fulfilling the letter of a condition of charitable status without inhibiting their necessary investment to be able to move with the times and safeguard their longer term activities.

FORECASTS

Thus far, the factually based elements of the management information package have been considered. Now let us look at the forecasts. The cynic would say that this is all pure or inspired guesswork, reading crystal balls, and so on.

Nevertheless, some attempt has to be made in order for the business (or life in general for that matter) to continue. The usual timescale is for annual, two-, three-, four-, five- and ten-year forecasts: but in practice they can be for as long or as short a timescale as you want, although annual periods sound sensible for many situations as their validity coincides with the next round of Trading Accounts and Balance Sheets. Sales forecasts have already been mentioned.

The principle for any forecast is simply to anticipate, with the most up-to-date and comprehensive intelligence, what is likely to happen in each of the next time periods (say each of the future 12-month periods). The farther into the future, obviously the less certain the figures can be, whereas short-term forecasts can be fairly accurate.

Sales forecasts are the starting point and these were explained in Chapter 10. What else is needed?

* firstly, deliveries
* secondly (as a consequence of deliveries), revenue.

This latter (whilst 'shadowing' the sales forecasts to some extent) will be *delayed* from the original sales by varying periods across the entire range of potential sales with a minimum of at least one month, in practice. Consider:

* Where goods are sold for cash and paid for immediately (often because they are simply in stock, on the shelves or whatever), the revenue forecast would be theoretically identical to the sales forecast.
* Where the goods are not in stock and need time for manufacture and design, as well as additional time to obtain suitable supplies from other businesses, a delay would follow (several weeks or months).
* In either case, if they were sold by invoice which is based on up to several months' delayed payments, for example, there is clearly going to be a sizeable gap between getting money in and getting the original order.

The object is to produce a reliable forecast of payments coming into the business (for each and every month), that bears some direct link back to the sales forecast – and that in turn was based, you will recall, on marketing and sales intelligence, and other projections.

This series of forecasts is so critical: it affects estimates for the receipt of money ultimately; and that in its turn determines when it can be *forecasted to be spent*. The spending of money might be on plant, equipment, wages or something else *that materially affects when the goods destined to generate the revenue are available for delivery*; and hence when payment can be reasonably expected. It could be a circle of course! Clearly, if spare cash is budgeted too tightly, this arrangement could be far too uncomfortable. So, forecast and budget working capital carefully. It is absolutely certain that a good and accurate *revenue* forecast (that is, when the *money will actually arrive*) and its earlier counterpart, the *sales* forecast, are both desperately crucial to the well-being of the business.

There could be a geographical split to be handled within *all* the separate forecasts, just to complicate matters a little; and also international transactions with currency-conversion embracing further delay factors. To avoid millions of sheets of paper during the forecasting process, empirical rules will emerge, as the forecasting procedures become more refined; notional average block delay figures, if fairly accurate, could be substituted and applied across all products and services to simplify the tedious arithmetic.

Also computer software for the whole series of forecasting is available, that saves an awful lot of time, especially when one asks *What happens if ...?* The computer, if the system model is set up meticulously and proved to be correct, is obviously fast and accurate; and represents an efficient way to go – but it still relies on top-quality human-generated information in the first place.

The programmes can be used again and again, as new forecasts and derivative forecasts are wanted. Perturbations (*What if ...?*s) can be introduced to highlight the effect of an unscheduled delay or a sale that does not materialize. It is effectively an off-line *experimental model* for devising strategies for the business and testing what will happen, without actually tampering with the real business – and the results don't take a year to produce. Only seconds.

You will get a very close insight into the business, if you do it yourself, and you will also save:

- professional fees – if the accountant would normally have done it for you
- time and frustration – for doing this work yourself, and getting results straight-away.

BUDGETS AND CASH FLOW

Two more sets of important management information arise from the above forecasts: financial information that relates to *budgets* and *cash flow*. You understand budgets, now we look at cash flow.

Budgets

Ideally expenditure should be planned ahead against all-revenue forecasts (not just sales revenues, but capital injections, loans, VAT receipts, advance payments, and so on) – but not too tightly as mentioned above. Planning individual expenditures (main items at least, augmented by lump sums for general miscellaneous expenditure and petty cash) and by month is actually an easier and simpler process than deriving all the forecast information. It is known by the familiar term *budgeting*. Most businesses have a budget (refer to the previous chapter and Figure 7); and many people have household domestic budgets (*see* Chapter 4 again). Budgets may be produced on a cumulative basis or not.

Cash Flow

Only one step away from budgets is the other set of financial information. This effectively consolidates the expenditure budget with the revenue forecast. The result is a cash flow forecast – much more useful than pure budget information.

This absolutely essential document virtually embraces everything about the enterprise financially, and could be presented on a computer spreadsheet document, similar in principle to the other forecasts.

Figure 11 shows a typical cash flow forecast (blank form) that could be tailored to suit your particular enterprise. It shows for any month, the detailed projected business income, expenditure and anticipated bank balance.

It carries forward from one month to the next, in a cumulative manner, the excess of income over planned expenditure (or deficit, of course) and hence shows the anticipated level of working capital and overdraft facilities – but it really only works in practice *if* sales live up to, or exceed, forecast or expenditure is maintained within or well below budget.

Cash flow forecasts should show payments for *all* known or anticipated expenses, including loan repayments, credit purchase instalments, taxes, VAT, PAYE and so on. Just as the revenue forecasts should accurately reflect the *actual* payment time, in preference to the corresponding sale month, so too should the payments be geared to the *actual* payment date, not the corresponding incoming invoice date.

Maximize Sales

The whole integrity rests on good sales forecasting; so, in this respect, be realistic – not optimistic or even pessimistic. Get as many sales as possible, and as quickly as possible! It's such a straightforward equation:

• more sales
• more (deliveries and) revenue
• higher the bank balance
• smaller the overdraft potential
• cheaper the borrowing
• higher the profits
• higher personal income potential.

Item	Dec' last	Jan	Feb	Mar	Apr	May	Jun	Jul	Aug	Sept	Oct	Nov	Dec
Invoice sales													
REVENUE													
Sales													
Invoices													
Other													
Assets													
VAT (net)													
TOTAL INCOME													
Materials													
Payments													
Suppliers													
Cash purchases													
Salaries													
Wages													
Other drawings													
Employer													
Tax													
VAT (net) estimate													
Rent													
Rates													
Vehicle HP													
Publicity													
Oil/gas													
Electricity													
Telephones													
Vehicle running													
Fees													
Equipment, plant													
Stationery, etc													
Bank Charges, Interest													
TOTAL PAYMENTS													
MONTH SURPLUS													
B/F from previous month													

Fig. 11   Bank cash flow forecast sheet.

Don't Borrow, If You Don't Have To

If businesses can manage without an overdraft, put the spare cash on short-term deposit (don't tie your money up for a lengthy period) and make it *earn* some money.

CASH FLOW EXAMPLES

Ground Rules

- Show every item of income and expenditure, under the exact month. Reflect the budget estimates.
- Cash flow forecasts are designed to anticipate the bank situation: individual VAT elements are not shown – *only the net remittances* to and from the authorities (reflecting cheques to and from the bank accounts).
- It is extremely important that all items are shown, and brought together to produce the most accurate and meaningful cash flow forecast. Timely revenues are exceptionally important to pay bills, and so on.
- Some items are *rigidly fixed* as far as payment dates and amounts are concerned, such as direct debits, instalments, bills of exchange.
- Certain items are *effectively fixed* each month – that is, not really optional in either amount or timing such as rent, insurance premiums.
- Some items can, and almost certainly will, *fluctuate* by definition – sales forecast figures (they are only a forecast, after all).
- Others *can be allowed to float* in time and amount, depending on busines conditions – personal drawings, owners' salaries, maintenance, repairs and new fittings.
- Use the flexible items to the best advantage to maintain liquidity.
- Don't run too tightly, and have contingency plans available, just in case something doesn't work out.

The Bottom Line

The bottom line indicates the spare cash availability (or alternatively, the working capital requirements, that is, the overdraft short-term borrowing requirements), that drive home the twin important messages of bank overdraft requirements and above all a crude indication of the business viability.

The cash flow forecast, assuming it was totally accurate, could be translated by the accountant into a projection of the next or first Trading Account and Balance Sheet showing whether your business is viable.

The bottom right-hand corner figure (the annual cumulative surplus) should, for comfort, be significantly positive. On the other hand, if the bottom line (the cumulative surplus or deficit) showed a substantially negative trend, the omens would not look good – although a professional observer might detect some better news and suggest several constructive changes to the financial framework of the business to make it much more robust. If the cumulative bottom line appears to indicate bad news, talk to the experts and let them apply their specialist expertise first. Don't be despondent.

Apart from the technical knowledge for the business, you can now understand why some sales, marketing and cash flow knowledge make a good combination to master as the business progresses. You may even come to enjoy understanding and creating cash flow forecasts, as a means to comprehending the business better.

Three Worked Examples

Cash flow forecasting should be second-nature when you get thoroughly familiar with business. To consolidate your mastery and confidence in this fundamental subject, here are three nominal illustrations:

- a freelancer working from home
- a small shop
- a small-to-medium manufacturing business.

In each case (it could be *your* business) the businesses have been started from scratch. Two years' projections are shown for the latter two. You should appreciate that each business starts with zero cash surplus/deficit, apart from investment money earmarked for specific purposes, in Year 1; but that the cumulative cash surplus/deficit at the end of Year 1 is used to commence year 2. Year 2 surplus/deficit represents the aggregate for both years.

You are asked to study them meticulously to see how they have been created and to understand the interrelationship of some of the figures. Staff and wages bills, including the owners', carry increases to reflect the gradual build-up of the businesses. Items like cars have been deferred until the businesses can truly justify the costs. VAT is shown periodically either as a payment or receipt (*net*); materials and stock that have been *invoiced* from suppliers are usually due for payment one month later (and hence the shaded line showing when stock and/or raw materials were assumed to be delivered).

When compiling such spreadsheets, remember that certain series of figures may have a *direct* relationship with another series elsewhere on the same document, as with the employers' figures; whereas other figures are almost or entirely independent of each other. No attempt has been made to optimize the forecasts, so you could try the effect of advancing or delaying some payments and revenues, and so on. Revenue has been split between cash sales and invoiced sales (in most cases).

Freelancer Working From Home

Figure 12 relates to a typical consultant, therapist or computer subcontractor working from home. He or she has no overheads, but a good lifestyle, as represented by satisfactory, but not brilliant, salary (at the moment).

A minimal investment (only £3,000) for computer hardware, software, office, and so on – or whatever – is planned; the business is not registered for VAT. A cash surplus of £8,115 is anticipated for the year, but remember this is not the same as profit, as profit calculations take into account depreciation, amortization (gradually writing off a debt or investment), prepayments, and so on. (You may feel it helpful to re-read this chapter to re-establish these basic principles.)

Item	Dec last	Jan	Feb	Mar	Apr	May	Jun	Jul	Aug	Sept	Oct	Nov	Dec	Total
Invoice sales		2000	3000	4000	4500	4500	4500	4500	3500	4500	4500	4500	4500	
REVENUE														
Sales														
Invoices – fees		0	2000	3000	4000	4500	4500	4500	4500	3500	4500	4500	4500	44000
Other														0
Assets		3000												3000
VAT (net)														0
TOTAL INCOME		3000	2000	3000	4000	4500	4500	4500	3500	4500	4500	4500	4500	47000
Materials	200	100	50	50	50	50	50	50	50	50	50	50	50	650
Payments														
Suppliers		200	100	50	50	50	50	50	50	50	50	50	50	800
Cash purchases		50	20	20	20	20	20	20	20	20	20	20	20	270
Salaries		1200	1500	1800	1800	1800	1800	1800	1800	1800	1800	1800	1800	20700
Wages														0
Other drawings														0
Employer		0	180	225	270	270	270	270	270	270	270	270	270	2835
Tax														0
VAT (net)														0
Rent														0
Rates														0
Vehicle HP						2030	330	330	330	330	330	330	330	4340
Oil/gas				75			60			45			60	240
Electricity			60			45			45		60			210
Telephones			95	95	95	95	95	95	95	95	95	95	95	1045
Vehicle running		50	50	50	50	60	60	60	60	60	60	60	60	680
Fees							500						300	800
Computer, office		3000								1000		2500		6500
Stationery, etc		200	100											300
Bank charges, interest		75			30			30			30			165
TOTAL PAYMENTS		4775	2105	2315	2315	4370	3185	2655	2670	3670	2655	5185	2985	38885
MONTH SURPLUS		-1775	-105	685	1685	130	1315	1845	1830	-170	1845	-685	1515	8115
B/F from previous month			-1775	-1880	-1195	490	620	1935	3780	5610	5440	7285	6600	
C/F to next month		-1775	-1880	-1195	490	620	1935	3780	5610	5440	7285	6600	8115	8115

Fig. 12   Homeworker cash flow forecast.

Commentary
As a crude yardstick, the final predicted surplus equates to 18.44 per cent of turnover or 270 per cent of capital investment. It appears to be a healthy business, but the consultant or therapist must not get complacent, and should keep up the effort.

Small Shop
Figure 13 represents a smallish shop in rented premises that buys and sells merchandise for 'cash'. In the first year its turnover is predicted to be £182,000, excluding VAT – averaging £3,500 per week or roughly £600 per day, all 'cash' sales. Its staff consists of the boss plus approximately two part time staff, working quite hard to get the sales figures – although this is partly contingent on the precise nature of the merchandise, the working hours, shift patterns and detailed staffing arrangements.

The initial investment of £80,000 is used for:

- initial payments in connection with the property
- fitting out the shop (£30,000 + £10,000)
- initial stock (£20,000)
- cash reserves to mitigate the large overdraft requirements (£20,000).

Commentary
There is a predicted £3,535 cash surplus over the initial £20,000 reserve buffer, which represents 1.94 per cent of turnover – not very high of course but at least positive, and hence just about satisfactory. All in all this is probably par for the course and should be compared with current building society and other investment interest rates.

Year 2
Refer to Figure 14. The turnover for the second year is predicted to build satisfactorily to £290,000, excluding VAT – averaging £5,600 per week or approximately £1,000 per day. This projected increase of 60 per cent will be achieved with the help of an additional part-time member of staff.

Year 2 Commentary
Although the business forecast a slow start, it is probably going to develop well with a cumulative cash surplus increased several times to a predicted £22,775 *over* the initial £20,000 buffer – or 7.85 per cent of turnover – a promising start; let's hope it continues.

Small Manufacturing Business
Figure 15 relates to a small (at the moment) manufacturing business in rented premises, that buys raw materials and produces finished goods. It employs between four and eight staff. There are some cash sales, but most are invoiced sales. The first year turnover is shown as £186,500, excluding VAT, after an initial investment of £60,000 for equipment, down-payments and so on. Explicit

Item	Dec last	Jan	Feb	Mar	Apr	May	Jun	Jul	Aug	Sept	Oct	Nov	Dec	Total
Invoice sales														
REVENUE														
Sales		4000	7000	10000	12000	14000	16000	17000	13000	19000	20000	22000	28000	182000
Invoices		0	0	0	0	0	0	0	0	0	0	0	0	0
Other														0
Assets		80000												80000
VAT (net)			5250											5250
TOTAL INCOME		84000	12250	10000	12000	14000	16000	17000	13000	19000	20000	22000	28000	267250
Stock	20000	5000	6000	7000	8000	9000	10000	10000	8000	15000	10000	12000	15000	115000
PAYMENTS														
Stock		20000	5000	6000	7000	8000	9000	10000	10000	8000	15000	10000	12000	120000
Cash purchases		500	150	150	150	150	150	150	50	100	100	100	250	2000
Salaries		1000	1000	1000	1200	1400	1600	1600	1600	1600	1600	1600	1600	16800
Wages		1400	1400	1400	1400	1700	1700	1700	1700	1700	1700	1700	1700	19200
Other drawings								200						200
Employer		0	360	360	360	390	465	495	495	495	495	495	495	4905
Tax														0
VAT (net)	estimate					2800			2900			3000		8700
Rent		1100	1100	1100	1100	1100	1100	1100	1100	1100	1100	1100	1100	13200
Rates		525	525	525	575	575	575	575	575	575	575	575	575	6750
Vehicle HP				830	330	330	330	330	330	330	330	330	330	3800
Oil/gas				400			300			200			300	1200
Electricity			150			160			140			150		600
Telephones			95	95	95	95	95	95	95	95	95	95	95	1045
Vehicle running		60	60	60	60	60	60	60	60	60	60	60	60	720
Fees							2500						1500	4000
Fitting out, etc.		30000					10000							40000
Stationery, etc		200	100											300
Bank charges, interest		100			60			65			70			295
TOTAL PAYMENTS		54885	9940	11920	12330	16760	17875	26370	19045	14255	21125	19205	20005	243715
MONTH SURPLUS		29115	2310	–1920	–330	–2760	–1875	–9370	–6045	4745	–1125	2795	7995	23535
B/F from previous month			29115	31425	29505	29175	26415	24540	15170	9125	13870	12745	15540	
C/F to next month		29115	31425	29505	29175	26415	24540	15170	9125	13870	12745	15540	23535	

Fig. 13   Shop cash flow forecast.

Item	Dec last	Jan	Feb	Mar	Apr	May	Jun	Jul	Aug	Sept	Oct	Nov	Dec	Total
Invoice sales														
REVENUE														
Sales		30000	19000	21000	23000	25000	23000	20000	18000	26000	27000	28000	30000	290000
Invoices		0	0	0	0	0	0	0	0	0	0	0	0	0
Other														0
Assets														0
VAT (net)														0
TOTAL INCOME		30000	19000	21000	23000	25000	23000	20000	18000	26000	27000	28000	30000	290000
Stock	15000	12000	13000	14000	13000	12000	12000	11000	16000	16000	18000	20000	10000	167000
PAYMENTS														
Stock		15000	12000	13000	14000	13000	12000	12000	11000	16000	16000	18000	20000	172000
Cash purchases		300	300	300	300	250	250	250	250	350	350	350	400	3650
Salaries	1600	1600	1600	1600	1600	1600	1600	1600	1600	1600	1600	1600	1600	19200
Wages	1700	1900	1900	1900	1900	1900	1900	1900	1900	2100	2100	2100	2100	23600
Other drawings													200	200
Employer		495	525	525	525	525	525	525	525	525	555	555	555	6360
Tax	estimate									1000				1000
VAT (net)	estimate		3000			3100			3200			3300		12600
Rent		1100	1100	1100	1100	1100	1100	1100	1100	1100	1100	1100	1100	13200
Rates		525	525	525	650	650	650	650	650	650	650	650	650	7425
Vehicle HP		330	330	330	330	330	330	330	330	330	330	330	330	3960
Publicity														
Oil/gas				440			330			220			330	1320
Electricity			190			170			150			160		670
Telephones		130	130	130	130	130	130	130	130	130	130	130	130	1560
Vehicle running		60	60	60	60	60	60	60	60	60	60	60	60	720
Fees							1500						1500	3000
Fitting out, etc.														0
Stationery, etc.														
Bank charges, interest		100			60			65			70			295
TOTAL PAYMENTS		21540	21660	19910	20655	22815	20375	18610	20895	24065	22945	28355	28955	270760
MONTH SURPLUS		8460	−2660	1090	2345	2185	2625	1390	−2895	1935	4055	−335	1045	19240
B/F from previous month		23535	31995	29335	30425	32770	34955	37580	38970	36075	38010	42065	41730	
C/F to next month		31995	29335	30425	32770	34955	37580	38970	36075	38010	42065	41730	42775	42775

Fig. 14 Shop cash flow forecast Year 2.

Item	Dec last	Jan	Feb	Mar	Apr	May	Jun	Jul	Aug	Sept	Oct	Nov	Dec	Total
Invoice sales		8000	10000	11500	14500	18000	20000	15000	13000	16000	17000	18000	20000	
REVENUE														
Sales		2000	2000	2500	2500	2500	3000	1500	1000	2000	2000	2000	2500	25500
Invoices		0	8000	10000	11500	14500	18000	20000	15000	13000	16000	17000	18000	161000
Other														0
Assets		60000												6000
VAT (net)			7000											7000
TOTAL INCOME		62000	17000	12500	14000	17000	21000	21500	16000	15000	18000	19000	20500	253500
Materials	4000	3500	2000	6000	2000	2500	3000	3500	4000	3000	3300	2400	3800	39000
PAYMENTS														
Suppliers		4000	3500	2000	6000	2000	2500	3000	3500	4000	3000	3300	2400	39200
Cash purchases		100	20	35	40	25	20	25	35	10	25	30	30	395
Salaries		500	1000	1000	1200	1400	1600	1600	1800	1800	2000	2000	2000	17900
Wages		4000	5000	5000	5000	5000	5000	5000	5000	5500	5500	5500	5500	61000
Other drawings								200						200
Employer		0	675	900	900	930	960	990	990	1020	1095	1125	1125	10710
Tax														0
VAT (net)	estimate					600			9000				7000	16600
Rent		1250	1250	1250	1250	1250	1250	1250	1250	1250	1250	1250	1250	15000
Rates		525	525	525	575	575	575	575	575	575	575	575	575	6750
Vehicle HP		1030	530	530	530	530	530	530	530	530	530	530	530	6860
Publicity		1000	500	500	300	200	200	200	200	200	200	200	200	3900
Oil/gas				400			300			200			300	1200
Electricity			150			160			140			150		600
Telephones			95	95	95	95	95	95	95	95	95	95	95	1045
Vehicle running		60	60	60	60	60	60	60	60	60	60	60	60	720
Fees							2500						1500	4000
Equipment, plan		40000			10000					7500	2500			60000
Stationery, etc.		200	300	100										600
Bank charges, interest		200			60			65			70			395
TOTAL PAYMENTS		52865	13605	12395	26010	12825	15590	13590	23175	22740	16900	14815	22565	247075
MONTH SURPLUS		9135	3395	105	-12010	4175	5410	7910	-7175	-7740	1100	4185	-2065	6425
B/F from previous month			9135	12530	12635	625	4800	10210	18120	10945	3205	4305	8490	6425
C/F to next month		9135	12530	12635	625	4800	10210	18120	10945	3205	4305	8490	6425	

Fig. 15   Manufacturer cash flow forecast.

publicity is to be undertaken to the value of £3,900 to considerably boost the business in the early stages (unlike the ventures in the first two examples).

Commentary
The first year's predicted cash surplus is a modest, but satisfactory, £6,425 or 3.44 per cent of turnover and 10.71 per cent of capital investment.

Year 2
Refer to Figure 16. The turnover is forecast to rise to about £330,000, excluding VAT – an increase of 77 per cent – which is to be achieved by having more people and hence higher labour costs. A further own-capital investment of £20,000, and a *reinvestment* of some of the profits (£35,000), are planned to try to improve productivity and efficiency.

Year 2 Commentary
The second year's cash surplus has been predicted at £67,925 although £35,000 is to be reinvested, which is 20.58 per cent of turnover. It will be hard work for the first year and a half, but the business hopes to be showing good progress later. The second year profits will generate a business tax entry on next year's cash flow charts.

Observations
The examples deliberately represent three completely different types, styles and sizes of business, with differing degrees of fortunes: your own venture will attract different figures. You should make sure you understand cash flow principles, and could produce such a document for your own venture. You must learn to understand them, and use them in running the business.

On the face of it, depending how the various businesses above have been established (and hence the governing rules and so on), *some* of the original investments could be withdrawn at the end of the periods forecasted: but further investment of 'profits' (or additional new capital) might be very prudent *in all three cases* to generate even more turnover and profits for the future.

Funding
No account has been taken of bank repayments in these examples because it has not been expressly established whether any money was to be actually borrowed from funding organizations. If it were, the repayments would have to be clearly shown, together with any interest and charges – and clearly they might make a considerable difference to their implied profitability and viability! But, in theory at least, it could have been created without recourse to external funding.

Summary: Cash Flow Forecasts
Cash flow forecasts are:

• highly critical documents for all businesses

180

Item	Dec last	Jan	Feb	Mar	Apr	May	Jun	Jul	Aug	Sept	Oct	Nov	Dec	Total
Invoice sales	20000	22000	24000	26000	28000	25000	25000	22000	18000	26000	28000	30000	22000	
REVENUE														
Sales		4000	3000	3250	3000	3000	3500	3000	2000	2700	2900	3200	2500	36050
Invoices		20000	22000	24000	26000	28000	25000	25000	22000	18000	26000	28000	30000	294000
Other														0
Assets					20000									20000
VAT (net)														0
TOTAL INCOME	24000	24000	25000	27250	49000	31000	28500	28000	24000	20700	28900	31200	32500	350050
Materials	3800	5000	4000	6100	3800	4000	4500	5000	5500	5500	5000	4500	5000	57900
PAYMENTS														
Suppliers		3800	5000	4000	6100	3800	4000	4500	5000	5500	5500	5000	4500	56700
Cash purchases		200	50	50	50	30	40	40	40	40	50	50	50	690
Salaries	2000	2000	2000	2000	2200	2200	2200	2200	2200	2200	2200	2200	2200	25800
Wages	5500	5500	6000	6000	6000	6000	6000	6000	6000	6500	6500	6500	6500	73500
Other drawings		500											1000	1500
Employer		1125	1125	1200	1200	1230	1230	1230	1230	1230	1305	1305	1305	14715
Tax	estimate									2000				2000
VAT (net)	estimate		12000			12000			12000			12000		48000
Rent		1250	1250	1250	1250	1250	1250	1250	1250	1250	1250	1250	1250	15000
Rates		575			625	625	625	625	625	625	625	625	625	6200
Vehicle HP		530	530	530	530	2000	1000	1000	1000	1000	1000	1000	1000	11120
Publicity		500	400	400	300	300	300	200	200	200	200	200	200	3400
Oil/gas				420			315			210			315	1260
Electricity			175			200			180			185		740
Telephones		125	125	125	125	125	125	125	130	130	130	130	130	1525
Vehicle running		60	60	60	120	120	120	120	120	120	120	120	120	1260
Fees							3000					1500		4500
Equipment, plan						20000						35000		55000
Stationery, etc.		200									100			300
Bank charges, interest		80			80			90			90			340
TOTAL PAYMENTS		16445	28715	16035	18580	49880	20205	17380	29975	21005	19070	65565	20695	323550
MONTH SURPLUS		7555	-3715	11215	30420	-18880	8295	10620	-5975	-305	9830	-34365	11805	26500
B/F from previous month		6425	13980	10265	21480	51900	33020	41315	51935	45960	45655	55485	21120	
C/F to next month		13980	10265	21480	51900	33020	41315	59135	45960	45655	55485	21120	32925	32925

Fig. 16   Manufacturer cash flow forecast Year 2.

- used and scrutinized by potential funding sources
- essential at the business plan stage
- used by the owners or directors to monitor and control their businesses.

Variances

The business fortunes should be rigorously monitored against the final versions of the cash flow and other documents. Variations (or *variances*) must be satisfactorily explained. It is important that the bookkeeping running totals for sales and expenditure keep in step with these *projected* figures. You must make very regular comparisons to ensure that sales forecasts are being met (or exceeded) and that expenditure is within budget (and preferably a lot less).

You should take fast and effective corrective action if matters are not as they should be. Alternatively, you should not sit on your laurels if the figures appear better in various respects. This latter scenario should spur you to do even better: it all helps the ultimate profitability.

EXERCISE

Prepare a cumulative budget, from the following annual information, making realistic assumptions about the individual monthly expenditure:

Cost of stock, raw materials	£39,595
Salaries, wages, etc.	£89,810
Rent, rates	£21,750
Publicity	£3,900
Fuel, etc.	£1,800
Telephones	£1,045
Vehicle	£7,580
Fees, etc.	£4,395
Stationery	£600
Total	£170,475

Hint: To do these three exercises, you will need to use your judgement [it is often like this in practice], making realistic assumptions about the monthly phasing of expenditure (and any income) where no data are provided. Produce the best monthly individual and cumulative surpluses/deficits (predicted bank balances) where applicable. This reflects real life, in that there are no absolutely wrong or right answers. If you get bogged down, you will notice similarities with the worked example in Figure 15, although some of the figures represent the sum of several entities, and some are omitted altogether – so as not to make it straightforward.

EXERCISE

Produce an appropriate sales forecast with annual sales totalling £186,500 (or copy the one used in Chapter 10). Use one of them, together with the above budget information, to produce a cash flow forecast for your own business.

FAILING OR SUCCESSFUL BUSINESSES

Businesses are capable of being both brilliantly successful and spectacular failures (and anywhere between those extremes). This small set of comparisons seems to fit better in this chapter rather than the marketing and sales chapters because of your appreciation of more aspects of the business, such as the critical importance of all forecasts and cashflow, and business management – and their close interaction. It seems to follow on naturally.

Let's look at some of the characteristics of, and reasons for, failed businesses. Perhaps:

- doom and gloom pervade the air, when you enter the premises
- minimal, if any, lighting or heating on (to save money, but not inspire sales to generate money from sales)
- customers put off by old stock, low *stock turn ratios*, wrong products – shoddy goods
- a new enterprise opened or there was simply a genuine, or at any rate perceived, collapse of marketplace
- a problem with the location – either a faulty choice in the first place or downward change as a result of general decay or redevelopment
- insufficient capital and lack of customers
- the business is overtrading
- an inability to adapt to changing times, or competitive pressures

- poor management, exercising poor or no control, and poor, uninspired, touchy or disgruntled staff
- staff fraud and theft.

You are urged to be on the lookout for all these signs (and others) in connection with your own venture!

Overtrading

On the face of it, overtrading seems to be an odd one to make a business fail. It's all to do with underinvestment and lack of resources generally, but trying to do too much business with *hopelessly* inadequate resources.

Stock Turn Ratios

Stock turn ratios, reason 3, provide another useful indicator. For example, if a supermarket sells greengrocery, no stock should be on the premises, at least unchilled or whatever, for more than a few days – say five. Therefore the shelves ought to be completely replenished (hopefully because of sales *not* wastage) every five days, or roughly 73 times a year, at least – 365 divided by 5 (both measured in days). 73 would be the stock turn ratio.

Conversely, a bookshop might keep its bestselling titles on the shelves for two or three months, and then make more room for other new would-be bestsellers coming in from the publishers; and this would represent a stock turn of between 4 and 6. (12 divided by 3 or 2, both numbers in months.)

If the shop carelessly left most of the books on the shelves way past their notional couple of months or so, it might only have an empirical stock turn of 2, 1, or fractional, indicating extremely slow stock turns where the stock remained on the shelves in excess of twelve months on average. Customers would always observe in the latter months very little new to interest them, and would not patronize the business – to the ultimate extent that sales would decline and the venture would have to close. Hence, other things being equal, from these few examples a healthy business is synonymous with a high stock turn ratio, for its type of business.

Again, there are industry yardsticks.

Successful Businesses

Conversely, the characteristics of successful businesses are:

- visibly bubbling and thriving, well-lit, welcoming atmosphere
- instantly noticeable happy and occupied staff, although not too busy to 'jump' when customers enter
- working directors or proprietors visible, getting their hands on the day-to-day practicalities
- the whole enterprise under the personal direction and management of owners or shareholders
- probably good cash flow, high turnover, high stock turn ratios, sufficient funding and other resources

- publicity machine (effective marketing) probably working overtime
- probably, a fortunate location and opening hours, attracting a plentiful supply of customers
- good products or services (if not the best) – relative to market expectations
- quality, friendly, knowledgeable and courteous staff, with correct personal qualities and attributes
- willingness to oblige, a *can do* attitude, where nothing is too much trouble.

A Silent Voice – First Impressions

Make your business seem thriving when customers arrive at reception or the shop. It's a silent evaluation, but it usually carries a wealth of information about the business. If you can pick up vibes about other businesses (and we all can), so too can the customer, representative or visitor – about your venture. It's quite obvious, but whatever feeling and perceptions customers pick up will endorse the original ones and accelerate either the decline or the lift-off of the enterprise!

BOOKKEEPING: THE KEY TO A SUCCESSFUL BUSINESS

You can see that good quality bookkeeping bears a heavy responsibility in the last analysis. It plays a vital part in compiling management information, and monitoring and controlling the business. So, the more solid understanding of the oft-maligned bookkeeping you have or acquire, the better! Whilst it is not necessary to become over-involved personally, as mentioned before, you are urged to know what goes on. Then:

- You will know intuitively what is going on in detail, providing you with an immediate means of assessing what is going on in the business as a whole.
- The Annual Accounts will not produce any real surprises, at year end, as you will instinctively know how the business is doing.
- There is a tighter management control on the enterprise.
- You will understand the business and the accountant's comments better.
- You can plan ahead better.
- You will save accountant's fees and be better able to steer around adverse cash-flow situations.
- Staff will be aware that the books are regularly scrutinized (a deterrent against possible fraud and so on).
- You can investigate matters further and quickly if suspicions are aroused, and instigate actions to compensate.

WHAT HAVE YOU LEARNT IN THIS CHAPTER?

★ What are trading accounts and balance sheets? Why and when are they produced? How can they help the business owners?
★ What other information is valuable?
★ Name the key forecasts.

- ★ What is a cash flow forecast and name the guidelines for producing one?
- ★ Why is it vital for businesses? What two aspects stand out immediately?
- ★ What are the consequences of ignoring the messages?
- ★ Why does a healthy business need to make a profit?
- ★ Bookkeeping produces valuable numerical data. How should this be used? What do you do with variance information?
- ★ Why do some businesses fail and why are some very successful?
- ★ What is overtrading and why is it a bad characteristic?
- ★ Why does bookkeeping play such an important part in operating a business?

16
Embracing Technology

The information presented thus far has enabled you to decide what business to enter and how to go about creating and running it. It has drawn on good solid traditional thinking and time-honoured principles, employing proven manual practices with modern tools like computers where helpful and relevant.

This chapter covers some of the electronic evolution and how it might help your venture. Specialist text books on the subject and IT professionals should be consulted when you get seriously interested *as it is a very swift-moving field* and potential minefield.

Full technology is not for every small business – especially if it is very small or even a one-person organization, perhaps arts-biased, maybe part-time and without very much technology acumen and interest. However, a growing interest (coupled with training in this area) might prove to be irresistible. Depending on the nature, scope and ambitions for your business, the predictions are that businesses embracing these developments are more likely to succeed – although this step alone is no substitute for the validity of the comments elsewhere in this book about building a successful business.

The ethics, moral values and fundamental concepts underlying any venture have changed very little down the ages (the need to build the business generally, maintain standards, advertising, customer relations, selling, good housekeeping, accounting ground rules, and so on): but the mechanics, tools and techniques have.

In addition, customer expectations have changed, time-scales have shortened, distances have shrunk, technology has come to our aid (or has it forced the pace?). Think about this; is it for you? Check how your business might benefit – either right now or else in the future, and by how much.

Historically, when time moved slower, people strove hard for quality and service, goods were made somewhat less efficiently in productivity terms, technology was much less advanced: the business world, our social values, our domestic situations and our living standards were completely different.

Developments are accelerating rapidly, so this chapter provokes thoughts on how these advances can be *applied* in your business (and the implications), rather than the technical detail. It represents yet another culture change.

In recent years, exciting new terms have emerged to supplement our lives: laptops, video phones, smart cards, cordless phones, mobile phones, digital GSM, Web phones, Webcams, WAP (Wireless Application Protocols) technology, audio and video conferencing, digital cameras, voice recognition, speech synthesis, voice mail, e-mail, armchair shopping, home banking, electronic cash, virtual warehousing, e-commerce, e-business, automatic voice response, voice and inter-active call centres, redirected follow-me telephone calls (and e-mails and faxes). These additional media or mechanisms are just as stimulating and provoking as the new fax machines, photocopiers, microfiche archiving and computers were in *their* day.

Although their roots point in somewhat differing directions, the current tech-nology of digital televisions, interactive (pay-as-you-view) television, cable TV, cameras, multimedia, fibre optics, digital communications, platforms, telephones, mobiles, faxes, computers and open network standards, is beginning to merge, especially when connected to telephone lines (computer telephony integration) and satellites: the convergent result is *capable* of communicating data with the outside world in *both* directions, enabling us to listen to CDs and the radio, and watch videos, films and television – virtually instantly. Essentially these are rela-tively low-cost (and getting cheaper) high-tech powerful communication advances serving voice, data and moving picture transmissions. Even the tradi-tional suppliers of the wires to your front door (the local loop) do not have a monopoly any more as this is open to competition now.

Whilst you may not understand how the technology works (any more than you necessarily need to understand a car or the human body) or the precise meaning of the terminology, it is critically important that you understand its uses, limitations and what it means for your business; because those businesses that adapt to the changes will be the ones most likely to prosper – and even survive. Customers will choose which ways they want to do business and (once again) *it's their voice that counts in the end.*

Although historically we have not *needed* computer-based technology, it has obviously helped in many cases. In the future, such developments will be less optional as customers will perceive them to be an essential tool for a thriving and growing venture – a positive discriminator in fact. They might even regard a non-technology business as a dubious venture! It has been suggested that the future division of individuals will be based on their understanding and use of technology (or not, as the case may be) rather than on geographical location – the traditional north–south divide.

In SWOT parlance, this technology progress presents business opportunities, not threats. It's just as easy setting up your business from the outset with this tech-nology as without it: to younger generations it will come quite naturally.

PRIMARY USES OF COMPUTERS

You will recollect that the personal computer (or Apple Macintosh equivalent) has already been suggested in connection with word-processing, forecasting, finance, databases, project planning and budgets. Another series of useful applications is in producing designs, graphics, production planning, plant control, automation gen-erally; but both hardwares can do a whole lot more as well.

Modern commercial computers are dumb unintelligent machines basically, albeit fast and powerful. They only come to life and do useful work when loaded with suitable software, storing lots of data, acting on voluminous complicated pro-gramme instructions, and working with extreme rapidity. Software has come many rungs up the ladder over the last few decades to enable computers to be very user-friendly and straightforward. Specific training courses and books are also readily available – at all levels of understanding.

Although special applications need special add-on hardware (such as scanners, digital cameras, video cameras, play-stations, musical MIDI interfaces, colour printers, sound systems), a normal business computer (as opposed to one for home use alone) consists of an electronic data processor chip together with supporting electronics and memory chips, rotating removable floppy discs, a large so-called hard disc, CD or DVD player, and a modem (all in one metal case), a QWERTY keyboard, mouse, display monitor and a fast laser black-and-white printer.

Computer magazines abound with articles and advertisements for them. Be careful about the specific combination of hardware subassemblies, depending what you want to *use* the computer for. *Computer usage determines the configuration*; and the configuration, together with the relevant software, determines prices. Outward appearances don't help much.

Modems connect to the ordinary BT telephone line – quite possibly a separate one from that used frequently in the business for speech. The purpose of modems and related hardware/software is to convert the computer messages into more appropriate electronic signals for analogue transmission over domestic phone lines, and then to convert them back again at the other end.

Other Applications

Phone Dialling, Organization and Personal Expenses

Standard business computers can be used (with suitable software and an appropriate database) as a telephone directory for simply storing numbers, and dialling con-ventional phone calls; keeping detailed records about customers, suppliers, designs or the business (cf. 'card indices'). The Data Protection Act spells out the legitimate ways personal data can be used in practice.

Computers can also be used for logging appointments and for alerting you to important dates and meetings (electronic diaries). Personal expenses can be item-ized and controlled.

Small Packages

Frequently CDs are available at low or zero cost for dictionary applications, route planning, encyclopedias, clip art, virus checks, utilities and a myriad of other applications.

Inventory Management, Sales and Invoicing

Other off-the-shelf packages will provide 'semi-automatic' inventory manage-ment (stock control, purchase orders and automatic ordering from suppliers), sales order processing, invoicing and credit control. These are necessary routine func-tions in most businesses that can be done by computer. Choose packages in conjunction with the accountant so as to integrate smoothly with the downstream activities (accounting and tax return packages).

Faxes and E-Mail

Faxes created directly using a computer can be sent without the need for a printed copy at the originator's end of the line. Use of technology this way effectively enables a conventional remote fax machine or *computer printer* to print out your locally constructed messages, reports, spreadsheets and drawings – for a distant person or business to read, and act upon the information.

Modems are used to connect *the recipient's* computer and its remote printer with *your* computer by making a 'phone-call' using conventional analogue technology. Alternatively, sometimes high-speed and higher quality ISDN (or even ADSL) digital telephone lines are used instead of ordinary telephone lines; and these circumnavigate the need for modems as such. Full digital transmission (without conventional modems at either end) is coming on stream, and this will improve reliability, accuracy, bandwidth and speed – the quality and capacity generally of data transfer (downloading for example).

You can utilize the computer for free or low-cost e-mails in a similar way, using your own and the recipient's e-mail addresses via networks. Your e-mail address should be published by you if you want people to communicate this way with your business. More is said in the next chapter about choosing and registration of e-business names and addresses.

The main benefit of electronically-produced faxes and e-mails can be a virtually instantaneous communication of any length between your business and another person or business; or a series of messages to and from the persons with whom you are corresponding or negotiating. E-mail messages are sometimes transmitted in batches (for optimizing costs and delayed as a result) to optimize the network time – and hence minimize cost. They are stored until the recipient turns on his or her computer and is ready to read them (thus also received in batches).

Fax transmissions obviously require a fax number for the dialling process: this assumes some form of prior arrangement and an implied physical address. On the other hand, e-mails only need the recipient's name (and notional, but unique, e-mail address) but no physical address or known whereabouts: they are thus much more flexible. There is a built-in database of chosen recipients and their respective 'fax' numbers (complete with redial facilities) to ensure the right connections are made.

Technology, backed by suitable software, is even tackling automatic responses to e-mails, faxes and voice messages, either formulating answers itself or pulling them to one side for personal replies.

When sending messages by e-mail or fax, if confidentiality is paramount, encryption and de-encryption devices (and other techniques) are available; but it does not prevent the documents being read by non-addressees or through misdialling – they could fall into the wrong or even competitors' hands! Multiple levels of passwords and other security arrangements can and should be employed for computer access and hence e-mail messages.

Browsing on the Internet

You can use the same computer hardware (or Apple Macintosh machines), as well as other specialist devices, including dedicated *Network Computers* (NCs) as opposed to general purpose *Personal Computers* (PCs), to communicate with the Internet. As well as using modems, telephone lines, and so on, you also need some organization like an Internet Service Provider.

Internet Service Providers (ISPs)

The very many (and increasing numbers of) ISPs and on-line services cause some confusion because they tend to offer broadly similar, yet different, features. ISPs generally (not universally) provide a basic connection to the Internet, several e-mail [names and] addresses, access to newsgroup computers, 'live chat', varying amounts of free personal Web space, some necessary software and user help lines; whereas on-line services provide access to magazine features with users' contributions, and additional Web links as well.

There are tremendous variations between the ISPs (and the package you ultimately choose from them); they should be selected carefully (perhaps by recommendation and/or reference to IT magazines) with particular reference to:

- ease of use
- convenience
- technical sophistication
- speed of access and delivery
- 'bandwidth' – effectively the speed of data transfer of the system
- performance
- free software
- additional services
- access to specialized information
- browser procedures and behaviour
- search engine design and performance
- communities of interest
- quality of news service
- contractual small print
- costs (for use and support):
  - how much access you want to particular communities, information or specialist services
  - call charges – usually local (low cost or free) call rates
  - preferred access times – time of day and likely duration
  - speed and efficiency of the search methodology
  - the degree of technical sophistication, web hosting, mail forwarding, and so on
  - support call costs
  - precisely what is included in the package
  - payment method (regular phone bill, credit card or bank account direct debit, invoice)
  - agreement details.

True comparisons are difficult: sustained experience ranks very highly and league tables are produced and published. Fortunately, magazines, books and IT experts are available to help you make a decision based on current advice about ISPs and e-business generally. Also, some ISPs *claim* to specialize in business usage, where certain operational parameters like Web page design services are available, and security, reliability and speed of access are better (in return for a higher charge).

Time spent trying to gain access can be a problem, as it is related to global demand (and varies throughout the 24-hour period) and size/configuration of the ISP's hardware and software, in relation to the number of surfers signed up.

E-COMMERCE AND E-BUSINESS

Promoting Your Business on the Internet
Becoming more adventurous, you can proactively promote your business to a global market, literally *worldwide*, on the Internet, so that international individuals and businesses can interrogate *your* files. This implies gearing up for cultural differences round the world, global economies, currency variations, time zones possibly and being prepared for limited multilingual scripts for the advertisements, although English is most widely used, and preferred in many countries.

Advertisements
There are several points to remember when advertising on the Internet:

- The simplest form of web site consists of conventional advertisements or descriptive text; but audio messages, sound clips, animation and images of, or video clips about, your business or products are frequently employed.
- This is another form of advertising, subject to all the rules of advertising that states it must be legal, decent, honest and truthful. It is conceptually similar to mail order business or distance selling.
- A web site usually takes the form of several or many individual Web Pages fronted by a so-called Home Page, with its own worldwide web address (http:\\www …) and 24 hour, seven-day access.
- Its design and content should be well thought out and attractive, reflecting the *customers'* point of view, just like any other conventional advertisement (*see* Chapter 9). If you are uncertain how to proceed, use the skilled practitioners in Web site design and maintenance. There are also myriads of specialist books on this subject specifically, and it is one of very fast-moving technology generally: consult them when you are ready.
- Facts can and must be easily updatable as situations, stocks, prices and designs change (to circumnavigate possible legal misrepresentation).
- Any information that you choose to make available can be noted and compared with competitors' information, for example.
- The more elaborate your text, designs and message, the more disc storage it occupies: the more time and costs will be incurred by surfers (potential

customers) to download and print it out: the more potential customers might be dissuaded from using the site.

- Your page must be free from errors and usage problems, as it is virtually the only way you can 'meet' your customer – a fundamental business relationship.
- You must provide all relevant details for a decision, as it is likely to be your only chance; and face-to-face or voice selling (albeit over the phone) may take a severe back seat!
- You must make it easy for customers to find you, to be easily accessible and user-friendly, to close in on their desired product; and buy it.
- You have some control on targeting, if you wish (and correspondingly, filtering out incoming junk mail).
- Some web sites can have the added benefit of providing a record of site visitors.
- Aim to get a good site visit rate and repeat visit rate; with a high interest resulting in large amounts of solid business. A good design will incorporate a facility for counting how many times your site has been visited.

Catalogues

Next are partial or complete on-line catalogues (not just advertisements) with 'three-dimensional' illustrations, specifications, text articles, colour photographs, sound and even demonstrations by video link. Products can then be selected; orders can be placed by the Internet of course, or by phone, fax, e-mail; or handled by invoice and so on, using conventional methods downstream.

Alternatively, customers could be presented with an attractive detailed on-line ordering system as well, that might consist of an electronic screen-displayed order form – armchair, home-based shopping technology in fact. The implied *two-way* transfer of data would use any of the following interactive systems:

- mouse-sensitive display screens
- touch screen technology
- the QWERTY keyboard, mouse and/or keypad entry
- some other input system
- call centres.

A form of payment method would be presented (see below) and then certain other actions would follow:

- Written acknowledgments and receipts would be generated automatically, and dispatched.
- The electronic system would automatically produce a picking list in your warehouse for someone to take the products off the shelf, pack them, arrange and ensure delivery – even in a different country.
- Alternatively, a *customer order* would automatically initiate a manufacturing process that would start to assemble the goods (like a particular combination of options selected for a car). A modular product or service greatly aids this on-line concept.

- Another concept of delivery is to download electronically – reports, books, documents, articles, information generally, software, music, ideas, intellectual property, for example.
- Automatic ordering from your supplier could be triggered if your warehouse stocks fell below a previously determined critical level.
- Suitable forms of after-sales service and warranty might be appropriate.

The next embellishment of the service is to grant and provide corresponding access to *your* manufacturing, dispatch and delivery system information (and anything else), via integration with your more conventional computer systems, so that customers can track progress of the goods. Parcel delivery tracking is widely used, a concept relying heavily on computer and bar code reader hardware.

Domain Names

If you are considering trading on the Internet, domain names are a critical factor in your web site and e-mail addresses. Registration of names will involve a fee, and can be handled by one of a number of such organizations, advertised in magazines. Although the control of these matters is somewhat confused and continuously under review at the moment, attention should be particularly paid to this choice (including name *acceptability* and *availability*) when decisions have to be made – as with conventional name selection. Refer to Chapters 9 and 17.

NETWORKS: INTRANETS, EXTRANETS AND THE INTERNET

Intranets

Intranets are more organized, but less flexible and lower-cost, ways of linking computers than by the Internet; and are particularly applicable to multiple branches or sites of the same organization. They broadly work in similar ways, except that they do not need any ISPs or other third-party intervention. They are more limited in their applications. Supporting telephone lines and other equipment can be for general use or for dedicated use (especially in business).

As a result, they offer much higher security because they only allow limited access to what is a restricted line of private communication: they are certainly no substitute for the Internet, for e-commerce or e-business, but are ideal for internal, interbranch or intercompany communications, linking computers or tills, their files and printers; and for sending faxes and e-mails to a limited number of known people. The actual size of the intranet (in terms of geographical coverage and numbers of computers) is not particularly material.

Sharing files works well, inasmuch as a particular user is able to read 'locked' documents, or to update 'unlocked' files. Different people might contribute to a major document by each subscribing a few paragraphs virtually independently of the other contributors, although being able to see (*read only*) what the others have written. Corporate edicts, memos and new product information can be circulated conveniently and 'instantaneously'.

Intranets transfer data both ways: they can be arranged to link an organization with its staff, offices, suppliers or customers (or any other organizations or groups of people with a shared interest) with the aim of mutual service support – for sorting out servicing and product maintenance problems for example, or for linking the INs and OUTs conveniently. They can also be typically used for submitting expense claims, arranging staff holiday bookings, updating personnel records, booking training courses, and so on; downloading data from tills sited in retail chain branches for extracting daily sales transaction – or uploading them with daily currency conversion rates or centralized pricing data.

Extranets

Extranets, also controlled by the organizations they serve, offer the same broad advantages and disadvantages as intranets except that they group a larger number of entities with a common interest. They are effectively *linked intranets*, enabling many more computers to be linked together.

Internet

In contrast, *anyone in the world with the right equipment* and 'authority' can gain access to the Internet (there is only one) and its World Wide Web (WWW): and hence its universal appeal for e-commerce. It became more formalized, accepted and acknowledged in the early 1990s, although created originally and primarily for computer professionals, serious academics and military use. It was at first conceived as a communication system that could withstand a nuclear attack, because of its deliberately dispersed locations.

The Internet (effectively a vast ramshackle network of voluntarily linked computers – of all different kinds) offers businesses and individuals several features – not only for sending and receiving e-mails, but also for exchanging information generally:

- acting as a library
- being bulletin boards
- acting as notice boards
- debating
- asking questions
- playing fully interactive games with real people scattered round the world
- providing entertainment
- browsing the World Wide Web
- *chatting* informally or in news groups.

Chatting on the Internet takes the form of written comments, questions and answers – a spontaneous keyboard-entered equivalent of a verbal conversation between two or more parties. Some users even express coded emotions to complement their chatting and newsgroup postings.

The users fall into two groups – the 'originators', that is, the people and organizations mentioned above (on the one hand) who prefer to continue to have the medium for themselves without commercial interests, and everyone else (on the other) – in spite of the fact that commercial money helped to develop it. Efficient usage (convenience, performance and speed) demands more capacity or 'bandwidth' (and less junk, rubbish or 'spam' – a term for unwanted information generally) to prevent the Internet from becoming clogged up. It is not owned by any one individual or organization: there is no one person or organization to act as arbitrator; but there are group conventions that effectively control it, aided by the ISPs or on-line organizations who control access to it.

It is almost a living entity and has acquired a culture, language, codes of practice, rules and 'laws' of its own, much of which is not documented, but understood through experience and hearsay. It relies heavily on unwritten empirical agreements, although hints can be gleaned from textbooks, magazines and the Internet itself (such as Acceptable Use Policy and Conditions of Service).

In spite of everything, it all seems to work in practice, although at the moment it doesn't operate very efficiently. It is of course continuously evolving – changing, growing, developing ... and getting better.

In practice, the Internet and most other networks utilize very powerful specialist computer systems called servers, some of which specialize in handling incoming and outgoing mail, handling web pages, passing data and information, and coordinating news and chat groups.

Surfing the Internet effectively enables you to read *remote files* on other users' large hard disks, via suitable automatic 'telephone' routing, the ISPs or other on line organizations, like AOL and MSN. A subscription for using the facilities is sometimes payable at a flat rate or time-based – which also covers the provision of relevant software.

Surfing, browsing or searching for information (tracking down data) is handled by your own 'manual' intuitive guidance using keywords, or by specialist software (called search engines); and the art is to choose the most effective method or combination. The search engine performance provided on-line or by the ISPs varies in sophistication, speed and effectiveness.

Other Examples Employing Modern Technology
To demonstrate the variety of current applications, here are just a few possibilities to get you thinking:

Networks Generally

- conducting research by universities, academics and others – one of the original purposes of the Internet
- collecting data from remote meters and instruments sited in distant locations, difficult access points, hostile environments, automatic process plants, and so on.
- sending data back again in the form of control signals, after processing, working close to 'real time'
- calling off consignment stocks, where the initiative of another party dictates what happens on *your* premises

- distributing information via 'automatic' built-in mailing lists
- technical design and discussion services
- holiday and airline enquiries through travel agents
- negotiations between various parties, concerning a multitude of subjects
- authentication and issue of various certificates – quality, product origin, and so on
- security systems and burglar alarms
- customer support generally
- questionnaires.

Internet Specifically

- Tesco Direct and others operate up-and-running home-based *point-and-click* shopping outlets
- businesses generally, and employment agencies particularly, utilize brilliant and cheap advertisements for staff, whether in this country or not, asking applicants to download further information, and then to actually apply, *on-line*
- brief applicant profiles are published from CVs held by recruitment agencies
- banking and call centre transactions
- tax returns and legal work are beginning to be conducted *on-line*
- *on-line* auctions
- ascertaining recorded delivery of conventional mail and parcels via specialist services
- electronic publishing of fiction and technical articles, books, music, and so on
- live discussions – serious, learned and informal
- train timetables and aircraft schedules
- direct sales of financial packages, travel, holidays, insurance, double-glazing, kitchens, computers, houses and similar products
- procurement of raw materials generally – searching for products (and suppliers), matching a particular customer 'specification' that can be fed into search engines – together with prices and other commercial terms: it can save purchasers considerable time, and hence would be very attractive
- placing of customer orders alongside users' or buyers' usual buying profiles, such that any proposed purchase for unusual or dubious products (medical drugs, dangerous chemicals, and so on) in relation to the usual pattern of purchases can be questioned or even filtered out first
- large company purchasing departments are demanding on-line buying. If you could satisfy their wishes and want to take advantage of their business, you have very little choice but to integrate with their procedures and systems – another application of e-business
- national telephone directories
- the Internet will be used by customers as frequently as Yellow Pages
- portal-style services, where one web site transparently links to others (and offers a few other facilities as well); the customer deals, almost unknowingly,

via the first one to other 'slave' sites. These are effectively 'search-engines' in a slightly different form; if the first site can't satisfy the need, it may know someone who can! It might make several links in practice

- reciprocally, using the Internet to your advantage to gain business, to evaluate competitive offers and to search for your own raw materials and supplies – even to find hotels, restaurants, travel deals and business equipment
- businesses use the Internet for supplementing core technical information or researching ideas for new potential products, services, applications, markets, and the like
- predictions are that long distance or international calls and data transmissions will be undertaken over the Internet from mobile phones, *and at local rates*; and offices as such will be irrelevant
- a touch of *1984* appears when you realize the Internet's potential. With appropriate hardware and software (acquired for broadly legitimate reasons), marketing profiles of you – databases compiled from seemingly innocent questionnaires amongst other media, your purchasing habits, other private and personal data and so on – enable others to make intrusive and subtle suggestions to influence you.

Advanced Networks, Satellite, Conventional Land-Lines, Fibre Optic Links, Infrared and Radio Transmissions of Data

- video or digital camera images – data transmission to a central location for newsgathering, reporting, broadcasting, and for use by newspapers, estate agents, security and so on
- land, air and sea navigation ulilizing satellites and sophisticated software
- space exploration and observation
- traffic monitoring and control
- scanning customer-signed documents (in moving vehicles) to trigger invoices generated at base
- data logging of on-vehicle air-conditioning equipment for pharmaceutical and food deliveries
- accessing and interrogating documents and information generally (figures, reports, software, drawings, diagrams, pictures, plans, and so on) whilst 'on the move'
- reporting the whereabouts of public transport and other vehicles on their routes
- reporting mechanism for security and other persons on their 'rounds'
- bar codes and shelf stock levels read by special intelligent 'guns' carried by supermarket staff (walking through the aisles), transmitting this to a central point within the store. The information is processed automatically, producing shortage or low stock lists, and critical shelf-fill lists. Orders are raised on warehouses for further deliveries (allowing for historical sales data, current sales data derived from the tills, and also weather forecasts). In fact the tailored computer software is simply a model to emulate the detailed store operation and optimize the stock levels and hence maximize profit. All the related stock and

sales reports can be produced for review, with thousands of lines priced and counted – bar codes are a wonderful invention
- automation and electronic integration of front and back offices, linked to call centres culminate in a concept known as Customer Relationship Management.

SELLING PSYCHOLOGY

Computer technology has of course existed for several decades: the broad principles have not changed, but the scope and technical ingenuity have seen very dramatic leaps that have to be admired and respected – truly an inevitable exponential growth in fact.

Developments from primitive beginnings have witnessed spectacular changes in the pace of the many advances in ingenious electronic circuits and software. The original computers have grown in sophistication, but diminished in size, from very un-user-friendly crude and clumsy machines bristling with valves, transistors, ferrite rings, masses of wires and very basic data storage and programming techniques (filling complete rooms) to the modern high-level software-driven devices that we know today (where the underlying computer and its peripherals is virtually transparent).

However, own businesses in the form of ancient traders, merchants (relying on sheep, salt, gold, various other 'currencies', animal transport, sea currents, trade winds and various forms of sailing boat) and more modern entrepreneurs have been around even longer – *centuries* and *millennia* in fact, both in this country and abroad. Thus the now-proven and best business practices for good profitable business have evolved too (the essence of this book) and must not be dismissed as irrelevant.

The upshot is that your business must constructively and thoroughly investigate any means of doing business at its disposal. It must not be automatically dismissive of proven practices; or equally, be doggedly dazzled by the image, glamour and status created by technology. The old adage *if the cap fits, wear it* comes to mind.

In the early days, Internet vendors had it easy. It wasn't difficult to generate a modest amount of publicity for an e-commerce web site, or to be reasonably successful without too much effort. But now, anyone setting up an Internet-based business, faces stiff competition from local, national and international competitors. Competition is only a mouse click away (not another time-consuming journey across town or to another city or country) – and that's more true today than ever before. The sheer necessity for selling, so that a business can become successful, is a clear matter of survival – not a luxury. Has this ever been mentioned before?

E-commerce sites are frequently ineffective in spite of slick presentation and vast amounts of money spent on the technology behind them. Stunning designs or clever graphics alone will certainly never persuade people to buy. Instead, you still need to apply old-fashioned tried and tested sales psychology. Whilst web site designers are expert in fancy graphics, fonts, colours and page layouts, they know nothing about the science of the most important thing that web sites have to achieve – selling! However big or small a site, it is essential to remember that selling is a complex psychological challenge (check back on Chapters 11 and 12): it is not simply a matter of displaying a comprehensive catalogue.

In any selling situation, the salesperson is trying to achieve a number of things. One of these is to overcome objections and another is to help the customer or buyer to make favourable decisions. In a web environment, these things are obviously a lot more difficult than are face-to-face situations. To attempt to do battle with human psychology using static web pages is tough for most goods or services that are sold: so that means finding other answers. Most web site owners just give up; they either do nothing or resort to publishing their telephone number in the desperate hope that if the customer is having trouble reaching a decision, he or she will pick up the phone and call them. That's very unlikely, because if he or she wanted to sit in a queue, listening to robotic voices, the customer would probably have phoned in the first place, and not first wasted precious time on the Internet.

A cunning subtle way of helping customers decide is to remember that people like the security of knowing that other shoppers must have thought the same way, and have then bought the same thing. So by highlighting one particular product as a *bestseller*, you will possibly instil visitors with sufficient confidence to plump for it too.

When users are presented with a web page that has boxes to fill in, the natural tendency is (not surprisingly) to fill them in. They will do this even before, and in preference to, reading the small print.

The phenomenon known as customer loyalty does not apply neatly on the impersonal Internet. All businesses (whether web-based or not) retain customers only because they find it too much trouble to buy from somebody else.

Another thing … fixing web sites is not cheap. Time is money and good web site designers aren't exactly ten a penny. So before anyone starts Internet-based business, owners need to understand precisely what message they wish to project, and then analyse what's wrong with their initial efforts. They need to measure what's going wrong, and where.

Interestingly around two-thirds of Internet shopping baskets, once started, are never actually purchased. If you had a supermarket where something approaching this percentage of your customers abandoned their part-filled trolleys round the store and then just walked out, you'd soon know you had a problem. However with the Web, many e-commerce site owners simply do not appreciate the scale of the challenge they face, because they don't carry out the appropriate monitoring and measurements – *see also* Chapter 21.

It's worth offering some incentive to get people to use the web in the first place – people love to feel they are getting a bargain (customer perceptions once more, discussed in Chapter 10). Airlines and train companies offer cheaper fares or, in another situation, perhaps you can include free postage and packing, or delivery, or gift wrapping.

The business as a whole must agree strategic issues, discussed in detail later in this chapter; and the technologists must explain the equipment needed and how it can be used. As the business leader you must spell out to the technologists in lay-man's terms, as it were, how it is envisaged using the technology, the precise mar-keting and selling messages and the image you require; and handle the psychology interface.

It needs a tremendous amount of thought and probably testing in practical use. The tail must not wag the dog! Have a user-friendly system that *you* can update easily, and that will bring in maximum business, *efficiently.* Dramatic and cleverly designed web pages must not be an end in themselves – but the *means* to it for the greater glory of your business.

CUSTOMER PAYMENT AND SECURITY MATTERS

As already mentioned, service expectations are considerably higher nowadays. Delivery is typically the next or the same day: therefore payment methods and contract details must be as tight and as foolproof as possible.

Payment Methods

Payment can be made by secure procedures (whose speed has a positive impact on your business' cash flow, debtor and creditor situations – no invoices this way). It might even create a useful *negative* working capital requirement – *see* Chapters 8 and 15. Getting paid before delivering the goods really is appealing! Payment methods might include:

- Conventional credit and debit cards that are widely used for payment by telephone or on screen. Although there is currently reticence about divulging confidential card information directly over the Internet, card-issuing banks increasingly state that they will indemnify customers against fraudulent use in such a transaction. Customers can help reduce this type of fraud by using low-value credit limits on their credit cards that are then assigned specifically for Internet use by the customer.
- Trusted third parties like banks, newly emerging clearing houses and other institutions can help, either to hold and distribute funds, or to break the problem confidentiality chain with 'super-secure' systems.
- Electronic Funds Transfer, known about for a long time, offers a secure method for moving large amounts of money about between parties and countries.
- A euro- or dollar-based credit card or bank account that might prove useful.
- Pre-purchased encoded cards (similar to vouchers), that are only valid and entered once instead of effectively many times as would be the case with credit or debit cards.
- Normal phone bill. The seller simply arranging payment this way with the buyer – via the medium of transferring to a premium telephone number.
- Other protocols, that are continuously emerging as technology progresses.
- Voluntary donations, instead of formal payments (honesty boxes!) surprisingly perhaps.

- Traditional relatively cumbersome manual systems, although it clearly detracts from the spirit of e-commerce and e-business.

Security and Legal Issues

On-line trading is expanding well, albeit patchily and somewhat confusedly. The critical points are data transfer accuracy, authenticity, privacy, authorization, integrity (have the data been tampered with at all?) and security – "hacker proof'. Even manual systems are not completely fool or fraud-proof. The art is to manage, control, reduce and finally accept and allow for the risk in the pricing.

Security is an extremely important and very complex subject. At the time of writing, security and privacy from hackers, nosy people and plain pranksters, as well as deliberate fraudsters, are not as tight as they should be, but they are improving. Some arrangements are *already* in place and others are being developed and tested. One day all security will be deemed totally reliable for all practical purposes. Auditors provide certain services for businesses to minimize financial irregularities: so too computer security systems should be audited professionally, *and their recommendations heeded*.

As a guide, existing national laws hold for e-business, but specific laws (a global legal framework) are being urgently discussed – especially with regard to security, electronic signatures, prevention of hacking, holding and obtaining sensitive data, encryption standards, and law enforcement agencies' possible legitimate access to private data (encrypted or otherwise). The government is broadly supportive (and is actively promoting e-business itself), so is pursuing safeguards for users.

ISPs and broadly similar organizations, continuing to operate in this country, are radically affected by the Regulation of Investigatory Powers Act that, amongst others things, obliges them to hand over data and encryption keys to such authorities as the police and government intelligence agencies under certain circumstances. In other words, *security of information is definitely not guaranteed* – regardless of any other deficiencies and vulnerability of the Internet! All Internet activity, including personal and business e-mails, routed through ISPs (and the like) are subject to scrutiny. Other countries are also adopting such powers.

Electronic contracts (shadowing their striven-for watertight paper-based equivalent documents), identifying whether a contract exists or not, electronic signatures, dates, evidence of transmission, consumer protection, payment terms, foreign transactions, copyright matters, trademarks, data protection, legal issues, which countries' laws are to apply, non-repudiation reliability, *implied* terms, and other small print, are gradually becoming resolved and accepted. (*See also* Chapter 18.)

Observation

Did you hear of the electronic-business deal using all the technology mentioned in this chapter ending up with the absurd (possibly electronically voiced) message: *Thank you for all your personal and other details, and for giving us the business. We will confirm it all in writing through the post and ask you to merely sign the form and send the payment by return?* What a charade! What a wasted opportunity and waste of everyone's time and money!

BUSINESS STRATEGY, RESPONSIBILITY, COSTS AND IMPACT

Technology offers to implement *additional* ways of doing business, supplementing or substituting traditional methods as seamlessly as possible, whether it be keeping up with the news, sports results, marketing intelligence, financial dealings, share prices, trading, travel and so on. It could be applicable to internal communications, business-to-business or business-to-consumer relationships (known, respectively, as B2B and B2C these days).

Speed and convenience are the key enablers (flexibility), with an ability to do almost any task, from any sort of terminal, anywhere in the world, whenever the user desires it (just like the modern phone network does for speech).

Technological changes will affect your chosen business in different ways, depending on what business you are in, your philosophy, your aims, your personality, the projected life of your venture and so on: but they *will impact* you and your business. But how?

The main purpose of this overview is to put technology options firmly into perspective for your business. It is not intended as a guide to the *detailed technical* workings to what is a rapidly developing and very explosive subject, or to advocate particular sites (that can just as easily and quickly appear and disappear). Neither does it duplicate the excellent detailed descriptions in magazines and specialist books on how to:

- choose and configure the hardware
- navigate the software
- choose ISPs and search engines
- determine acceptable security systems
- design and set up web sites
- fully exploit the technological capabilities.

Your Strategy

- Participate in this new industrial revolution somehow, even if the dust *hasn't* settled.
- Technology provides an excellent opportunity for competitors to sneak up, and overtake – and *vice versa*!
- Plan your technology strategy thoroughly.
- Consider its consequences.

The Internet, for masses of businesses and individuals round the globe, has become a convenient Aladdin's cave, a tremendously rich source of invaluable personal and business information embracing all manner of data including software, music, games and entertainment. It is constantly being updated and joined by an ever-increasing number of users. Some of it is subject to copyright restrictions; some is not.

As a potential purchaser, be wary of web sites whose offers seem too good: they probably are – to your cost!

All the examples cited in this chapter represent electronic business situations. The idea of a real *Big Brother* is not too far away! Controlled risk-takers stand a better chance of gaining more profit than the non-risk-takers. The twin priorities should be to improve customer service and to cut costs; so as to increase sales, revenue and hence business profitability. You'll be relieved to know that the whole subject can be handled by outsourcing – either just to set up and maintain, or to be totally responsible for everything – whilst *you* continue with the *core* thing that you are probably best at.

Responsibility

Decisions must be handled by the directors or partners, not by technologists. All in all, it's a very large step calling for adequate research, commitment, investment, resources, budgets, training, change in culture, and so on. The board (or you alone, along with your key managers if appropriate) must decide on the goals and authorize realistic budgets. You should:

- regard the technology as an enabler, rather than an inhibitor
- recognize a potential transformation from a local business to an international concern, with considerable changes in the ways your business will operate. (Is this what you really want?)
- examine new opportunities for trade, product research, competition, business partnerships, and for searching for supplies and procurements
- seek better methodology for core aspects and supporting infrastructure (*see* Chapter 19), where useful and cost-effective
- undertake a SWOT aimed at the new technology (*see* Chapter 2)
- evaluate new markets
- consider additional marketing ideas and new competition
- talk to established business partners and customers – to gain their likely reactions
- consider cultural issues
- obtain full employee support, commitment and 'buy in', to minimize risk
- arrange adequate training for the new environment
- remember you will be more exposed and open to much more comparison as a result
- discuss:
  - the cost of implementation (hardware, software, ISPs, set-up, web page design and ongoing maintenance, staffing, training)
  - the extra profit potential
  - the penalties or lost opportunities
  - the effect on customers, suppliers and staff
  - the overall effectiveness.

Costs

Costs associated with this form of trading will be offset by a reduction in those for traditional methods, cutting the net costs significantly – and hopefully giving much better service to customers. Since, it's relatively easy and low cost (so much so that many potential competitors could also do it quite painlessly, but to your cost), you might be virtually forced into Internet ways of working.

Impact

It might be helpful to re-read the chapters on getting business because the principles are extremely important, even if the medium has changed – Chapters 9, 10 , 11 and 12. You should also reconsider the impact on:

- image
- marketing
- selling
- customer service
- after-sales service
- warranties
- research and development
- finance
- profit
- inventory reduction
- production
- purchasing
- distribution methods
- risk management
- internal communications
- ability of the rest of the organization to respond sharply
- integration across departments
- resources generally
- other expansion or investment plans.

Side Effects Of Using the Internet

Apart from the benefits to the business, there are also side effects to be borne in mind:

- You are operating in, and exposing your business to, an international environment.
- Even a small business (yours?) suddenly appears through a computer display to the vast world, as a much *larger* international player with enhanced consumer expectations. They will, therefore, expect international standards: much faster service, better service, lower prices probably and swifter delivery: they will expect the same rapid response as from the rest of the Internet. Are all these things too daunting?

- A common failing when businesses change their trading pattern this way, is that they gear up only for *average* trading conditions; and then crack under the strain of *peak demand*, like Christmas or holidays (when either staff, computers or both cannot cope).
- In all cases of electronic trading and derivative computer actions, some equipment and systems duplication should be employed as many of the business eggs will critically be in just one basket (customer service and access channel). Your business could be seriously at risk.
- Regular back-up routines should be automatically produced. Specialist organizations (for example so-called data-warehouses) will maintain secure back-up copies of your data and software *off your own premises* as part of a comprehensive disaster recovery service – a fire on your premises, perhaps!
- Viruses will always be about, but can be mitigated if the correct precautions are taken and procedures followed every time.
- The use of so-called *fire walls* between your business and the outside world, implemented in a multitude of ways, aids data security, authenticity and screening generally.
- Where private use of an employer's Internet is explicitly sanctioned or just condoned (turning a blind eye), the *employer* could be liable under legislation for sexual harassment, libel (amongst other things) or merely a financial cost of several thousand pounds, as a result of the employees' use and/or abuse of the system. If in doubt, talk to a solicitor and instruct your staff accordingly.

VIRTUAL BUSINESS

Business Organization and the 'Hot' Desk

Whether or not you fully embrace the technology discussed above, there is dramatically less need for an individual to actually *travel* to work in the traditional sense: he or she could work from home for example, only occasionally visiting his or her base – because of the advent of advanced computer technology, the convergence of technologies and the mobile telephone explosion.

Staff and owners can still do business with customers and be in touch with their offices, field staff, managers, e-mails, voice mails, 'paperwork', sales figures, business performance statistics, and so on – whether at home, in the car, airport, hotel or when travelling (that is, geographically independent) without the need to be *at the office* or *factory*. This translates into a considerably more flexible working environment to match social, domestic and personal needs, as well as aligning better with global trading patterns and time zones.

You (as an employee, for example) would log in to any vacant computer terminal and phone, either at your base in person, or via a network of some 'transparent' sort with an identification code and password(s); the system will know where and who you are, routing appropriate internal and external messages to you automatically. Your physical location is immaterial: your 'business' status is not, but is looked after automatically. Your business contacts do likewise, and you both begin your day! Progress in WAP technology (aimed at linking mobile phones to the Internet, with all that that implies) will hasten these events. You may not realize it, but mobile phones (if switched on) already track and record your whereabouts in order to serve you.

Implicit Enterprise

The upshot of all this is that you can sit in your armchair, using your computer(s), without a shop front, a manufacturing business or warehouse in sight, selling and buying over the Internet, getting and receiving some form of money thousands of miles away. You are running a *virtual* business with minimal overheads – co-ordinating the achievements of other people! This puts a new slant on the previously mentioned requirements for choosing premises, arranging finance and managing the business (Chapter 8 particularly) – but not on responsibilities and accountabilities. Don't forget that reliable and independently audited records and Accounts still need to be kept for various reasons as stated in the previous chapter.

Finally, don't get carried away with technology as the ultimate goal – it's *only* a means to an end! Your judgement must be firmly based on what is best for the business – achieving its revenue, profit and other goals within the acknowledged constraints, and using the lowest possible cost structure. When considering the use of technology, keep firmly in mind the basics of creating a successful business spelt out throughout this book, whatever actual mechanisms you use:

- the fundamentals of creating and running a business
- what you and your staff are best at doing
- your longer-term plans and ambitions
- how you want to get business and handle customers
- your image in the marketplace
- customer relations and service
- in what aspect of your business the profits really originate.

The critical overriding questions are very simple:

- If technology were employed, would it improve your business?
- What differences would it make and how much difference would it make?
- What are the advantages and disadvantages?

Whatever your business, it will probably benefit from using computers, and from electronic trading to some lesser or greater extent. A recent survey conducted by Andersen Consulting showed that 97 per cent of European businesses were engaged in e-commerce in one form or another. It is claimed that e-business is not a passing fad; it is a profound economic change that has implications for us all. Think about it during the outline planning stage: accept that it is almost certainly the way to go, *sometime* (except for a minority of ventures). It's a case of moving with the times – *see* Chapter 21. You cannot ignore it completely, even if the technology and confidence *are* still unfolding. History never has stood still! Ultimately, the likely opinion change catalysts for you will be:

- image
- falling sales or rising costs
- falling profits
- uncompetitive selling prices
- lost opportunities
- competitors.

EXERCISE

What basic functions could, and would, be performed on computers, if any, within your business? What sort of packages would be employed?

EXERCISE

How could other technology assist aspects of your business? List the concepts and the manual systems they might supplement or replace.

WHAT HAVE YOU LEARNT IN THIS CHAPTER?

★ What technological changes are gradually taking over our lives and businesses?
★ Why should you seriously think about technology?
★ Group these into proactive business promotion facilities on one hand, and useful internally focused business aids on the other.
★ Discuss: now that technology has taken over, the traditional ways of doing business can be ignored.
★ What benefits and drawbacks are associated with technology for businesses?
★ Which businesses are less likely to benefit from a deep infusion of technology?

17
Exploring the Legal Framework

The slight, but essential, deviation started in Chapter 9 has now finished: the main thrust of starting a thriving business can now resume. It is hoped that you can better understand how certain personal attributes considered in Chapter 2 are virtually essential to run your own business in the light of the last chapters on marketing, sales, bookkeeping, management information and technology. So to continue Stage 2 ... you should now be prepared to take professional advice. The venture is ready to tentatively put its head above the parapet.

Businesses can be created in several ways from a legal point of view. Each has its place, characteristics, advantages, disadvantages and appeal – relative to the concept of the proposals. Ultimately the member(s) or owner(s) make the main operational decisions because they legally *own* the respective businesses. The main choice is between:

- sole traders
- trading associates
- partnerships
- cooperatives
- private limited companies
- public limited companies
- limited liability partnerships
- franchises.

Some are effectively sledgehammers to crack nuts, and inappropriate for the smaller end of the spectrum; whilst some demonstrate business standing and offer some protection for the owners, if the business ever gets into difficulties; some can be established with the minimum of formalities.

Questions will be asked of you: the choice between the various forms of business status should be made in conjunction with the chosen accountant, solicitor or banker. Between you and your chosen professional, several key factors will be discussed to make this decision. The main points arise from a consideration of:

- preferences
- nature of the proposed business
- roles, nature and number of participating potential 'owners'
- size/anticipated turnover
- roles and number of staff
- proposed growth potential
- methods of obtaining finance and raising money generally
- business startup and disposal or transfer later

- nature and value of assets
- business credibility
- security
- the position with (and vulnerability from) creditors
- the accounts formalities
- possible audit requirements
- taxation (both from a personal and a business point of view; taxation levels; capital gains; handling any losses; and when the tax is due for payment as this affects the cash flow arithmetic)
- National Insurance Contributions and corresponding benefits package, personal pensions, the relative complexity in setting up and running the entity weighed against the comparative benefit
- pension provisions for you and your staff.

TRADING STATUS

Sole Trader–Self-Employed

The simplest way of all to start a business is to become a *sole trader* or a *self-employed* individual working from home, a small shop, a rented office somewhere or even a vehicle! The two terms are somewhat interchangeable and tend to be used identically. The nominal turnover limit is usually relatively small, though not necessarily so; and VAT registration may or may not be compulsory or desirable – *see* Chapter 14.

This style of operation is typical of individuals just embarking on going it alone, for example, as:

- window cleaners
- gardeners
- decorators
- domestic helps
- childminders
- consultants
- photographers
- software writers
- subcontractors

- authors
- bookbinders
- artists
- musicians
- secretaries
- professional people (architects, accountants, and so on)
- barbers and hairdressers
- market traders.

Many more complex businesses operate this way as well, such as many smaller shops:

- butchers
- cobblers
- corner-shop grocers
- wool shops

- baby-wear shops
- ice-cream kiosks
- fish and chip vans.

Usually only *one* person is legally responsible for the business, although he or she may employ staff – who then become conventional employees and not its legal owners.

The business can be run as a part-time concern (growing it simultaneously to become fully independent later), whilst still being in a conventional full-time employed situation, if convenient and contractually acceptable to the present employers. This status is most likely to be applicable in those cases where there is minimal turnover and risk, perhaps starter and/or part-time situations.

Essentially, the business and the individual person are one *legal entity*; so that the financial fortunes of the business impinge directly on the individual owner and his or her family. Sole traders often have limited assets (apart from some stock, a [second-hand] vehicle and some equipment, perhaps), and a property that often serves partly as the family domestic dwelling house, with its own attendant running costs; and few liabilities.

Sole traders are at the mercy of business creditors (refer to Chapter 8): *you and your family* (if you choose to set up your business this way) take *all* the risks. In other words, if creditors pursue the business through the courts, the owner and his or her family, personally, are next in line. If necessary, the owner will be declared bankrupt. However, be comforted by the fact that there are many sole traders still around, and doing very well.

Proper bookkeeping, right through to Management Accounts in some limited form still has to be carried out – *see* Chapter 14. All the 'books' still have to reflect the business operation faithfully with agreed apportioned figures for facilities and services shared with the domestic home (heating, lighting, rent). A word of warning though … any part of the house used for business purposes might inadvertently impinge on planning regulations, household insurance policies, council tax and capital gains liabilities (this latter applies if and when the house is sold). Care must also be taken with insurance policies concerned with anything used by business and the individual – respective liabilities, premiums and cover.

Sole traders are the simplest of the businesses to set up, but the ability to raise finance is usually restricted to bank overdrafts or individuals who might lend you money – usually stemming from security, credibility and commitment factors.

Working From Home
There is added personal freedom: but it must not be at the expense of the business. For those for whom working 'from home' and 'at home' is a novelty (as opposed to the enforced pattern of working directly for an employer on his or her business premises), experience dictates that you must:

- maintain a professional customer presentability and image
- work with discipline, to a strict regime, with good time-keeping
- plan your time, but not necessarily on a nine till five basis
- foster a suitable work pattern to suit you, your family, your other commitments and, above all, *your customers*
- even organize a dedicated room if possible (as an office or workroom

substitute, a telephone, fax and computer if applicable, complete with spare chairs for visiting customers, if any,)
- have a form of transport, if relevant – second-hand perhaps.

Sole Trader Status?

Whether or not you are eligible for this business status (as opposed to normal employment) is determined by your preferences and the rules of the Inland Revenue. They will consider:

- nature of business
- mode of working
- whether or not the *self-employed* person is effectively being *employed*
- where the business actually comes from *in practice*
- responsibility for allocation, control and correction of work done
- responsibility for provision of major items of equipment
- independence when staff and other resources need to be acquired
- turnover
- size of assets
- finance arrangements
- whether the public enter the premises
- number of employees, if any
- number of hours involved.

Taxation and National Insurance

Taxation will probably be under Schedule D, a more involved system based on profits and losses within specified accounting periods, which the accountant can deal with, or Schedule E (the familiar PAYE) for very simple businesses.

You may be able to pay the reduced National Insurance Class 2 Contributions (that are lower than the Class 1 equivalents for employed persons, but so are the benefits). There are no subsequent benefits of the unemployment type, job-seekers allowances or when off sick. You also have to check the effect on accumulated contributions towards the State Retirement Pension, even if it is a long way off, because it's too late afterwards. Class 4 profit-related contributions will probably be applicable when the business develops); but your accountant and the authorities will advise on the details.

There will be no automatic provision for holidays, pensions, sickness, private health insurance, and so on. Times when you don't or can't work will cost you irretrievable income – a point worth remembering. It may be of interest to note that the author took holidays (sometimes alone because the family could not all be away simultaneously in a small retail situation – in the early days) but was usually too busy to be ill.

Trading Associates

Groups of apparently self-employed individuals or sole traders in similar or complementary businesses set up separate businesses, and often work together informally, calling themselves something like XYZ Associates. They are separate businesses from legal and accounting points of view.

They provide mutual support; and share expertise, resources and possibly client contracts, especially when overstretched. If this arrangement is an option, it needs careful thought. Often they are in related but not identical businesses, acting either informally and independently or as a subcontractor to another associate concern.

Partnerships

Where there is more than one person involved in the ownership of the business, or matters become much more complicated, business *partnerships* are sometimes formed. These help share the duties to a limited extent. Their assets usually take the intangible form of highly qualified professional people with their own:

- knowledge
- expertise
- skills
- experience
- customer base.

They are normally associated with professional or commercial practices, like firms of:

- vets
- doctors
- private medical centres
- financial investment advisors
- stockbrokers
- accountants
- solicitors
- surveyors
- insurers
- architects
- design studios
- business consultants.

Partnerships can be regarded as a formalized version of the XYZ Associates, actively sharing premises, infrastructure, staff and some responsibilities. Important business agreements between partners setting out the business and personal ground rules hold it together. Partners (as owners) normally meet periodically to review the business as a whole and make policy decisions.

Each partner does not necessarily have an equal share in the business; and some firms have many partners who have joined or left at varying times – running into a hundred or more. Partnership businesses carry more standing, responsibilities and liabilities than smaller businesses. Legally, partners *jointly* and *individually* share risks, responsibilities, liabilities, benefits in accordance with their individual agreements, and partnership legislation: so if you or any of them default in any way, you *and your family*, might well feel the powerful backwash. Partnerships usually have considerably more assets than XYZ Associates like:

- computers
- specialist software
- office equipment
- other equipment
- vehicles
- property
- stock
- possible investments.

The turnover can be considerable, where a seemingly expensive fee for its services (selling price), that effectively includes a profit and an overhead element, is usual. Bookkeeping and production of formal Management Accounts are undertaken as an entity. It is obviously prudent to take out professional indemnity and other insurance cover, *as with any form of business status – see* Chapter 18. Schedule D taxation is the norm for the partners, although the numerous staff would be handled under PAYE.

Your business *could* be this type of legal status, if the nature of the business is appropriate. You would either start your own partnership or buy into an existing one, with an appropriate agreement. However, if your proposed business were as significant as these partnerships imply (or larger), albeit not otherwise of partnership character, then the most likely status would be that of the private limited company, as discussed later.

Cooperatives

Sometimes these multi-ownership organizations take the form of cooperatives (not partnerships in a legal sense), where all members are more or less equal owners. Decisions are taken by the owners or members (often the entire workforce), and can be cumbersome and not necessarily in the interests of best business practice. The objectives will vary with the aims of the cooperative, which might be for marketing purposes, production, social, political or ethnic reasons and so on. Familiar names here are the well-known store group carrying that name, some farming marketing groups and effectively the John Lewis retail group (although not strictly behaving as a cooperative).

There are special rules applicable to this form of business, and these should be clarified before any initiations are implemented. In practice, this is not likely to be the chosen route for your venture however.

Private Limited Companies

These are the next most likely option for your venture after sole trader status, assuming the implied qualifications for partnerships are inapplicable. They take the chosen business name (mentioned elsewhere) and add the legal word *Limited* after it (often abbreviated to Ltd).

Limited companies are blessed with a considerably higher public perception, image and credibility that helps to demonstrate serious commitment in the eyes of customers, financiers, suppliers and creditors generally. They usually represent the most expensive option for you.

They enjoy a separate legal and taxation identity from the individual, which means that the two entities are, and must be kept, very strictly separate; and have separately named bank accounts. Monies cannot be arbitrarily transferred between them. They carry certain legal protection from many creditors, which is more comfortable for the family of course; but also carry certain obligations.

Company status is particularly applicable to, and associated with (in the eyes of the general public), larger concerns, or more complex business operations. However, businesses can and do range from individuals, through small and medium to larger businesses. The common denominators are empirically deemed to be high, or relatively high, stock levels, high values of projects or work in progress and/or high outside contracting obligations.

In return for the aforementioned limited liability immunity, these businesses have obligations to the public at large, society in general, authorities, creditors and to the shareholders in particular. The liability immunity really applies on the premise that the directors have complied with several critical clauses in the Companies Acts – which means, among other things, that they have:

- complied with the Companies Acts generally
- carried on the business honestly and in good faith
- not traded illegally
- not intended to defraud or deceive creditors, shareholders, staff and the general public.

Certain formal meetings have to be held, minuted (often by specifically pre-worded forms), sometimes submitted to Companies House in Cardiff, where details of all companies, their directors and members (shareholders) are filed, and where virtually anybody in the entire world *can* have access to them, if they want to of course – usually for a fee.

Formalized Annual Reports and Accounts also have to be produced and submitted each year, which may increase the accountant's bill slightly; but remember most of these documents are already needed for taxation and management information reasons anyway. Additionally, there are certain audit requirements – that are often based on annual turnover and other factors, but the rules vary from time to time. Details of Audit and Account Requirements (for this and another form of business) should be obtained from your accountant for your particular business.

Companies have to be *incorporated* or *formed* (but there are professionals to handle this, if you do not want to do it personally – for example, accountants, solicitors or specialists in company-formation). There are certain forms to complete and formalities to attend to, and a registration fee to pay. You have to choose the business name and have it vetted and approved at this stage. For this, all the necessary consequential details and documents are produced automatically.

- The company has to have a minimum of one named shareholder, although there could be several or indeed many.
- They elect or nominate at least one named *director* (but there could be several, in which case one, usually the driving force or founder, becomes managing director).
- They elect or nominate a named *company secretary* (who does not necessarily have to be either a director or a shareholder).
- There are a number of restrictions placed on qualification and eligibility of potential directors, but these can be established in advance. To most people they are no barrier.
- The company needs a stable address for the so-called Registered Office, in the UK.

The Registered Office could be that of the venturer, the accountant, solicitor or almost anywhere else for that matter, corresponding to the country of registration; but the company can also have other premises, and operate from other addresses.

Shareholders must provide at least a nominal sum of money for their shares (and that is the usual limit of their individual liability in the event of business disaster), but larger amounts of capital to fund the business can and would be raised as discussed in Chapter 8. It is worth stressing that all money the business needs does not have to be raised through shares. Creditors like to see a higher, rather than a lower or purely nominal, figure for share capital as it gives them more confidence in the company's standing, the shareholders' and your commitment.

Companies are governed ultimately by the various Companies Acts; but within themselves, by various documents setting out the ground rules, known as the Memorandum of Articles and Association, and the so-called 'Table A'. These documents have to be agreed by the members of the proposed company first, then formally submitted to, and approved by, the Registrar of Companies in Cardiff. In practice, agreed and very wide ranging off-the-shelf formats of these documents abound, allowing the members considerable freedom. These are effectively called up as required at the incorporation stage.

Typically, you become one of the directors of a *private* limited liability company, if not the only one, whilst the shareholders could be you alone, or in conjunction with a spouse, partner, colleague or anyone else by and large. But in essence it means the chosen named company, followed by the word *Limited*, is created, established, registered and recognized as a legal and separate entity from the individual.

If you decide this is the best route for the business to follow, you will usually become a Company Director as defined by the Companies Acts, inheriting all the obligations, responsibilities, liabilities, privileges, that that status accords. Along with any other directors, you, and any staff, as individuals, usually become employees of the company – being taxed under PAYE, and so on, and paying Class 1 NI Contributions – just as you would in an outside employment situation.

If *any* directors' names are published, then the *entire* list of directors has to be shown (not just some of them); it's all or none, although generally there is no obligation to publish *any* names.

Certain other obligatory information on official stationery must be carried, including where it is registered and the registration number. (It should also carry the VAT number, but for different reasons.)

Company taxation will be governed by corporation taxation rules, and any shareholder dividends will attract personal taxation. If the company closes for any reason, there are formal winding-up rules and procedures to follow.

Summary
Under certain conditions it's the right course of action – the main business considerations being:

- the nature, image, projected turnover and complexity of the business

- risks involving third parties
- the potential size of creditor liabilities and stock levels
- amount of work in progress
- financial arrangements
- business and personal taxation.

Private limited companies are more complicated to set up and operate than some forms of business, chiefly because of the protection afforded by the Acts from various liabilities in the case of problems. The protection is primarily against the business running into bad trading conditions or being exposed to unexpected third party risks; not reckless and irresponsible attitudes, with persons dubiously running the business and trading illegally. Public disclosure and legal obligations ensure as much transparency as possible.

You should not be put off this approach just because it seems complicated:

- There is so much practical help available.
- Forming and running companies appears to have got simpler in recent years.
- It could prove to be an extremely prudent decision downstream, because of the financial protection this status provides, as the business is a *separate legal entity.*
- There may be cost-saving benefits relating to the taxation system invoked.

The information above summarizes the 'bottom line' in company formation to show the broad picture in the context of the other trading situations; you are urged to read one of the specialist books on the subject and to *unequivocally take professional advice* about this and other forms of trading status – then discuss the options with the professionals. It will cost money, but at this stage you should have fairly complete outline plans with which to make informed confident decisions.

The Companies Acts are voluminous; but fortunately, authoritative, helpful, concise and practical guidance books are available on the entire subject; so there is no need to be alarmed or unduly worried about the complexities.

It is interesting to note, but probably surprising to learn, that the vast majority of companies (hundreds of thousands, and growing) in this country come into this *Private* Limited Company category, whereas there are only a few thousand in total of another sort of company – the *Public* ones! Only the two most commonly used company variants have been mentioned.

Public Limited Companies
Large public concerns account for a massive aggregate annual turnover, high employment numbers, national and international conglomerates, image and so on, but numerically there are relatively few Public Limited Companies.

A *public limited company* – carrying plc, not Limited, after its name – *usually* attaches to multi-shareholder concerns and complicated operations – even higher risk and exposure. They are usually associated with the major household and other

High Street names, although they may have originally been formed as *Limited* concerns. However, some High Street names still remain Limited, in spite of their apparent size – where they still represent close-knit family businesses. If your business is very successful and expands considerably, and then considers a stock market flotation to attract more capital for expansion (for example), and hence multiple shareholding in due course, it might prove to be the right approach one day.

They will probably not be applicable to your situation, right now, which is why the stock market is also beyond the scope of this book.

There are several distinguishing features, but one of the main dividing lines between private and public limited companies is the *minimum* value of the share capital – the amount of joint personal liability if things go wrong: the minimum for a plc is £50,000 (as compared with £1 for a private company). All companies, public and private, must raise their capital before they can start trading or borrowing; and plcs must have a minimum of two directors (not one).

There will be changes: it's worth noting that the Companies Acts are currently under heavy review. Watch this space.

Limited Liability Partnerships

Another form of trading, applicable to both larger and smaller businesses, is designated limited liability partnerships. Talk with the professionals to establish their relevance to your particular circumstances. All businesses previously working as conventional partnerships should at least consider their options. Because new legislation was only enacted by Parliament in the year 2000, limited liability partnerships have barely been encountered – and thus have no real track record yet as regards their practical operation. The name of these partnerships must end with 'llp' or 'LLP'. The sphere of such enterprises is not limited to the so-called professions and commerce, and can in fact relate to virtually anything.

Their status is a cross between a partnership and a limited company; and their status, rules and so on reflect both forms of trading. Whilst they are not dissimilar to partnerships in principle as described above, they offer some peace of mind in the form of limited liability for the *individuals*, as with conventional companies.

The Act sets out broadly similar obligations and restrictions to those applicable to limited companies with regard to their being treated as a completely separate entity from the individuals. It is generally aimed at flexibility for the partners with obvious adequate public and creditor protection. The Act covers their creation; their limitations, their accountancy and auditing requirements; their closure, their individual members' deaths, their taxation, and so on. Although taxation is assessed collectively, liability to taxation is limited to any one individual for his or her dues only, and not for the full partnership. Typically, this business status is applicable to those businesses who would previously be candidates for conventional partnerships – listed above.

Llps are governed internally by formal properly-drafted agreements and the incorporation documents (that have to be delivered to the Registrar of Companies and must include the partners' names, addresses, the registered office, the name and nature of the venture, and so on) The subscribers to the incorporation are the original members of the business, although others may join and some of the originals may leave, with suitable later agreements and approval of the members.

Franchises

Franchises are another option, but they are discussed in Chapter 22, when you are better able to appreciate the differences after reading about conventional businesses. It will be better if *non-franchised* businesses are completely understood first.

EXERCISE

What is the most appropriate business status for your venture, and why?

MORE ABOUT BUSINESS NAMES

Closely allied to the status of a business is the subject of business names that will have a very strong connection with the image and prosperity of the business. So it's important to choose the right business name – *see* Chapter 9, which discusses the marketing angle. This chapter considers the legal situation.

Name screening processes *must* be undertaken for the purposes of finding a suitable and available name for a formal company: certain keywords are not allowed. Some names, logos and descriptions might be registerable under certain conditions as *trademarks*: these therefore should not, and cannot legally, be duplicated.

There are currently no practical watertight ways to protect a name, although the prospects are better if the business is formed and registered at Companies House. As electronic trading on the Internet evolves, this situation may well change – so this point needs careful monitoring.

In choosing a name, you must search trade directories, telephone directories and the Internet as best you can; and any lists relating to trade marks and company names (even if you will not trade as a company in the end). More information on this particular subject will be available in books, or at business and general libraries, and organizations like the Institute of Trade Mark Agents, the Confederation of British Industries, the Institute of Directors, the Federation of Small Businesses and various trade associations.

There is also a whole raft of equivalent information on *patents*, which might be relevant. This should be checked out at a very early stage in the research, preferably using a recommended Patent Agent – whether one wants to patent a product, or to avoid infringing someone else's patent, or to find a way round another patent, or simply to enquire about a business name.

Take professional advice, once more, since any infringements could be expensive, even if not intentional. From your trading point of view, let alone the so-called *infringed party*, it could be very embarrassing, inconvenient, confusing and expensive to have similar or identical names – and so is best avoided using all the research avenues and tricks at your disposal. Conversely, if your business has become an *infringed party*, there are remedies through negotiation or the courts; but take professional advice.

Think very hard about your business name (if official screening doesn't eventually preclude it), as it will have to be lived with for a long time. Any slogans, logos and trade marks should also be considered, *and registered if possible*, at the same time.

Although it is possible to change names, the image building and marketing has to be started again. This smacks of inefficiency, mergers or takeovers. The PR machine will need to work overtime and cost more money.

Electronic names mentioned in the last chapter are equally important – whether e-mail [names and] addresses or Internet web page designations. As a precaution, you should take very great care in choosing, acquiring and registering *all* your possible Internet sites and domain names, so as to secure their reserved use for you and your business from the outset. Agencies will assist with this process for a fee. Innocent names seemingly are being created, logged and *registered* by less scrupulous people (with a keen eye for deliberately making money by selling the names and their rights back to the legitimate owners or users). At the time of writing this book it is not apparently illegal, although morally unjustified. However, some legislation to outlaw the practice is likely to emerge sometime.

One very obvious point to watch is *not* to get any printing done (office stationery, business cards, advertising and general publicity) until all these matters have been settled and, if necessary, authorized. This comment goes for things like telephones, fax numbers and e-mail addresses. Don't print until the last moment – a double run is very expensive, just because a name will change or a number's wrong for example! However, one way to meet the problem, as it were, would be to get a *small* quantity of some items of stationery from a low-cost supplier at first until matters settle down. Then get the proper stationery ordered! Even use your computer and 'business card printing' machines.

When these numbers (or names) are allocated or chosen, ensure that they are as memorable as possible, and not too similar to a competitor's or another big business' number. Not only should you strive to get 'good' numbers, but you must not suffer loss of business, frustration and wasted time as a result of being subjected to repeatedly misdialled calls if your particular number happens to be similar to those of a major call centre, for example.

Comforting hunches will emerge on the subject of closely related numbers for the first weeks or months, but things might change afterwards, as future applications from other businesses seeking new numbers are allocated; so you have to keep on your guard.

Subject to a charge on your business, special phone numbers (like FREEPOST postal addresses) are available to give your customers free calls. Numbers can be replaced by letters (a memorable *word*, rather than a telephone *number*), premium rate numbers and so on are available.

EXERCISE

Try out about two dozen business names on colleagues for their reaction. Reduce them to a short list of three.

WHAT HAVE YOU LEARNT IN THIS CHAPTER?

★ What are the eight principal trading status options? Indicate the more likely options?
★ What factors influence the choice?
★ What are the advantages and disadvantages of being self-employed or a sole trader?
★ What are the main advantages and disadvantages of trading as a limited company?
★ What are the basic formation requirements of a private limited company?

18
Engaging
Professional Support

Finding out about the personal and business issues of setting up and running your own venture by yourself for the first time can be very exciting, tinged possibly with what seems to be the enormity of the problem. Not only is it fun, but it is also challenging, adventureful and deeply educational. During these euphoric days, pre-launch risk and expenditure must be kept to an absolute minimum by efficient self-learning through courses and reading – as you are doing at the moment – and by doing as much of the groundwork as possible yourself.

This chapter discusses the role of the professionals first, and then some legislation that might affect you.

Ultimately you must get help: professional help is called for in roughly this order (although there will be slight variations in this lengthy list between various situations – and not all of them will be needed for every venture):

- libraries – for preliminary and general feasibility research, and for sorting out business ideas
- trade associations
- trade contacts
- potential suppliers
- project management
- accountants
- IT and e-commerce technologists (if applicable to your concept)
- Companies House (for helping to establish matters like business names, trade marks, and logos, possibly)
- banks
- other lending sources, maybe
- estate agents
- letting agents
- local authorities (for rating figures, planning and building regulations)
- surveyors
- solicitors (for personal agreements, property conveyancing and so on)
- insurance brokers
- architects
- builders
- shopfitters
- designers

- VAT office, if applicable
- Inland Revenue (for taxation generally, self and employees PAYE, NIC)
- bookkeepers
- credit and debit card companies
- finance houses (as appropriate)
- service providers (for phones, faxes, water, electricity, gas, oil)
- external printers
- design houses
- advertising media and/or agencies
- Chambers of Trade
- Chambers of Commerce and Industry
- copyright and patents organizations.

PROFESSIONALS' FEES

It will start to cost serious money, and the business won't be earning money yet! As each professional organization is contacted, work out precisely what will be sought from them. Do as much as possible to help, in a tidy and organized fashion. You should be fairly certain about your venture concept. It should be supported by structured logic, thinking, back-up details, accumulated factual or numerical data. It's almost your first draft at the business plan.

Be absolutely clear about what you expect from the professionals; and they will be best placed to give an estimate of the fees, both for the immediate task and thereafter when the business is up and running.

Always ask first what the fees are likely to be (and is VAT payable, additionally?). It obviously varies, depending on:

- who you engage
- conciseness of *your* thinking
- complexities of the assignment
- size of your organization
- size and reputation of their organization
- time involved
- *their* methods of charging
- rates of charging.

PROJECT MANAGEMENT

Professional project management, included here for completeness, should not really be necessary, except where the venture is very complex.

Nevertheless, one of the big challenges of the detailed planning stage is precision coordination of everyone's involvement, including that of the professionals, so that no precious time and money are wasted, or efforts duplicated – especially when you have to go round some parts of the same loop many times. Careful juggling of the meetings with the various professionals will be called for.

All fact-finding and implementation matters take time and cost money: so they must be built into the detailed planning of the venture – a master plan. This is all to do with initiating matters in the right sequence (and phasing) so that they all dovetail neatly, after allowing for the vagaries of each element or activity.

You are strongly advised to become conversant with project management techniques to an appropriate level to get the job done:

* effectively
* ensuring that the targeted opening window(s) are not missed
* minimizing inconvenience
* within budget
* without duplication
* without omissions
* without unnecessary waiting around
* without secrecy being compromised.

Even simple manual ones are helpful, although there are computer solutions. If the computerized versions don't appeal, or appear expensive and complex, some mastery of project management skills at this stage right up to launch date is very valuable – and can save you time and money.

Mishandling these early stages, and acting in a non-professional manner could somehow wrong-foot the venture and generate bad publicity. If the word escaped too soon or was heard by the professional adviser of a competitor, the venturer could be scuppered before even starting – being pipped at the post. Only divulge to others the minimum of information, compatible with giving enough for each person to be able to advise properly – a need-to-know basis.

ACCOUNTANT

The most important and long-term professional is your chosen accountant: he or she plays a key role, and should be selected very carefully – preferably by recommendation from other well-satisfied clients or the bank, for example. Your accountant should be formally qualified as a certified or chartered accountant – ensuring that they have passed the necessary examinations, know their stuff, and are experienced. Curiously not all businesses have an accountant and, strictly speaking, you do not have to have one, but …

Why have an accountant, anyway? After all, on the face of it, businesses could save a considerable amount of money by not employing one.

It must be indelibly written somewhere that:

* You can also *save considerably* larger amounts than his or her fees by engaging a good, proactive and constructive-questioning accountant.
* The accountant will generally have gained considerable experience with various clients across a wide range of businesses and industries.

- He or she will have encountered many broadly similar situations, and will have a huge collection of contacts for all those business-related matters that aren't directly within his or her sphere of knowledge.

On the other hand, careful discretion between clients must clearly be upheld – as in fact is usually the case. There might even be business *opportunities* as a result of introductions made between clients – another example of networking.

The primary reason for your accountant's involvement is for professional advice on a whole range of issues from:

- initial feasibility of establishing the venture on the best business footing, including forming a limited liability company, if relevant
- tax planning, tax wrinkles, tax negotiations and avoidance
- compiling official paperwork and taxation returns
- having the Accounts presented professionally minimizes the risk of tax investigations – which would cause extra hassle and possibly involve extra expense anyway
- keeping within the financial legislation
- sharpening up cash flow forecasts
- putting the business case together professionally, to achieve the best results
- seeking finance
- bookkeeping, if applicable
- payroll, if applicable
- personal taxation
- ensuring compliance with the Companies Acts
- advising on legal positions
- auditing, if applicable
- being an independent sounding board for ideas
- being a business mentor as, in the last resort, two heads are better than one!

Five further important points:

- You will recall that outsourcing matters that were not your real interests or areas of expertise was generally advised in previous chapters, unless you or your staff happen to have indigenous skills in those directions, coupled with spare time – so that your business' foremost revenue-earning efforts would not suffer.
- Audits for the Companies Acts, VAT and other taxation returns, have deadlines. It is time-consuming and voluminous. Such paperwork is legislation-based; tardiness, and incorrectly completed documents will trigger automatic fines on the business or person – another worry worth off-loading! Accountants have the computer software that deals with these matters accurately and automatically.
- However, one advantage of you keeping the primary stages of bookkeeping is your ability to register all the details that occur; it's a tacit form of hands-on management. Come to an agreement as to who does what in this connection.

- Although not legally responsible as such for the business (as the owners are), accountants are effectively, but unofficially, a sort of silent partner or non-executive director. In his or her dual role, that embraces pure accountancy matters and their derivatives, as well as their non-official standing, they are almost uniquely very intimately concerned that the business is well-run and given the best possible direction and management advice. It's a case of the onlooker seeing most of the game.
- Finally, there are times when life at the top is very lonely: it's good to have someone else to talk to – who understands you and your business. Your accountant is the main confidential and independent 'consultant'.

Summary

- A good accountant is really worth searching for, and worth his or her weight in the proverbial gold.
- Don't try to manage without one *to save money*: you probably won't in the long run.
- Although quite reasonably they want their fees, they do provide a valuable service to your business – and can *save* you money.
- Not all the professional help you encounter will be of such a deep and long-lasting relationship: or in your business' best interests.

Longer-Term relationship

In the early stages of your venture, only a little knowledge of accountancy should suffice: but as the business grows, more awareness on your part will be useful and interesting. If you are able to anticipate the answers to your questions, there will be far fewer small matters that need to be discussed directly with the accountant. You will learn how he or she thinks which will make you more self-reliant in this area. It will be cheaper for you.

So, an important valuable fourfold skill for you to develop in time is to:

- learn from the accountant
- understand his or her way of thinking and viewing the business
- think as he or she does
- argue constructively and discuss the business issues on an equal footing.

There are several specialist books available to get you off the ground, covering the detail of an accountant's craft that reflect different types of businesses, such as distribution (which includes shops), manufacturing, catering (which includes, pubs, guest houses, hotels, and so on), self-employment and so on. The accountant will almost always be required, but you will become less dependent on him or her.

The first step (after the basic confirmation of concept and viability) concerns the business status that will certainly embrace the services of an accountant or solicitor.

It is important to get some feel for this at an early stage and get the matter sorted out before going too far down the rest of the road, because of the hassle and costs entailed in changing things afterwards. Business status is determined by the considerations referenced in the last chapter; and, to some extent, your business status will influence how others treat the business and its transactions.

PROPERTY MATTERS

You will need to encounter several professionals in connection with property dealings.

Local Authority Planning Department
Soon after sensing interest in a property, the local authority planning department will need to be consulted to establish whether or not there are likely to be any difficulties using the particular site for the particular purposes that you want. The authorities are usually very helpful and will give guidance on the procedures.

The authority's plans for the area should be revealed and interrogated by you (or your solicitor if necessary). Find out whether there will be any adverse developments anticipated (such as demolition work, developments, buildings, road systems, past or present underground workings, liability to flooding) that might impinge on the fortunes of your venture.

Present and proposed uses of the property could be discussed directly with the authority's planning department officers who will advise the next steps and whatever forms and fees are required. Usually basic advice and various helpful maps and leaflets are all free, or available for a nominal cost.

If building alterations, new shopfront, new shop sign, or change of use, and so on are involved, a planning application will have to be submitted and approved before go-ahead; and if building work is needed, an application with regard to building regulations will have to be submitted as well. Filing these forms entails a fee.

Where a complete change of use is planned, there could be considerable building or fitting out work to be done – and this could entail very large sums of money. Remember that:

- Funding will be required to get the property in the first place.
- Additional funding will be needed for the alterations.
- Written permission may be necessary from a third party for alterations, like the landlord, mortgagor or lessor, and insurer, before the alterations can be carried out.

Business Rates
Not far away from property discussions will be the subject of business rates. Get and understand the precise figures from the council for the rating side (and consider monthly, quarterly or annual payment figures for the cash flow forecast).

Leaflets and guidance will be readily on hand – but bear in mind that different properties will attract different rates. They could be largish figures and will embrace wide variations between properties.

Town centre shops, offices and other premises tend to be the most expensive properties to acquire, and attract the higher business rates in proportion; but they can attract large volumes of customers and sales as well – with constructive effects on profitability.

Property Surveyor

The services of a property surveyor should be sought once the choice of property has been almost settled (and provisional funding plans have been made and approved), to establish the constructional state or condition of the proposed property. They will also arrange special surveys of drainage systems, central heating, electricity wiring, dry and wet rot, and so on; and provide written reports on:

- the property condition
- whether it represents value for money
- its suitability from a constructional point of view for the purpose for which you intend to use it
- any work that is necessary or prudent
- whether or not anyone is likely to lend money against it, if required.

Usually, contractors' estimates for any work are free, although the eventual work may be expensive. Costs could range between buying:

- literally a new shop front (to give a unique and fresh image – but don't skimp this *if it helps the venture*)
- extensive new fixtures and fittings and/or building work internally that could amount to substantial sums.

Architect

An architect's services may be appropriate to provide image or practical building changes. Architects and surveyors will also specify, obtain, evaluate and recommend estimates; and then be prepared for an additional fee to supervise any work that is required.

So cost factors (for rent and purchase as well as rates) in relation to turnover are important and could vary considerably. Keep all factors relating to property choice in mind, and make a league table for the short-listed sites. It's a good idea to undertake several alternative outline sales forecasts if several different properties are being considered to establish their contribution towards costs, for each case. This is not an easy comparison to make of course, but you must try.

SOLICITOR

Personal recommendation is again a good guide to a trustworthy firm of solicitors, in relation to qualifications, experience, proactiveness and legal specialization fields.

Conveyancing

The legal moves to acquire property should never be started until the preliminary property and funding discussions have taken place, and solutions, if any are needed, are on the horizon.

When factors like property, finance and legal establishment of the business (however this is done) have been properly considered and concluded with your business partners, fellow directors and accountant, a solicitor should always be engaged for the actual legal transfer of the property (*conveyancing*) and perhaps some related matters.

Personal Agreements

A solicitor will probably come in handy at some stage to draw up any personal agreements between the individuals, stating their relative stake in the business, their terms of contract or engagement, and so on; alternatively, the agreements may be between the business itself (however it is established in a legal sense) and some or all of the individual key players. If you have ever received a service contract or conditions of employment relating to an employed situation, the clauses contained therein will be broadly similar to those the solicitor should incorporate in these own business agreements. The degree of formal legal jargon will be higher.

Discuss with a solicitor the necessity of such agreements, and their precise clauses, but bear in mind that solicitors would probably tend towards them because it is their business – even if it is a good idea really.

Wills and Business Transfer

In due course (although probably somewhat premature at this early part of the business' life), the solicitor should be involved in drawing up appropriate documents relating to personal Wills, Trusts and other provisions for passing on the business at times of a death of the owner(s) or a key player(s) to avoid ambiguity and to minimize the various duties, taxes and capital gains taxes.

Informed professional advice at the outset (and later as well) to keep up with the constantly changing rules, is called for. It will vary with different legal standings of the business, and its consequential impact on the individuals – and inevitably, the tax situation. Hence another need for careful business status considerations at the appropriate time.

Litigation

Although they will not be needed initially, the services of the legal profession – both solicitors and barristers – might be sought in connection with any bad debts, disputes, civil and criminal court cases or litigation generally (as plaintiff or defendant) at some time in the future.

INSURER

Businesses must be adequately covered by insurance. Talk with the accountant in the first place about all insurance matters. There may be special risks associated with your particular business, for which specific insurance cover should be sought. The strategic aim should be to limit the risks for the business as a whole, from wherever the risks appear to come.

Take advice and shop around for the best deal – not necessarily the cheapest – with regard to cost, settlement, minimum hassle and so on. Matters like the following should be positively considered, although not every aspect is necessarily applicable to your proposed business. Some are people-related: some are business-related:

People-Related

- For anyone on the premises, including customers, visitors and subcontractors
- for you, and your business partners or fellow directors
- for other key people, who make the business work and earn revenue
- for other employees – as required by law.

There are special policies applicable to business partners and company directors (for their specific liabilities under the Companies Acts).

Consideration should also be given within remuneration packages to optional personal insurances, PHI (permanent health insurance) and pensions.

Business-Related

- General comprehensive business cover, including loss of profits in the case of certain contingencies
- all business risks, including third-party liabilities
- professional indemnity
- stock
- properties
- plant
- equipment
- machine tools
- furniture
- contents
- fittings
- vehicles.

Professional Indemnity

Self-employed persons, and small and medium businesses generally, should not forget the professional indemnity cover. This could be vital in the case of a professional person advising clients, where things go wrong after the advice has been heeded. Ultimately, your client could sue the business or you, or both. Your head is on the block; because the damage figures could well exceed the value of the original fee, and even the business assets (killing the business). Two examples to bring home the point – one you are sued, and one you sue.

Example One

Suppose you, as a freelance consultant, are working on computer software solutions or another business problem for your large international corporate client, and get it wrong somehow, upset an existing arrangement with third parties, with large-scale consequential disruptions to production, or whatever. No doubt, in the interests of good and continuing business or sales relationships, you will do your best to resolve matters, but in the last resort, you could be faced with, and sued for, a general claim for damages for professional negligence, amounting to millions of pounds – a sum which far exceeded your original fee.

Example Two

Suppose a fully qualified surveyor examines and provides a written report on a different personal or business property that you are contemplating buying, as his or her client – valued at around two or three hundred thousand pounds. You handed over professional fees amounting to several hundred pounds.

On the basis of this, and other, supporting information, you decide to proceed with the purchase. A few months later, perhaps, a serious structural fault shows up, and you sue the surveyor (whether it is the surveyor's direct responsibility or not). The huge legal fees, litigation costs and compensation will far outweigh the surveyor's original fee, and probably bring financial ruin to him or her surveying business, and personal life – unless he or she has taken out a suitable form of personal indemnity insurance

TECHNOLOGY

Rest assured that if you don't understand technical matters, there is help available to tell you what is and what is not possible at any particular time – and when it might be available. All you have to do is generate the ideas, discuss the concept and how you think your business could possibly benefit, with your accountant and business partners.

Revise your understanding of technology, its ramifications, selling psychology and hence web page design in Chapter 16. Discuss practical visions, listen to colleagues and professionals; and only *then* call an IT specialist. Once you've got the broad nod, get the technical opinion on how to go about it.

He or she will advise on the feasibility, what hardware is required, when it is needed, what else is needed, terminals, headsets, costs, installation, maintenance, software, design of the best and most effective web pages, ISPs, e-mail addresses, web pages, dedicated phone lines and so on – and confirm how it can be used to help your business.

Get up-to-date recommendations about system capabilities, how easy they are to work with, and names of reliable and knowledgeable computer experts, systems integrators, such as when and where they were trained, certified and qualified, whether they be individuals or businesses. They should all be familiar with costs, data integrity, security, load balancing, integration with other future

231

developments, installation, testing and all other technical issues. Check out other clients' installations and experiences.

This area is just as important to your business (the influence it has over the image and prosperity); much as a good accountant is. It needs very careful thought and referrals from colleagues probably.

EXERCISE

What professional help and advice will you seek for your own particular venture?

LEGISLATION, RULES AND REGULATIONS

This part of this chapter takes a general overview of some aspects of legislation that might affect businesses generally – and your business in particular; but as on other occasions, it might depend on a variety of factors such as the: nature; size; turnover; ownership; trading status; whether it employs people; a multitude of other qualifying or disqualifying points.

Various instruments of government control could come from, and are continuously being created daily by, our government, the European Commission, local authorities and other bodies. A *tremendous* number of laws that are perpetually changing and being augmented are being announced continuously, so it is virtually impossible for any one individual to maintain up-to-date information on every legislative matter. Check the latest situation with the professionals.

In general, questions for the professionals do not change, but the answers might, depending on timing. It has frequently been stated that this book sets out to raise flags and pose typical questions; but points you, at the particular time when you need to know, to the professionals, part of whose job is to keep up with relevant changes in the law and regulations, supporting case law and expert predictions. Timing is crucial.

How a particular change assists or adversely affects your business is a question you must monitor, enquire about sometime and then take professional advice:

- *at the appropriate time*
- not too early, because of the constant necessity not to waste money
- not too late either, because that could *cost* your business money, too.

Only matters that are of immediate interest to us, make us sit up and listen:

- whether openly being discussed in the newspapers or by the broadcasting authorities
- whether they emanate from London, Brussels, Washington or locally
- whether they are in the form of a Bill being debated in Parliament, a Green or White paper, and so on.

232

Sometimes they affect everybody, sometimes just a section of the population or business world. If they don't immediately affect our lives, we temporarily or more permanently ignore them. But what is certain, is that somehow we all have to keep abreast of changes; and that, as individuals and businesses, we have no choice but to comply with the various laws in the end.

Laws, rules, regulations, directives and codes of practices can be segregated into, and considered in, two different groups – based on the generality or otherwise.

General Legislation, Regulations, Codes of Practice, Guidelines, Rules

Certain items of legislation and forms of regulation affect *virtually all* businesses. Here are just some of the Acts, European Directives, Codes of Practice and Regulations that most businesses will be affected by, to some extent or other:

- ACAS procedures
- British Code of Advertising
- Companies
- Competition
- Computer Misuse
- Consumer Credit
- Contracts of Employment
- Copyright
- Dangerous Goods
- Data Protection
- Disability
- Discrimination
- Economic and Monetary Union
- Electronic Communications
- Employment generally
- Employment Relations
- Employment Protection
- Environmental Protection
- Equal Opportunities
- Equal Pay
- European Charter for Small Enterprises
- FPS
- Fair and Unfair Dismissal
- Factories, Shops and Offices
- Fire regulations
- Harassment
- Health and Safety
- Human Rights
- Intellectual Property
- Insolvency
- Late Payment of Commercial Debts

- MPS
- Mail Order Protection Scheme
- Minimum Wages
- Noise
- Nuisance
- Oftel
- Patents
- Pollution
- Part-time Employees Regulations 2000
- Race Discrimination
- Redundancy
- Regulation of Investigatory Powers
- Sale of Goods Act
- Sex Discrimination
- Social Security
- Supply of Goods and Services
- Taxation (budgets)
- Tenancies
- Trade Unions
- Trade Descriptions
- Trade Marks
- Unfair Terms in Consumer Contracts
- VAT.

Specific Legislation, Regulations, Codes of Practice and Rules

There is another set of matters that affect specific businesses or groups of businesses, such as:

- ABTA (travel)
- Aviation
- Children
- Dangerous Goods
- Drugs
- Food Handling and Preparation
- Labelling
- Hotel Proprietor
- Hygiene regulations
- Licensing Laws
- Shipping
- Transport.

There are also a number of conventions and miscellaneous matters that are of concern to businesses, depending on the business, although they are not necessarily directly based on regulation or legislation. Applicable businesses should take note when it comes to things such as:

- product fitness for purpose
- goods being of merchantable quality: *is it capable of doing the job?*
- safety of merchandise (for example, electrical goods)
- consumer rights in general
- care when giving advice
- labelling
- marking country of origin
- dated products
- shelf life
- display and use-by dates
- sale or return stock
- assorted customer loyalty schemes (cards, stamps, points, redeemable vouchers, tokens from newspapers and previously purchased packaging)
- gift and book tokens
- extended warranty policies
- opening hours
- pricing
- accounting in both the euro and other currencies simultaneously, possibly.

Not all these matters will affect every business in quite the same way: and in any case some businesses are excused compliance because of the nature of the business, location, ownership, turnover, how many are employed, relationship of employees to owner, and so on. If in doubt ask! This whole subject is very complex – and it could always change!

In practice, the realistic way to keep up to date is to establish the current situation with your own business (as a base line, using some of the methods mentioned above); and then empirically to keep up to date on a slower timescale as points change.

TERMS AND CONDITIONS

A topic that crops up many times, and that will be different in detail for virtually every business, is the one on your own Business Terms and Conditions (T&Cs). The irony is that, with just a few exceptions, and until there is a dispute, nobody apart from those who formulate the T&Cs really reads them. In any case, each party associated with a particular deal writes their own T&Cs (and then assumes mistakenly that *theirs* alone will always prevail) – whereas T&Cs between supplier and purchaser often conflict when read together. Be wary of T&Cs from other parties who expect your business to agree to their T&Cs. A solicitor's help, maybe?

Writing your own terms and conditions of business is quite simple. For your business:

(a) study the T&Cs from competitors if the chance arises;
(b) talk to trade associations (part of their *raison d'être*);

(c) think about various possible clauses (special, almost unique, situations) in outline for your venture;

(d) *then* consult the professionals to put them into 'legalese'.

As litigation cases are on the increase, these matters must be sorted out before trading starts – assuming that there is sufficient indigenous knowledge about the particular trade already to properly understand and address the issues. The more complex the venture, or the more potential third-party liabilities, dependencies and consequential damages, the stronger the case for watertight contract terms at the earliest opportunity. It could be disastrously too late afterwards. It's not what you believe and think – it's the *courts'* view that counts!

Some contracts and agreements are drawn up specially for each customer project, and some are printed on the back of other documents as a 'permanent' feature. Nevertheless, here are some key points to form the basis of your thinking:

- names and addresses of the contractual parties
- nature of the products, services and business
- duration of contract
- price, price variations
- payment terms, late payment provision
- finance instalment arrangements, if any
- title
- acceptance or rejection arrangements of products or services, and time period (particularly in the cases of unique designs, unique manufacture and projects)
- inspection, test and delivery arrangements
- copyright and trade marks
- warranties and guarantees
- installation
- insurance
- limit of liability
- third-party involvement (installation, servicing, off-site working)
- termination and cancellation
- *force majeure*
- disputes
- any special conditions
- date of agreement possibly
- signature of the parties.

Generally these matters should be expressed in properly constructed contractual format by solicitors, other times as 'grey print' on the back of quotations and order forms or even occasionally unwritten – although the latter can be dangerous if it came to a dispute! Endeavour not to let matters get out of hand in the first place, and try hard to settle out of court or, better still, over a cup of tea. Any litigation, however far it proceeds is *very expensive*, totally unproductive and very time-consuming (when there are other more profitable and revenue-generating things to do) – except for those in the legal profession!

In drawing up T&Cs, contracts, agreements, notices and the like, the law says that certain types of terms, phraseology, wording and statements may be deemed to be unfair and possibly illegal. Guidance in these matters can be sought from the Director General of Fair Trading and solicitors. These so-called unfair contract terms can apply to your business and to your customers.

Unfair clauses can be inadvertently incorporated into other agreements – like personal Service Agreements – as well that might seek to affect staff rights or their protection from unscrupulous employers. Similarly, employees want fair deals.

CUSTOMER AND CONSUMER RIGHTS

Customers have rights – by law: so you should ensure familiarity with them. Not just because it is the law, but because it shows professionalism and good business practice, if you are aware of them. In any case, most traders will want to stay in the clear. It's a classic case of being forewarned, and hence forearmed. These rights typically relate to most goods or services, their implied or stated fitness for purpose, how to deal with second-hand, exchanged or faulty goods, advertisements, accuracy of statements and responses to customer questions about the products and services, safety, buying on credit, mail order business, direct marketing, financial services, building work, and so on.

So again you are urged to become familiar with all the organizations mentioned in this chapter: any potential advice they are likely to give, in advance, will help avoid any possible trouble and bad publicity through the press and other media. There are also Codes of Practice, 'best practice' recommendations and procedures. Nevertheless, the customer has the ultimate right to seek legal redress for his or her grievance or concern.

The fields outlined in this latter part of the chapter are extremely complicated; but the following people and organizations thrive by keeping various businesses informed about the essence and impact of new laws, so as to help the inexperienced and the 'too busy':

• the professionals, mentioned above
• the Institute of Directors
• the Confederation of British Industry
• Chambers of Trade, Commerce and Industry
• the Federation of Small Businesses
• the relevant Trade Associations
• the Office of Fair Trading
• Enterprise Agencies
• Business Links
• local authority Trading Standards Departments
• Citizens Advice Bureaux

- Libraries
- County Courts and Small Claims Courts.

You should be reassured, not overwhelmed, because help is at hand to advise you about all the matters contained in this chapter – both current situations and potential changes. It is a major part of the various organizations' roles in relation to businesses. These are often the major reasons businesses join trade association and other similar bodies. Another source of information is exhibitions, trade magazines, journals, the Internet, newspapers, radio, television and books of various sorts including encyclopedias.

EXERCISE

Write down the specific, or rough areas of, legislation that might affect your venture.

EXERCISE

Which trade organisations should you contact, and why?

WHAT HAVE YOU LEARNT IN THIS CHAPTER?

★ Give the reasons for not contacting the professionals in the early stages of contemplating a business.
★ Why is it necessary to approach the professionals eventually?
★ What additional advice and help should you seek, and why?
★ What could be the consequences of not getting professional help?
★ List the key professional contacts.
★ What are the many advantages of having a first-class accountant?
★ List the jobs the accountant can do for you.
★ In what areas should a solicitor be consulted?
★ How should you find a first-class accountant, solicitor or other professional for that matter?
★ What sorts of legislation affects most businesses?
★ Name the most usual business organizations?
★ Why do they exist and how can *they* help?
★ What are the main T&C points?
★ Name some areas of consumer law?

19
Supporting the Business

The focal point of any business is its core activity, responsible directly for producing products and services to generate revenue. If businesses could thrive under these rudimentary conditions alone, they would presumably be running near maximum efficiency.

The Internet and fax machines can transmit information, but not physical items. The country has an infrastructure of roads, motorways, rivers, canals and railways to make it work (just imagine trying to do business if goods and raw materials couldn't be moved about easily). Correspondingly a business should have supporting features.

Depending on the precise nature of your business … to support the core responsibility, an infrastructure of some sort (refer to Figure 3 in Chapter 6) is likely to be needed:

- people with supporting technical skills, perhaps
- people with underpinning expertise in selling, marketing, finance, technology and management
- people who can handle other people
- people who have good communications and telephone skills
- people who themselves are not directly responsible for revenue-generation – such as receptionists, catering staff, drivers, cleaners, office and administration staff
- suitable accommodation, systems and various forms of equipment.

SPENDING THE LIMITED FUNDS WISELY

A problem that is worth spending a lot of time on is deciding the best way to spend the very limited funding resources to best advantage. Address the overall range of facilities, so that the customers get the best impression and range of stock or facilities, bearing in mind the usual tight financial constraints.

Image and Business Balance
The key point is to balance a genuine business need, functionality, convenience, safety, smart image and cost effectiveness with funding availability, space utilization and other physical constraints in the property. In the case of customer accessibility and visibility, it must look and feel inviting, interesting and to some extent

intriguing: customers must be made to feel wanted. Overriding all these points, is the need to have welcoming, courteous, friendly, polite, knowledgeable, well-dressed (or at least appropriately dressed) staff. All the foregoing should be in place by Day 1.

As money can be allocated in several conflicting ways within the business as a whole, the art is to get the best balance – and this might entail several attempts. Overall business targets will determine the best balance of total spending within the practical constraints of the business. The usual internal arguments centre on what are seen as:

- image
- premises – raw, but not completely ideal
- premises – alterations to, and fitting out
- essential plant
- necessary equipment
- obligatory furniture
- indispensable working vehicles
- vital stock or raw materials
- initial working capital
- ongoing wages/salaries.

In terms of overall space allocation, space effectively costs money (both to acquire in the first place, to adapt, to operate and maintain – it isn't free). Consequently, it must be assigned to particular tasks where it will be fully utilized, contributing the maximum to the business as a whole so as to be cost-effective and to maximize the overall business output, 'production' and revenues. Space allocation needs careful assessment.

Although subsequent changes and minor adjustments *can* be made, it will cost time, money and disruption to trading – and probably a lot of carrying or manhandling of heavy items. Whatever constitutes the business core (that includes accommodating customers, of course) must have an overwhelming priority call on space – to maximize the revenue-earning capability.

When considering the infrastructure, there are design houses working with 'shop-fitters' that together can be employed to make the customer areas as appealing and conducive to relaxation and buying as possible. Correspondingly, second-hand furniture and fittings abound (some of which are perfectly respectable or can easily be made so) – if these are acceptable behind the scenes to save some vital money, perhaps.

So, summarizing … when thinking about and planning the infrastructure, make sure it reflects the target core capacities, business turnover targets and priorities

Ensure that it figures on the main project chart for the venture, mentioned in Chapter 18. In the detailed planning stage, organizing these details and planning the physical implementation (and *in the right order*) is often very complex and hence time-consuming – so organize the whole subject meticulously and carefully.

ESSENTIAL FACILITIES

All parts of the infrastructure are important (whether they be people or 'things'). Their relative priorities will also differ between different businesses and industries: some might not be too relevant to your business. All parts, if they are deemed necessary in the first place (however large, small or virtually non-existent), must be functional and earn their keep. Whilst being very important to the business, they cannot possibly be considered luxuries.

You must interpret the following thoughts as appropriate to your individual venture. The shape, size and lubrication factors of the infrastructure clearly contribute to the ultimate capacity and turnover abilities of the business. It is important that all parts of the infrastructure fully support the business: the tail must not wag the dog, or *constrain* the core activities in any way.

Customer-Visible Infrastructure

Some parts of the infrastructure are always *visible to customers*; some are not. You must separate these areas from the behind-the-scenes ones. The customer-visible parts in particular have their image to maintain, that must be of stylish appearance, exhibiting businesslike impressions.

Care must be taken to ensure that the support is appropriate to the needs of the business and its customers, and that it is appropriate in respect of size, scope and nature of business. It must not be over-the-top (otherwise it will give out the wrong image signals and have a negative effect on the fortunes of the business).

Although not classified as infrastructure as such, there is a situation that comes to mind whereby the owner of a small local business parks his car (a Rolls Royce) right outside his shop, which sends out the wrong signals to his customers. Whilst he might indeed be justified in having one as a direct result of his efforts, it is not really a good idea to rub his customers' noses in it.

Access for everybody – customers, visitors, staff, owners, including the disabled – is very important – staircases, lifts, toilets and kitchen facilities, as well as all the other areas mentioned below.

These thoughts are directed at:

- shop-style businesses of all sorts, showrooms, including design studios and other creative concerns
- businesses where customers spend a long time at the establishments, like hotels, restaurants, pubs and health clinics, although the weighting and terminology will vary
- non-shop style businesses including manufacturing and repair concerns.

Commensurate with your business and its desired image, you must create a smart showroom, shop or other 'work or relaxation' space dedicated to customers, with appropriate tills or terminals where applicable. This area must not be ostentatious, but not frugal either, for best results. It must be welcoming, and should be carpeted if appropriate to the image, with seating and other customer-related facilities – even the smell of coffee brewing possibly.

A fully equipped attractive reception area, a private area, small meeting room, tidy office or small boardroom should be provided for receiving visitors and customers (to suit the situation). Good quality lighting, heating, air-conditioning and functional communications equipment such as computers, fax, phone, e-mail, Internet, mobile phones, pagers are all important so far as they are in keeping with the image of the business; as are a very discrete tannoy system, if there aren't better ways of contacting staff and making customer announcements – without the global interruptions.

The main design, drawing office, production, assembly areas (that customers should be encouraged to see, since it represents the *raison d'être* or soul of the enterprise) should be a good quality visibly productive area – tidy, functional, well-lit, safe *and busy*!

Finally, the customer-visual image should extend to professional well-designed business headed notepaper, invoices, business cards, pricing tags and all other important stationery; and also to suitable uniforms and clothing, either for protection, hygiene, image or otherwise to match customer expectations associated with certain business activities (for example health related, medical, entertainment, shops or sports ventures).

Infrastructure 'Not Visible' to Customers

Behind the scenes, it is just as important to have a good, tidy, well-lit and safe working area for the areas that are *less* customer-visible. Do not assume that customers will never see behind the scenes – and don't forget that it might put them off for life, if they did. The need is for essential but minimal office and back-room support, suitably fitted out with:

- carpets or good quality safe flooring (as appropriate)
- furniture
- office equipment such as a computer, typewriter, photocopier and shredder
- separate clean and tidy staff toilet facilities
- a small secure room with fireproof safe for cash, and safekeeping of confidential information (personal data, patents, designs, and customer-owned material left whilst a project is being worked on by your venture).

Toilets, cloakrooms and the backyard, if any, should be smart, and clear of untidy rubbish (hire, and regularly change, skips, if that's your way of disposing of unwanted materials). Be as safe as possible, with organized car parking provided for visitors and staff (in that order of priority). Have efficient warehouse facilities for storing materials, stationery, equipment, finished goods and a dispatch area; and employ appropriate transport for deliveries and internal movements such as hoists and forklift trucks. These might call for garaging and recharging points.

There needs to be an appropriately sized kitchen and staff rest area (even in house sleeping accommodation in some situations), equipped with: clean work-tops; cupboards; sink; water; microwave cooker; toaster; tea; coffee; biscuits; crockery; cutlery; first aid.

Implementing the infrastructure plans could well be phased to fit in with the anticipated sales and business development. This less sensitive part does not all have to be implemented straightaway, although the more complete the overall facilities are, the more pleasing they will appear, and the more conducive they will be for both staff and customers.

STAFF AND CUSTOMERS

Infrastructures, like business as a whole, need the right staff: all your staff are your day-to-day proxies. They can make or break you: look after them and listen to them, at grass-roots level. Get the best staff the business can afford, *because you only get what you pay for.*

- Staff may remain with the business for a very long time, can be a good investment, and can generate revenue, quality, customer satisfaction (or otherwise).
- Happy, contented people make loyal staff; and the 'infection' spreads directly to the customers.
- Happy customers make for a thriving business.
- That, in turn, makes for a happy boss.

Staff and customers should be nurtured right from the beginning. They represent a short-, medium- and long-term investment. Care for them both as they're part of the total investment in the business (although they may not realize it).

Just as with the staff, always listen very carefully to customers, because at the end of the day they have *the* major influence on the effectiveness of the enterprise, its future direction and continuing viability. They also effectively pay the wages – both the immediate ones, and the future wages, salaries and dividends.

As your business grows, stop and consider the hidden profit potential of your staff. Encourage a well-oiled two-way communication between you and your staff, seeking out new and better ideas for doing business. They will improve your business' performance – if you listen at the coalface!

OCCASIONAL STAFF RESOURCES

Certain resources may only be required spasmodically. They may have to be hired as and when required – from someone else's own venture, possibly.

Computer Repairer

Example One cites a temporary resource, normally working freelance as a specialist computer repair engineer. Software houses and many other businesses, using computers as tools in their trade, might call on him or her only when their hardware goes down, but don't need their services all the time.

Consultant

Example Two relates to a special adviser, very knowledgeable in trade-peculiar legislation and regulations. This industry consultant is only needed occasionally – but is vital on those occasions when he or she is called for.

Other Specialist Skills

Example Three could similarly relate to someone with secretarial, bookkeeping, translation or computing skills, in which he or she sells their time to your business by the hour, as and when you need them.

All these people could be paid a retainer as independent consultants, or just be engaged as temporary staff or subcontractors for the work they do. Money is likely to be scarce.

- You won't want to spend it unnecessarily.
- Staff are not a luxury: staff costs must be budgeted for, to make the business equation fit. Staff (and owners) have to earn their keep!
- Check the application forms, personal history forms, SWOTs, likes, dislikes, and so on for useful secondary skills.
- Check for useful personal attributes as well, to get the maximum internal horse-power and loyalty.
- Fill your resource gaps (whether technical or otherwise) with whatever skills, experience and expertise you can command – in-house first (you, your partners, your staff or your family).
- All these people could be paid a retainer as temporary staff, subcontractors or as independent consultants, but money paid out to family members (and effectively retained within the family) should be considered first. It's usually the most efficient way of sourcing these skills.
- Family members can be paid from the business, as employees via the PAYE system, if they genuinely work for the business and receive realistic and fair remuneration for that work; it must be declared by the individuals, as if it was their only job (or, if part-time, one of their jobs).

Job Descriptions

Proper job descriptions should be given to each employee, setting out precisely what is expected of him or her, who they report to, their objectives, responsibilities and accountabilities; and how and where they fit into the whole enterprise. They should accurately describe the tasks that they are expected to perform and the ways their success is to be measured. There are detailed guides on these techniques in various specialist books.

Before attempting to prepare them individually, start by creating a comprehensive outline function list showing each and every operation in the business, and how they integrate and interrelate. This way, not only will job descriptions help the individual, but they will also challenge you, as owner or whatever, to justify every position in the business. It will make you think Scrooge-like about who and what is needed, wanted or just on the wish list.

Start at the top, and consider how necessary each function really is. What is it for and what will it achieve for the business? It will focus your mind, highlight staff costs and identify skill and knowledge deficiencies – in relation to the business as an entity. Decide who does what, and decide whether the jobs are: really necessary, first of all; permanent; temporary; full-time; part-time; agency; subcontract; whatever.

STAFF TRAINING

However good the staff are, training is the minimum they could expect; and you will benefit as well. Ultimately it's your responsibility. You are strongly reminded that every member of staff should know the following topics backwards:

- the various procedures and routines for use in customer-related matters
- appropriate attitudes and dress code
- operation of equipment, computers, software and facilities
- where things are kept, including all major stationery and office equipment
- the stock, how to use it and where to locate it
- the business' capabilities and catalogue
- fire and safety procedures (staff and customers)
- how to handle and deal with customers.

If there is a chance, have a role-play dummy run with the staff before going live, and make it as realistic as possible. Explain the purpose, objectives and context of any training, role-play or delegation activities – it does help considerably.

EXERCISE
Work out where everyone in your particular venture fits in, their employment status and the consequential approximate staff costs. How does this reconcile with your cash flow staff costs and sales forecasts?

CLEANING AND DUSTING

Part of the infrastructure is to maintain clean, tidy and dusted premises. Cleaners are implicitly responsible for helping gain business, if they do their job well. Like bookkeeping, payroll and accountancy matters, cleaning is an area that could be, and often is, outsourced. The main points to watch are the trustworthiness of the person(s) so engaged, as they are *in the building alone* either at night or early in the morning. Access into a security area may be another matter to resolve. On the other hand, it's a job that you can do for yourself with any employees.

CORE VS. INFRASTRUCTURE

This chapter is deliberately short to reflect the fact that the infrastructure, whilst exceptionally important, knows its place in the context of the business as a whole. The business core is unquestionably king, and the 'unfortunate' infrastructure represents only a very necessary but money-consuming servant merely to oil the wheels for the greater glory.

EXERCISE

Think about and plan your own business' infrastructure.

EXERCISE

Prepare your own purchasing plan (business drivers and objectives, where and how much to source from each supplier, secondary or back-up suppliers, phased deliveries, contracts, desired credit and other terms, quality checks, consequences of non-delivery or inadequate quality, and so on).

WHAT HAVE YOU LEARNT IN THIS CHAPTER?

* ★ Why is a business infrastructure needed?
* ★ What are the consequences, if it is not in place?
* ★ What is the delicate financial balancing act to be performed in considering infrastructures?
* ★ What support is needed, in particular?
* ★ Differentiate between the customer-visible and the rest of the infrastructure.
* ★ What purposes do job descriptions serve and why should they be prepared?
* ★ Staff should be well-trained – what in, exactly?

20
Launching the
Business

You will now be aware of the solid principles of what has to be done: it's now time to move into Stage 3 – the detailed planning stage that should not of course be undertaken until the first two have been almost totally agreed upon, because serious money will need to be spent and committed.

> **EXERCISE**
>
> Complete the business plan for real, commenced as a draft in Chapter 8.

This is the final countdown to launch – it's a very busy time: it is also full of excitement and anticipation. Time for final detailed work to underpin the venture. There are a myriad of tiny things to do and attend to, superimposed on the bigger jobs that form the framework of the venture. The secret of creating your own business (like decorating or gardening) lies in the thoroughness of the preparation.

The first two stages together probably constituted about 45 per cent of the effort, depending on how much actually gets covered, *and how well it is documented*. You may have invested much more effort, time and possibly money such that there is actually somewhat less than the nominal 55 per cent left to do. To some extent, the two stages concerned with outline and detailed planning overlap in the sense that one builds on the work, research and note-taking done in Stage 2. All that really remains is to dot the Is and cross the Ts.

Practically speaking, this chapter is a recapitulation of Stage 2, but at a deeper level. No apology is given for repeating the message, but this time more concisely to emphasize the important points. It's a final checklist, effectively triggering the multitude of the various intricately connected detailed activities; it makes sure they actually happen on time and in the optimum sequence.

When undertaking an unexplored path for the first time, certain physical and navigational aids are used, and markers or pointers are inserted that can all be reused the next time to save doing the job twice from scratch. Stages 1 and 2 will have taken several months; but the contacts, know-how and essential ports of call, the research and spadework will already have been done. That's why this task may not be as burdensome as it may have seemed at first. Avenues of exploration undertaken in Stage 2 that, with hindsight, have proved to be fruitless, can be eliminated from Stage 3, of course.

Start off by concentrating on and recapping on the specific venture, going over the basic ground once more. In the general excitement, there is a tendency to rush to the end point and not give sufficient time and effort to the vital intermediate matters. Also in the general excitement, matters could get missed if no independent audits were undertaken. So, double check every detail by bouncing all the thinking off a colleague or business partner, if there is one, and/or your accountant; review and confirm what has been agreed so far.

PROJECT MANAGEMENT

Chapter 18 forewarned of this subject: for this stage, these skills are definitely needed.

- List practical actions that have taken place to date, using all the notes, minutes and checklists made after each earlier visit.
- Think about what *still* has to be done, and in the right implementation order;
- Present the thoughts on a project diagram showing the interrelationships of activities and achievements, or *events*, with other activities, and their timescales.

It is interesting to note that some actions operate serially (one after the other), others in parallel (simultaneously).

The diagram should clearly identify what specific resources are required at each step, and what enabling factors must be in place before each can be commenced – the resources referred to are not those for the business, as such, but merely for the *detailed planning*.

The objective is to clear the way for the following project planning activity to go ahead as smoothly as possible. For example, one such enabling factor might be a specific reply from one organization to enable the following activity to proceed with another. Keep an eye on critical deadlines and issues, or potential hitches which could jam some subsequent activity.

SORTING OUT AND PLANNING THE DETAILS

It is easier to identify specific things from a list which *haven't* been satisfactorily completed, rather than compile the list in the first place. That's why a trusted partner, colleague or accountant will be useful in this respect, even if he or she does want paying for the privilege. It is obvious now why prolific note-taking in earlier chapters was recommended.

It is sometimes very difficult to see beyond the end of your nose in the exciting atmosphere and understandable confusion, but you must think hard about the remaining tasks.

The ultimate fourfold objective for the detailed planning stage is to ensure that every:

- essential job gets done in time

- gap gets plugged in a positive way
- facility is programmed to be in place before launch
- resource is or will be in place before launch.

No excuses are permitted! That last sentiment is worth repeating: no excuses at all are permitted – for the simple reason that if it's not done prior to launch, it may be fatal to the business. *You're the boss, you can't be wrong; nor can you be seen to be wrong!* You, your business partners and the professionals should discuss and ask:

- Who needs, or *still* needs, to be contacted?
- Who specifically is going to contact them when and about what, in particular?
- Would a letter, formal meeting or telephone call suffice?
- Are all prerequisites in place?
- Are there any specific points relating to the uniqueness of the venture?
- What would the primary and secondary purposes of the meeting be, and its objectives?

Think back to the space launch analogy: once the rocket engines have ignited, it's too late for last-minute changes of mind. You should purposefully create new action lists, with accountable names. As potential boss, it is your responsibility to make it happen, and to check that it does, even if it is not your assigned task to carry it out *personally*. This is management and delegation in practice, of course.

- These activities could well take the form of consolidation or confirmation steps whose foundations were laid in earlier meetings, as in, *Well just give me a ring when you've decided what to do* – or whatever.
- One result might depend on the outcome of another. Hence the sequence is important.
- Check thoroughly that no stones have been left unturned.
- Just in case of a problem (a missed appointment or some other potential catastrophe), have timely contingency plans in place – to minimize the risks.
- Go round the loop several times, if necessary.
- Carry out the actions, *in the correct sequence* to achieve full satisfaction of the declared objectives for the individual meetings.

Management Tips

Sometimes helpful underlying rules can help forge a forward path through otherwise impossible forests. The would-be managing director, or whatever, might like to recall these thirteen principles from time to time – when doing almost anything, let alone planning and running a business.

- *Know what you really want to do*
  When performing any tasks, never lose sight of your true objectives. Rome was

certainly not built in a day, and neither will your venture be; but it certainly was eventually built. Even if the completion of the job in hand takes a long time, don't get side-tracked. Keep the real objectives in mind.

* *Enormous, seemingly horrendous, tasks are merely groups of smaller, much more manageable, tasks*
  Break up huge tasks into a series of smaller acceptable steps, and just go one step at a time. (Jumping from floor to ceiling obviously appears horrendous, but installing a staircase effectively breaks the overall task into manageable steps.) Get a firm foothold on each one before going to the next. It won't take too much effort, *then*, to complete the original. The same technique should be used on project diagrams, by breaking larger activities into their lowest common denominator – mini-sized tasks.

* *Time management – don't overwork yourself (or others)*
  Well-intentioned effort alone can be self-defeating, if it becomes over-burdensome. The glittering prize is not for trying exceptionally hard, or for trying to do it all oneself and maybe failing: but for *winning* within the timescale, with whatever strategy, methods and resources it takes. Never get bogged down in a task when it seems utterly impossible to progress (it may be through tiredness, mental blockage or simply that you can't see the wood for the trees, perhaps). Intersperse one job with another.

* *A change is as good as a rest*
  You can tell when you are failing to make real progress. There's no point in going on applying more of the same technique or strategy when it would benefit from a fresh start or another approach completely. Come back to the task later, with a brand-new mind and the immediate problem will have disappeared, or seems manageable again.

* *Ways of working or methodology*
  Often when faced with another huge, seemingly insuperable, problem don't work overtime on it. Instead, find a better *method* of solving the problem. In other words, simply work much more cunningly and cleverly – not just longer and 'harder'. Keep thinking of ways to improve productivity. The key to high productivity is not necessarily in sheer hard work and long hours, in the vain *hope* that the job might get done satisfactorily on time; it's in the methodology – that is, devising the best way to do the job! It's worth thinking about – and will save time, frustration and effort in the long run.

* *Plan ahead*
  Plan ahead deliberately and with purpose: anticipate what *could* happen. It may not happen exactly that way, but at least you'll be prepared with a contingency plan. In similar vein, plan your workload, create some space during the day and have some real thinking time. If you're very busy, delegate, trusting other people to do things responsibly.

* *Learn to prioritize*
  Differentiate between *important* jobs and *urgent* jobs; and again delegate (giving guidance where necessary); and merely check that the result has been

achieved satisfactorily. For example you must remember to phone a customer back (it's important that you do), but, because he or she is not available 'till late afternoon', it's not urgent that you do it first thing.

- *80/20 rule*
  Frequently, no one has time to do everything; so endeavour to achieve the most effective and productive 80 per cent of the job in say 20 per cent of the time; and leave the less-necessary remaining 20 per cent that might otherwise take say 80 per cent of the time – a disproportionate amount of time in relation to the extra it can achieve. Similar opportunities for the application of this so-called 80/20 rule crop up more often than you think – so employ it as often as it takes. The remaining 20 per cent can be handled another time, when the desk is clearer – or maybe delegated. Perhaps the rest's not terribly important anyway? This is why one is often urged to make lists of tasks; then prioritize them before tackling them.

- *Think quickly, on your feet*
  Practice making *good rational decisions*. Weigh up the evidence; what more might be needed and why; endeavour to get it or ask when it will be forthcoming; then make a reasoned decision for which one will usually gain respect – either *yes, no, or insufficient information at the moment, for the following reasons … and then a decision can and will be made.*

- *When promises are made; keep them!*
  Don't make them in the first place if they can't be kept.

- *Keep cool: don't panic or get flustered*
  Obviously much easier to say than do; but try, and try hard, to be rational – perhaps applying one of the other helpful rules as well.

- *Cooling off period*
  If things get a bit hectic and fraught (and you would otherwise get your revenge or dissipate your irritation on an innocent member of staff, or worse still, a customer) – thus exacerbating the original problem – just take a short break as soon as you can: go for a short walk or have a short time away from the hot-seat until you feel more relaxed. Do something completely different. This apparent walking away from the problem is not permanent, only temporary – for the greater glory of the business as a whole.

- *Discipline*
  A quiet word in someone's ear or a more serious disciplinary interview *is* necessary sometimes. Act firmly, politely and authoritatively as soon as possible to redress the situation. Part of your role is to anticipate, diffuse and solve possible difficulties. Handled the right way, they can almost always be dealt with professionally and satisfactorily – and with a neat and tidy solution. Any instructions must be given concisely, unambiguously and clearly. Whatever arises, from whatever direction and on whatever subject you must:

  - instantly assess the situation
  - methodically investigate it
  - understand the precise problem

- act decisively and authoritatively
- act within the law.

Almost Fully Prepared

You now have the theoretical background against which to plan the entire venture. If you feel there is still room for some improvement, or have a nagging doubt as to whether everything has happened correctly, you should go round the loop again and again, as necessary, until you are satisfied that everything possible has been done. This is a frequently encountered occurrence: nagging doubts over one's faculties, capabilities and suitability – that seem a weakness, calling for further reassurance (another form of prudence really). Check every detail twice with colleagues. All this detailed planning may be repetitive, tedious and not always easy; but nevertheless vital for a good launch.

In spite of all this really hard concentrated effort, some things will still be missed; but ultimately you will have to admit the omission – hopefully only a small one!

FINAL COMPREHENSIVE CHECKLIST

Here's a concise but far-reaching practical 17-point checklist in a punchy summary format. It covers many aspects of creating a business, but adjust its sentiments to your own specific venture. It is really asking (as appropriate to the venture context *and its genuine need*): *have all these things been considered, attended to, planned, ordered, arrived, been installed, and actually ready for customer inspection, as it were?*

- *Background information*
  Reading magazines, books, trade journals, Internet; visiting trade associations, exhibitions, trade fairs, craft fairs, car boot sales, seminars, competitors; doing market research, SWOTs, soul-searching, establishing concept; having family discussions.
- *Planning*
  Doing detailed homework; sorting out personal and business goals, core business(es), objectives and targets, range of products and services, undertaking sales forecasts, delivery and revenue forecasts, budgets, cash flow forecasts, contingency plans; determining throughput capacity infrastructure to meet turnover targets.
- *Resources*
  Seeking out premises, finance (banks, other lenders, capital, overdrafts), people, technical matters, key people, suppliers, equipment, subcontractors, cleaners, occasional help, plant.
- *Professions*
  Deciding on a logo, trade mark, business name, product and brand names; undertaking searches, business and company formation; finding an accountant, solicitor, surveyor, architect, bookkeeper, payroll undertaker, insurer, public

relations management; finding product designers, engineers, technologists, web page designers, project managers; talking to local, planning and rating authorities.

- *Suitable sites*
Looking for types of premises, locations, specific premises, buildings, land or whatever; considering convenience and access for customers, staff and transport; discussing fitting-out, heating, air-conditioning, stairs, lifts, shopfront, signs, car parking; planning building work; obtaining planning consent; adhering to building regulations.
- *Infrastructure*
Making choices and decisions about decoration, flooring, lighting, 'production' equipment, furniture, kitchen, toilets, first aid, access.
- *Finance support*
Arranging credit cards, debit cards and credit facilities, bank accounts and bank stationery, and HP-type facilities; arranging credit and debit card communications and sanctioning equipment.
- *Insurance*
Arranging comprehensive cover for buildings, contents, plant, equipment, stock, raw materials, loss of business profits, professional indemnity, self and key people, other employees, third-party liabilities.
- *Vehicles*
Choosing cars, vans, fuel, acquisition; considering need for HGVs, transport, tailgate lifts, delivery mechanism; arranging 'HP', servicing schedules, MOT, tax and insurance.
- *Communications*
Having enough telephone lines, fax machines, mobile phones, pagers, answerphones, telephones; choosing good telephone/fax numbers; acquiring and installing computers, software, networks, ISPs, computer stationery and consumables, technology, Internet.
- *Service providers*
Arranging gas, electricity, oil, water; arranging disposal of sewerage, refuse, industrial waste.
- *Stationery and printing*
Having pre-discussions with suppliers; designing and printing invoices, statements, compliment slips, business cards, leaflets, brochures, labels, price tags, bags, ordinary stationery, wrapping and packaging .
- *Stock and raw materials*
Having advance discussions and orders with suppliers, price guns.
- *Staff*
Considering and arranging job descriptions, budgets for staff, advertisements, recruitment, interviews, start arrangements, uniforms, badges, staff contracts of employment, payroll, personal agreements, tentative succession planning; having dry runs; doing *adequate* training; imparting product knowledge.
- *Precisely who does what?*
Assigning personal responsibilities and accountabilities.

253

- *Training*
  Arranging the initial and recurrent training – very, very important. Where, when, how, what?
- *Publicity*
  Marketing considerations generally especially Yellow Pages, telephone directory, Internet, e-mail addresses, making opening arrangements (*see below*), advertisements, leaflets.

Ensure all these matters are planned properly with sufficient time.

EXERCISE

Compile a sequenced list of the main activities to establish your own business.

EXERCISE

Carry out the detailed planning (Stage 3) for your own particular venture.

PLANNING 'PRODUCTION'

Just as it is crucial to meticulously plan the business as a whole (and have contingency escape routes in place, just in case), it is clearly necessary to think *everything else* out and plan it carefully. Earlier rough plans must be firmed up at this stage or 'final' plans checked to ensure that they will withstand your own and third party professional scrutiny. This is your last chance before opening.

For example, it was stated earlier that marketing (including any export activity, if applicable), sales strategy and the purchasing framework need to be considered, justified and quantified against the *business* goals, timescales, manpower, available finance, other resources and technology (that is, plans must be spelt out to exactly meet the business objectives).

Equally important, whatever form your core 'production' takes (as defined by one of the five pointers given at the end of Chapter 3), that, too, must be thought out and planned meticulously so as to be able to meet the other targets – sales, marketing, deliveries and revenue – derived ultimately from the business plans. You must plan 'production' to meet the other plans and business objectives – with timescales, shift system employed, availability of equipment and machines, product mix, priorities if conflicts should occur, contingency work-arounds, availability and quality of raw materials, staff, and so on, in mind.

EXERCISE

Draw up your own 'production' plans.

OPENING PUBLICITY

Opening publicity is aimed at announcing the business for the very first time: a sort of fanfare; whereas ongoing publicity (with or without special promotions) has a different purpose. Consider any or all of the following, depending on the nature, and desired image, of the venture; and also on budgets. Don't blow the first budget – or any other for that matter.

Twin Objectives

The *major plank* in the opening publicity programme must be the introduction of potential customers, or influential people who might be in contact with potential customers. The *secondary objective* as far as the owner is concerned is to get contact names, telephone numbers and addresses and then to make follow-up phone calls, and a return visit. So encourage potential customers to:

- see the premises and facilities
- find out what the business does and could do for them
- get their hands on the products, as it were
- meet the boss and the key staff
- talk further with the business either on their own account or on behalf of others.

All this needs to be organized to take place in a nice congenial atmosphere; remember a prime selling rule: get the customer relaxed.

As a solid guide as to what media to use, how to shape the event and who to invite, bear in mind the objectives of the occasion. Think of the customers your business wants to attract; try to enable them to hear or read about the business (and what it can offer) through a medium that you believe *they* listen to, watch or read.

Who To Invite?

- Known, interested and potential customers
- local dignitaries and local business organizations (whose help with additional publicity would be most welcome)
- neighbouring businesses
- professional sources
- any middlemen involved with the business such as distributors, agents, dealers, even suppliers
- local, and if appropriate, the national press
- local radio, TV channels and if appropriate the national programme producers and advertising controllers (but at least two/three months' advance notice is usually required).

It might also be appropriate to pay for the engagement of a famous personality as part of the hype or build-up, either a celebrity or a business-related colourful figure (bluntly, a crowd puller) – but it must seem a *very natural* choice and will depend on the image projection ideas.

House-Warming

Another good supporting idea is to invite these people to an official house-warming event – an open evening (at a convenient time for *them*, like immediately they close their own doors at 6pm, for an hour or so in the evening, or at lunchtime). The event has been known to be piggybacked as the venue for another official evening, like a Chamber of Trade or IOD monthly meeting. If this is the choice, the hosting can be arranged with the appropriate body, and additional publicity be gained that way.

Whoever the host, some form of snack eats and drinks will help to seal the invitation – in which case, glasses, plates, and so on may need to be borrowed or hired. A lot depends on what sort of customers the business is aimed at, but in general any publicity is useful; but remember, there is no such thing as a *free launch*!

Radio, TV and Newspapers

Press advertisements, with perhaps some form of opening offers, and corresponding editorial features should be high on the list of options. If cards are played carefully, for the price of an advertisement a lot more space might be available as well as through the editorial. The newspaper will interview you for the business (so prepare the story and take advantage of the opportunity, being careful to tell the potential customers what *they* want to know, which is not necessarily what the egotistical venturer wants to tell them).

The newspapers should be encouraged to take useful (not gimmicky) photographs or accept some from the venturer. Offer them professional quality photos with 'smiley' people!

Getting Close

Whatever opening publicity is arranged, organize it to perfection. After all, if the business can't even do this, how can customers have faith in the business for other more important things?

- How's the adrenaline and excitement doing so far?
- Are the nerves still holding?
- Time is running out and the Day 1 deadline is getting close.
- It'll soon be open for business!

The Actual Opening

- A *very short* personal thank you and welcome (and mini-presentation about the business capabilities, capacities, staff backgrounds perhaps, depending on the business) would not go amiss – but keep it short (five minutes maximum), memorable and *don't get them bored*. Try to leave them wanting more. Ensure that there are plenty of staff around to handle customers, to deal with queries and to gently 'sell' the business. Professionalism once more.

- Hire in extra people for the special occasion, if necessary; but make sure they, too, are thoroughly trained. Another good source of extra temporary help is suppliers' staff because they are product-trained, sales-trained, have a vested interest in your success, reputation and so on – and they're free!
- Give the visitors and prospects something meaningful about the business to take away with them. They can look at it or play with it afterwards, but make sure it's of professional quality and it's got the venture business name and phone number on, if not the address, fax number and e-mail address. There are many businesses who thrive simply by making and selling give-away business gifts.
- Some part, or even the whole, of this particular event and publicity generally could be organized by a professional public relations firm, but this tends to be more for the big boys.

Customer satisfaction is all-important: the launch or the start of the business proper concentrates the mind and becomes a suitable reminder. This relates to promises, quality of products or services, and to customer service in particular. Quality, it was observed, only happens when you care enough to do your best.

EXERCISE

Write down the pre-opening publicity and opening PR plans for your venture.

WHAT HAVE YOU LEARNT IN THIS CHAPTER?

- ★ Whose responsibility is it for preparing and ticking off the items on your final checklist?
- ★ List the thirteen management tips.
- ★ Final checklist – why is it necessary?
- ★ State the main points of the 17-point action summary.
- ★ In what principal way does opening publicity differ from other publicity?
- ★ What are the twin objectives of the 'house-warming', and the five matters potential customers should be encouraged to do?
- ★ How should the actual opening go and who should be invited? Key objectives?

21
Looking to the Future

OPENING TIME

Day 1 has at last arrived. Time to put the paint brush away, unlock the doors and welcome the first customer! The dream has come true. It's very exhilarating – open for business, after long months of planning, sleepless nights, meetings, explorations, and so on. You must be congratulated – you've made it! Just imagine the day, the excitement, the start of a new life and way of living.

You have started to build your own business: you really are the boss! Now look like, and behave like, the boss, the managing director, chief executive officer, president, or whatever. Smart office and new suit maybe? In practice, of course, the opening event may be still to come – in the early evening, perhaps.

- What are your expectations?
- What possible problems might crop up?
- What had been overlooked in all the last-minute panics?

To be sure, there *will* be things – even if it was only the milk, sugar, tea, coffee, biscuits, crockery, cutlery or toilet rolls; and if it's nothing major, that's all right. You might be more worried if *nothing* appeared to be forgotten, of course!

Just think about what likely events might be encountered on Day 1 –

- the smiles
- the congratulations
- the welcomes from the potential customers
- the flowers, visitors and well-wishers
- the visits from family and friends
- the comments – verbal, fax, e-mail, telegrams
- the *Best Wishes* cards
- the challenges
- the first sale
- the first awkward customer
- peoples' curiosity
- even a cake!

Perhaps a glass of champagne is in order at this point.

MONITORING AND CONTROLLING THE BUSINESS – FINE-TUNING

After the euphoria, now to continue …

- Life must go on.
- There's always more work to do.
- You haven't made your fortune, yet.
- It's certainly not possible to put your feet up.
- This is where the ongoing commitment and drive are relevant.
- It is where your business management expertise comes to the fore.
- You must make the dream a lasting reality.
- You have to monitor and control your venture.

In this chapter (Stage 4) the immediate day-to-day activities are discussed, and the future.

Making a business plan and eventually opening are only very important stepping stones. Businesses, like gardens, do not run themselves: they need a gardener! The fact that a successful launch has taken place does not offer any guarantee of the future prosperity, although without it, the chances would probably be severely diminished. Corrective actions, as with the rocket launch, will be the norm, and will need to be applied, depending on precisely what you observe about the venture. So you should continue to make solid, constructive, positive decisions.

Running a business (as distinct from *setting it up*, which is effectively all that has been discussed so far) means four main things:

- continuing to demonstrate a listening and positive attitude with customers, business colleagues and staff
- continuing to show a 'can-do' approach with flexibility, adaptability and whatever time it takes
- responding constructively to demands from customers, funders and fellow businesses but with reasoned arguments for maintaining the status quo and for not making hasty, *unnecessary* or emotional changes
- being unquestionably in charge – but with sensitivity, coolness and authority.

You, personally, must still do what you are best at – whether it be technical matters, selling, customer contact or whatever. You must of course be visible to customers and staff. You must continue to give 100 per cent of your effort in this direction, but you must *also* provide supervision and guidance to everyone else (as required) and manage the business as a whole; or else it will not completely remain under your control and direction – and then what might happen?

The story goes about a garage proprietor who had built up his successful business over several decades. As the business grew and he got inevitably older, he relinquished his technical skills, as he could not keep up personally with the new car technical advances. So he left the dismantling of engines and tweaking of car electronic systems and so on to younger minds.

By now concentrating on mundane jobs like mending punctures, dealing with the telephone, organizing the workload for his staff, managing his business and so forth – without interrupting his otherwise very meticulous highly complex technical work and possibly causing disastrous and dangerous mistakes – his declared aim was simply that he could supervise his other people better. Possibly a laudable and sensible attitude in the changing circumstances.

Progressive Business

- A very experienced account mentor and colleague asserted that business performance could go up or down; but that it could not remain on a level path. This, he affirmed most adamantly, meant that if the business wasn't visibly improving and going up, it was declining. In the long run this path would prove to be disastrous, if it wasn't rectified.
- Expressed another way, having accelerated to, say, 70mph on the motorway, try safely taking the foot off the throttle pedal. Eventually the vehicle *will* come to a halt, even with a following wind, or a gentle downhill slope.
- Alternatively, the fact that you might have been steering the car to keep in a particular forward-looking straight line is no guarantee that that course will be maintained when hands are removed from the wheel.
- You have got to put energy (in a scientific sense) into any system to counteract the fact that science does not support the concept of perpetual motion; and, however minute, the frictional and other forces will take their effect.
- The humble example of a child's swing in the park should make a visual reinforcement in that, if it is not 'pushed' occasionally after it has got going, it too will also come to a standstill in time.

Your skills will improve dramatically (almost without noticing) as the business develops, in management, business matters generally, sales and marketing, finance and technical matters. The *technical* core competence will improve naturally, because of the enhanced personal interest, concentrated use and experience: it simply *has* to progress for the business to grow in an expertise sense and overall stature. Correspondingly, the business enterprise will grow as well.

All those other subjects that were not originally second nature to you will gradually improve, too, through use and a growing interest supporting the core activity.

Five Critical Areas
There are several primary areas that always need constant attention, apart from the indigenous technical matters of course, and for which practical help is indicated.

Business Image, Reputation, Customers and the Marketplace Generally
It is very easy to let standards slip unwittingly, and one way to help prevent this is to ask independent observers about their impressions. You notice (or will do from now on) how other businesses fare and keep their sharp businesslike image, or

otherwise; you must train yourself to be permanently critical of your business' appearance – but in a positive and constructive way.

Listen hard to that highly valued and much-to-be-sought-after feedback from the marketplace in the widest sense of that word – in other words, customer and public reaction, and local/national media. Concentrate very hard on the public perceptions of the business using all the techniques mentioned earlier in the book about spreading the word, marketing the business and capturing customers, business and sales.

How the customers and potential customers view the business at the end of the day, ultimately determines the destiny of the business. In practice, consider:

1. Is the business getting enough of the right customers?
2. What are their reactions?
3. How did they hear of the business?
4. Ensure that they, as another level of ambassadors for the business, are fully conversant with the capabilities or stock range.

Always keep the customer environment attractive, inviting, well-decorated and welcoming; and keep the stock clean, free of dust, tidy and in good working order. Similarly, smartness, currency and frequency of give-aways, including brochures, leaflets, business cards and so on, and the mechanical quality of samples comes in this category as well.

With some commodities like flowers, food and certain packaging, it is exceptionally important to maintain freshness and quality of merchandise, especially in window and internal displays that can get genuinely forgotten. Scruffy stock (whatever excuses might be offered), faded pictures, posters and curled-up printed notices, like untidy personal appearances and disrespectful personal attitudes, put customers off immediately, and of course kill the business.

If the business is constituted round a service, the standards must be rigorously and noticeably upheld. It needs constant vigilance – and this cannot be overstressed!

- Strive to maintain public interest in what is going on.
- Keep public awareness high on the agenda with appearances and informative articles in the press, magazines and radio with telling reports and quality photographs – even reports and pictures on TV.
- Don't allow complacency to creep in.
- Keep stoking the fire.

Business Performance

Even before the first Annual Accounts are produced, it is always possible to monitor the main performance indicators for your own venture, if the official books are expressly set up to note the key parameters (as they probably will be). The vital things to look out for are:

- numbers of customers or even enquiries – sales prospects

- conversion or success rates (how many enquiries or browsers actually become true customers who buy)
- tightness of cash, or bank balance
- turnover figures
- profit levels
- cash flow
- sales
- expenses
- budgets
- direct and indirect costs
- how long customers take to pay their invoices
- quoted share prices, if applicable
- share earnings ratios, if applicable
- a few more as well, depending on the type of business.

It is even possible for you to note *rough* values of key figures, like sales figures and number of enquiries. You will find that the daily, weekly or monthly comparative figures become very exciting and almost a god (unofficial targets to beat) in themselves!

- Compare them as the days go by with their previous counterparts.
- Compare actual performances with every official or unofficial forecast – sales (by product, types, models, colours, size, specification and so on), incoming supplier orders, their deliveries, outgoing deliveries, problem areas associated with the core products.
- Watch times (and hence costs) of design, manufacturing and 'production', product lead times (that is, how long it takes to produce, deliver and install them).
- Keep abreast of business trends and news, noting how your business is performing by comparison.
- Be as objective as possible. Don't simply use the rose-coloured spectacles.

Anticipating and Managing Problems

Problems can start off, merely as little points that need attention. If dealt with early enough, most problems can be solved, or dissipated (with proper and timely planning). The obvious way to tackle them is to be constantly vigilant about spotting them in the first place – on the horizon – and dealing with them ahead of time. They:

- might arise within the infrastructure, or even in the core aspect of the business
- might relate to falling foul of legislation, regulations, directives, the authorities, and so on
- might relate to unhappy, and hence not fully performing, staff
- might relate to you or your staff simply not responding to phone calls, letters, e-mails or faxes; personal, financial or health matters; or just forgetfulness
- might sometimes get forgotten or ignored in the hope that they will go away

- should always be anticipated to pre-empt them, and kill them early on. That's what management is all about – whether related to customers, staff, suppliers, creditors or anyone else
- may fester and grow enormously in a short period to become huge management problems
- might be potentially serious complaints raised by customers (which is even worse).

Furthermore:

- Don't delegate responsibility for customer problems.
- Don't ever be too busy to deal with them.
- Deal personally with them, prioritizing where necessary.
- Handle and resolve all complaints *quickly and personally*.
- *Be seen* to be interested enough to handle them – with a win-win outcome (the customer should emerge happy with the outcome; the owner should be happy as well).

All problems may be somewhat masked – however they eventually get noticed and what they really refer to: they are still very active working away below the surface. They could represent a whole variety of matters; but in every single case, find out not only the superficial problem, but also the deeper problem.

A lot of persistent digging may be called for, but problems of any type represent potential issues to be resolved by you with all sincerity, haste and permanence.

- Solve them all somehow – quickly!
- Be on the lookout particularly for the levels of verbal and written complaints, faulty goods and returns, poor supporting paperwork for goods supplied and/or manufactured by your venture, incomplete follow-up documentation and service and so on.

Complacency
Complacency problems specifically could relate to your staff, or could even relate to the boss *deliberately or unwittingly* losing interest for some reason or other – perhaps a personal or financial one. If you become disinterested (even temporarily) the customers and the rest of the staff will quickly imitate this behaviour in a chain reaction; and again the business will collapse like a series of dominoes! Take time off, as the business allows, to help mitigate this problem – have another hobby. Strive to maintain the freshness you presumably started with (or should have done).

Leakages
The last area to watch out for discreetly is what is euphemistically referred to as *leakages*. Leakages are, sadly, own goals in a sense: theft by staff, partners, fellow directors, and customers, and effectively business fraud. It's no use you kidding

yourself that *your* business will be different. It won't. Leakages are all somehow and insidiously related to lack of keen observation, and meticulous interest in the bookkeeping. They can often be detected or mitigated by an exceptional, photographic and accurate memory, sharp observation, carefully scrutinized recruitment procedures, staff training, carefully constructed and self-checking internal procedures, recording security cameras and display monitors.

Make sure all employees are trained to watch customers *discreetly* (especially when customers arrive in groups). Correspondingly, staff must be firmly but politely aware (by virtue of their employment contracts right from the outset) that they, too, are being observed: that no dishonesty or other misdemeanours will be tolerated whatsoever. This must be strictly enforced of course, and be seen to be enforced – but fairly and impartially. Serious actions must be dealt with within the law of course, calling in the police, security staff and employing dyes and ultra-violet light sources with suitable 'inks'.

Summary

Occurrences like losses, theft, fraud, not dealing with customer comments and slipshod business performance parameters are all strong possibilities within any business, whether as a result of: just plain apathy; genuine oversight; being far too busy and preoccupied; insufficient interest in certain aspects of the business.

It's so easy: be vigilant, look out for them and act immediately. *Routinely* scrutinize the horizon along with every nook and cranny in the business for the danger signals *and act immediately.* These matters will be eliminated before they become ogres. You should be: visibly watching for signs and asking pertinent (but often discreet, sideways and double-checking) questions.

CONTINUOUS REVIEW

Within the timescale of the business, time has now moved on – beyond Day 1. Based on the fact-finding and observation since Day 1, you should continuously ask yourself the following and other derivative questions.

- Has the business continued to adopt the right strategy and policies?
- Is it located in the optimum location, bearing in mind all the financial and other constraints?
- Is it promoting and actively selling the right mix of services and products?
- Are they being sold at the right prices and terms?
- Is the pricing strategy right?
- Are the right markets being targeted?
- How have the resources and infrastructure stood the strain?
- What's the trade feedback?

Take soundings amongst the staff and of course a *few* strategic customers, suppliers, the accountant, bank manager, fellow businesses and local newspapers – in the knowledge that the latter group have got their ear to the ground, and are in regular contact with mutual customers and clients.

Business SWOT

Within a few weeks of opening it is worth performing another SWOT analysis – if you recall Chapter 2; but this time think about the *business venture* as a whole, and not about you or any other individual. It will help to answer some of the questions; and provide guidance for the future of the business.

Think very carefully about the following four questions; write down the multiple answers in the four quarters of the SWOT analysis sheet of paper – as before, but this time in connection with your business. Be aware of comments passed by and through the people mentioned above – not just your own views.

- *What are the* **strengths** *of the business?*
- *What do you perceive as the* **weaknesses** *of the business?*
- *What could be additional* **opportunities** *for the business?*
- *Where are the* **threats** *coming from, if any?*

Collectively, the answers to all questions identified in this chapter will form the basis of the future (a possibly revised) strategy. However, don't change it for the sake of change; and if it is too early in the life of the business to give meaningful information, shelve answering some of the questions and doing the SWOT for another few weeks; and then try again.

In some ways you might say it is too late now: all these points should have been addressed much earlier in the planning stages. Hopefully they were, as far as it was realistically possible.

Notwithstanding this view, if the answers with hindsight were *not* correct, it's far better to change course, even now, than to be ostrich-like. After all, one has to look forward, adapt to change – or die.

In any case, another opportunity might have now been spotted, the competitive situation may have changed, or business trading conditions might have altered, with the passing of several months – any of which could suggest further sales opportunities or slightly different approaches, beyond the original thoughts. This openly constructive attitude is also in line with expansion and market-following thoughts – whether major changes or fine tuning.

- There could be extra and new business sources.
- There could be new customers resulting from a positive marketing effort.
- A competitor might have closed down or another opened up.
- There could be some new products and new designs after the passage of time or by public demand.

Business soul-searching is vital for a strong healthy business and should be sufficiently forward thinking (either to implement immediately, or over the next few months as a preconceived and structured plan). This is especially true

265

with the practical benefit of a real opportunity to put the original theories to the test.

It's considered much more effective and professional to get it sorted out in just one *single* step if possible, because it doesn't create customer confidence and a good image to have too many bites of the same cherry.

In the meantime, fine-tune the operation, as required; but tread carefully. Don't leave it too late on the one hand, but don't make instant changes on the other. Give the impression to customers, staff and the funding organizations that these proposed changes were all programmed for and part of the grand plan!

The techniques to increase business, mentioned above, fundamentally comprise organic growth; that is, increasing the range of existing products or services, and numbers of customers, by internal means and relatively gradually – broadly keeping within its existing organization and structure. Suppose your business has been created and operated successfully for some time; then you decide to look for more dramatic ways to expand.

Another thought is to contemplate deliberately buying out a competitor (eliminating this influence and effectively buying his/her customer base), opening another similar branch, or (more radically) some vertical and horizontal integration – *see* Figure 17.

EXERCISE

Undertake a hypothetical business SWOT, assuming the business has been operating for a few weeks.

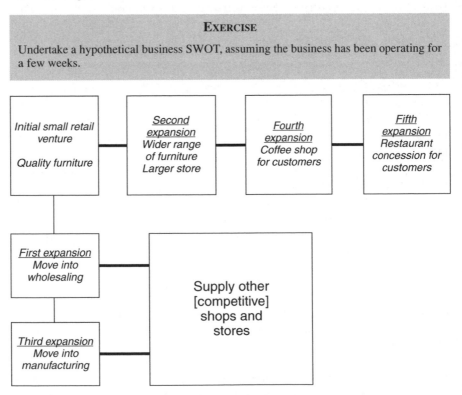

Fig. 17   Vertical and horizontal integration.

VERTICAL AND HORIZONTAL INTEGRATION

Vertical Integration

- One way is to add *an entire extra business*. In the case of a retail furniture operation, for example, it could buy one of the shop's supplier businesses, and move into furniture *wholesaling*.
- The wholesaling arm, still an *independent* business for most intents and purposes, would continue to supply all the shops that it did before, including some ranges of furniture to the original retail shop.
- Buying a wholesaling business would mean the original retail shop should be better placed to demand absolutely minimum cost prices for its furniture from this particular wholesaler (and thus help the profitability of the shop).
- The wholesaler-specific benefit is a guaranteed base level of sales to the retail outlet, as an aid to smoother production runs, and so on. (Think of the advantages towards meeting fixed costs in Example Three, Chapter 4.)
- There might be another learning curve for the owner, and there will certainly be additional investment.
- The combined arrangement would probably run as two distinct businesses (as described in this book) and, then at the highest level, 'merged' into a *group* for accounting and tax purposes under the original retail owner(s) and founder(s), perhaps.
- You would probably become the *group managing director*, if you were previously the original shop managing director, for example.

The retail customer is a customer of the original furniture shop (stating the obvious of course); and your shop continues to be a customer of the wholesaler. Because the business of wholesaling and retailing are very much in the same line (probably not totally identical in practice) in a supplier/retailer relationship, they are considered to be linked *vertically* – a small chain between similar businesses but at different 'customer' levels.

- Another vertical expansion, in due course, would be for the *group* to acquire a furniture *manufacturing* business.
- This would extend the link, whereby the manufacturer would supply a series of independent wholesalers (including the one already in the group that would continue to supply several independent retail shops, including the owners' *original* business).
- So the group is now even larger, comprising *three* vertically integrated businesses.
- One strong advantage of this arrangement is the overall integrated control of costs and sharing of overheads.
- The same advantages mentioned above that apply between wholesaler and retailer, apply now between manufacturer and wholesaler, as well.

- So, all in all, the general cost savings and economies brought about by the combined scale of the group operation, should boost the profits for the entire group.
- Notice the key feature: a chained sequence of customers – where each respective customer is serviced by the next higher level of business, all within the single group.

There is a major (but not insuperable) disadvantage though. The other wholesalers supplied by the manufacturer (on the one hand), and the other retailers supplied by the vertically integrated wholesaler (on the other), might feel aggrieved that they cannot purchase at such favourable prices, and on such favourable terms, as the owner's original or group business(es). These impressions of 'favouritism' may reflect real problems; or they may be simply presumed and entirely without foundation; but the effect might be a loss of business to the individual companies, and some loss of turnover and profits to the group as a whole.

Horizontal Integration

- The corresponding examples of horizontal integration rely on the fact that the same 'level' of customer is being served instead of the vertical chain, mentioned above.
- The customers of the business are all retail, not a mixture of retail customers and wholesale customers (other shops, in practice). As a consequence, there is of course no hint of the 'favouritism' concept, either.
- The basis is that the original shop either takes over another retail business that may or may not be in a directly similar market, and/or expands *radically* its own range of products or services.
- In the example cited, the original furniture shop increases its range of products quite dramatically, effectively growing out of all recognition as far as the original shop was concerned (although it didn't get directly involved with another retailer, as such).
- Then, by way of trying to relax the original furniture business customers, it felt that a small coffee shop might be a good idea.
- So there were two shops, effectively, on the same premises, each a business in its own right, and part of a new group; although the major emphasis was still on the furniture retail arm (in this case, but not necessarily so).
- The art in situations like this is to balance the costs, space requirements, and so on with turnover and profit contribution for each business, such that each supports the other but is equally self-reliant – which can be a tricky balance.
- Another consideration is that one acts as a business loss leader for the other. In other words, provided sales of furniture increase as a result of having the coffee shop on the premises, profits from the coffee shop as such are secondary.

In the example shown, it transpired that the coffee shop was sufficiently successful that a full-blown restaurant became the next form of horizontal integration.

Although the sentiments behind the coffee shop still applied, a real positive profit-centre in its own right was perceived by the management for the restaurant.

So, over the years and from modest beginnings, the overall expansion has embraced a furniture wholesaler, a furniture manufacturer, an enlarged retail furniture operation from a shop to a large store, a coffee shop and finally a restaurant – although, as will be noticed, not in that order!

Increased Group Profits
The broad objectives for either form of integration are usually to make overall cost savings or to make increased group sales, and hence increased group profits.

Of course, the extra business potential requires more investment and other resources, although the investment could come in part from retained profits over previous years – putting the money back into the business. Another way to implement the coffee shop or restaurant would have been simply to have rented the space to a specialist catering firm (back to the shop-within-a-shop concept): although the outlay and the profit potential would probably be less.

If all this sounds a long way off for you at the moment, don't worry. If it's going to happen, it will happen quite smoothly and naturally! Think back to the early days of organizations like Marks and Spencer, Tesco or any of the other entrepreneurs mentioned in Chapter 3.

EXERCISE

Anticipate the provisional growth and expansion ideas for your own venture.

BUSINESS DISPOSAL

Businesses can, and do, last for years – a fact that is easily verified by looking at headed notepaper, premises and advertisements – *Established in 1844*, for example. On the other hand, some don't last long at all. But what is certain is that no business lasts for ever. Eventually something has to happen, and this part of the chapter looks briefly at the various alternatives. There are four main destinies – the first two are voluntary, and the other two, distinctly less so.

When the business is no longer needed (perhaps through retirement, loss of personal interest, health reasons, financial difficulties, death or whatever), it could simply be closed down, assets sold and creditors paid – in theory at least; alternatively it could be sold either in a run-down state, just ripe for new management and revitalization (even another would-be entrepreneur might be looking to buy such a business), or as a going concern (in a take-over situation perhaps). It might be offered for sale either as a complete entity or in smaller parts.

Decision To Run a Business Down
When businesses are deliberately run down, it's advisable to discuss the matter in detail with the accountant and implement the agreed strategy over *several* years,

in advance of the planned closure. Tax planning and interaction with personal finances go behind a lot of the thinking.

The accountant should also be involved in the case of a sale, and will constructively advise accordingly. As always in business, don't make major moves without seeking professional advice. The size, status, precise circumstances and nature of the business have an influence on the best way to deal with it, and the procedures to be followed.

Decision To Sell the Business As a Going Concern

Businesses are sold via careful and discreet advertising in trade papers, newspapers and commercial 'estate agents'; word of mouth is another method. Be discreet and endeavour not to publicize the fact to potential customers because they will become edgy and the business turnover might fall away just when you are trying to maximize it, along with the subjective worth of the goodwill.

It's possible to 'put the word about' amongst suppliers and the trade generally, and even positively offer the business to likely possible contenders, but there will be a fairly restricted number of clients.

In the case of a positive interest, the latest Annual Accounts would be sought by a prospective purchaser to establish the health of the business and an estimate of its value. This information, when formalized and presented in a consolidated document with other relevant information is a form of prospectus. This comprehensive document *is* occasionally encountered in smaller businesses; but it is more likely to be found where larger concerns are being sold or where they need to raise capital.

Some of the following items have fairly explicit tangible values: others are more a matter of negotiations with the respective professionals involved. A prospective purchaser will be seeking information on the cost of the business, and so on, so as to evaluate the overall worth (to him or her), of:

- any assets (like building, plant, equipment, vehicles, stock, raw materials, work in progress, the business debtors, cash reserves, and so on)
- any liabilities (like creditors, loans to be cleared and tax liabilities)
- bank statements
- trading accounts
- minutes of board meetings
- key staff
- customers (not personal details, of course)
- turnover and cash-flow projections
- details about licences, patents, trade marks and goodwill shareholder interests
- debentures
- dividends paid
- details about suppliers
- many other things besides.

Business in Serious Trouble

If a business gets into serious trouble (usually financial), there are ways to handle it so as to minimize problems and to attempt a full recovery. A formal so-called business administrator takes legal control of the business away from the owners, and endeavours to meet its liabilities as a first priority while still trying to keep some form of the business going. Businesses have been known to recover. In extreme cases of financial trouble, the business has to be compulsorily sold, closed or officially wound up. This book will not go into precise details for three main reasons because:

- It's hopefully unnecessary, probably premature and potentially too far away.
- Your accountant should always be involved, and as early as possible, to advise on the best way forward in the light of the circumstances; and there are formal procedures to follow.
- The procedures are liable to differ depending on the legal status, size and nature of the business.

If all else fails, a liquidator is called in who sets about closing the business speedily (or even trying to sell all or part of it) and winding up the business affairs with the sole objective of getting the best return for the *creditors* (which includes the authorities, but not the owners, directors or shareholders) as his or her main priority – the so-called formal liquidation and disposal of assets. The financial and other interests of the original owners are abandoned!

Because there will be signs that the remedial efforts mentioned in this chapter will not have borne fruit, there will usually be plenty of warning of these moves. Observing the fruitless and strenuous efforts to try and resolve the difficulties gives you time to accommodate to the fate, in many cases. Also, if matters are very serious, it's a big relief when it finally happens – even if a little disappointing.

Business Inheritance

Lastly, if death should intervene, *and* wills or trusts are already in place (*see* Chapter 18), the business could continue. It *could* be legally inherited or transferred either as a whole or in parts.

This is very complicated, and is certainly susceptible to changing rules and legislation – and beyond the scope of this book. You should protect your interests and those of your successors by discussing the matter with both accountants and solicitors, well in advance – just in case. Accepting their timely advice could save your potential beneficiaries a lot of trouble, taxation and family financial problems. Again the usual factors dictate the ramifications and procedures.

WHAT HAVE YOU LEARNT IN THIS CHAPTER?

★ Discuss the following statement: once started, businesses can be left alone to run themselves.   *contd.*

★ What four things does running a business entail?
★ Why should businesses be progressive?
★ What are the five critical areas after the launch?
★ What are the danger signals to watch for after launch, and their remedies?
★ What could be the consequences, and who cares?
★ How and when should you reflect on the newly launched business?
★ Why should a SWOT be used in conjunction with a newly established business?
★ What is the objective of this review, and why should it be necessary?
★ What are vertical and horizontal integration? As a business owner, when should you consider it?
★ Outline four broad divisions of business disposal, and their relative characteristics.

22
Buying Franchises

Now that the concept behind a conventional business has been established, it is an appropriate time to examine another form of business, the *franchised* business, which has been left until you had a better grasp of traditional enterprises. It is claimed that franchises are of growing interest to potential business entrepreneurs and others who want to relinquish their employed status; and there are worthwhile magazines and exhibitions devoted to the industry.

The outward looking list of both familiar and relatively unfamiliar trading names is not too dissimilar from that for traditional businesses, although they will turn out to be in fact franchises. You would probably express surprise at some.

They cover a wide range of industry sectors – retail, sales, distribution, investment, management, legal, accountancy, caring organizations, cleaning, catering, vehicle repairs and job agencies; although most of them seem to operate in the service sector where stock demands are minimized. Virtually every type of business is a valid candidate whether providing a service or a product of some sort.

The list of franchises is constantly growing and changing, and there are thousands of them, but only a relatively few continue for a few years. Two consecutive straw polls, conducted a year apart recently, revealed that only about one-third of the names sampled in the first poll appeared in the second. There were too many new names for comfort, instead of the old ones. This is worrying.

A franchise might not necessarily apply to the whole of the business implied by the name, but only to a part of the organization.

WHAT IS A FRANCHISED BUSINESS?

Just imagine for a moment that you have pioneered a very successful business enterprise based on the broad principles of the other chapters in this book.

One expansion choice is to add another branch, as it were – *but not under the direct watchful eye and meticulous management of the owner.* Instead it will be managed at arm's length by a paid employee manager, who ultimately reports to the owner of course. If *this* business, too, proved to be equally successful, you might be tempted to invest in several more such managers, each running their own separate but virtually identically fitted out branches.

Conceptually (although not actually described as such), you, the original owner have developed and refined a business, and said to each of the specially-recruited managers:

Faithfully copy everything that I have done to make this first business successful – you can't fail! I will provide the lion's share of overall support by way of an enhanced form of infrastructure based on the first business, including all the know-how and expertise in the form of manuals, full brand image, advertising and other marketing support, pricing policy, equipment, plant, basic raw materials, stock, payroll, accounting, management, *your* training, staff recruitment, and so on. All you've got to do is to generate sales business, and run the mini-business just as if it were your own individual business, and pay the normal running expenses.

In return, all I ask is that you pay me a non-returnable advance lump sum as a licence fee, a series of management fees, royalties or whatever, for all my initial research and investment, central marketing, goodwill; pay me for the physical stock, etc. that you find you need; pay me a percentage of the sales or profits; and finally pay yourself and the staff that you'll need to recruit – and train along with yourself in the corporate company's ways and image.

In essence, this is how a franchised business operates and what a franchised business is all about, with the 'original owner' becoming the franchisor, who controls the whole chain.

CHARACTERISTICS

The concept has tremendous benefits for the true owner (the franchisor). It has its merits for the manager or local boss (the franchisee) as well, but it also has corresponding drawbacks.

- Franchises offer more scope for independence than a normal employed situation.
- The work has already been done for you, and of course this might be very attractive even if less exciting. The risks are reduced dramatically, because of the national or international infrastructure and support (supplies, equipment, stock, training, some marketing and so on). Sales (the harder part) of course are not included, although some notional, but questionable, leads might be offered.
- Unfortunately, the franchisee will certainly need a medium to large sum (to be found from savings, redundancy payouts, loans, mortgages, inheritances, and so on, as before), replacing the conventional capital.
- The franchisee (you) is effectively buying into the national or even international organization. This means that either you or the franchisor (or both) could be based in this country or overseas.
- Most emphatically, you do not become the boss – *you are definitely not your own boss*, not *the* boss, in spite of any contrary suggestion given in the recruitment publicity material (neither in spirit nor in legal terms). This is spelled out in the franchise Agreement.
- You will need to devote a large amount of time and effort (as with an own venture).

- Family involvement will often be necessary, in being available most hours of the day and night to learn, build up, maintain and expand the business effectively as you would expect in the true context of your own business.

There are positive advantages of a franchise business:

- Most of the resources have been found and supplied, including funding, premises, décor and expertise. The business pitch is all set out for you.
- It takes a lot of the initial fun and excitement away; your true independence, the conceptual and research work disappear too (compared with a true own venture).
- It is a plug-in ready-made business: most of the thinking has been done and most of the risk has been removed.
- All important supplies are arranged.
- It's certainly a possible way to taste being your own boss but to a very limited extent.
- It's definitely not the way to build your own business, as described in this book.
- Nevertheless franchises are quite popular, well-established and appear to be growing.

Whilst there are attractions, there are also disadvantages.

- The basic ground rules are set *in stone*: the franchise is not, by any stretch of the imagination, your own business.
- The real entrepreneur behind the franchised enterprise (whose brainchild, risk and reward it is) is *using* you to help his or her business and personal profits.
- You are definitely not the boss, and do not control policy, strategy, profitability and so on: nor do you have any major decision-making authority or any real control whatsoever over the franchised business.
- There is probably less financial commitment on balance than with your own business (although careful research and planning in this exercise will even eliminate most of that risk).
- There is less scope (if any) to really demonstrate any entrepreneurial leadership.
- You will probably consider yourself to be self-employed or a sole trader, at best – but with handcuffs on to some extent!
- You become effectively a puppet manager, drawing a much lower remuneration package, that is likely to be heavily biased towards commission or bonus, over which you have little control!
- If you're the sort of person who wants to get away from an employed situation, you will certainly give yourself a grand superficial *illusion* of being your own boss. That's all. Not much of the extra effort and revenue comes directly back to you.
- Centralized training sessions and meetings necessitate your attendance.
- Inevitable rigid paperwork and forms need to be completed and submitted on time.
- Stability appears to be a major problem for some franchises – but which ones?

If you wanted to be released from your obligations sometime:

- It is very unlikely that you could dispose of your part of the business without reference to, and consent from, the franchisor.
- You would not be allowed to set up a comparable business in competition!
- You might have spent your own hard-earned money on the franchise, having none left for the next possible enterprise.

FRANCHISEE'S QUALITIES

Being your own boss in the conventional sense must be the ultimate in commission-only jobs, *effectively* – if you think about it. But the big difference is that you do have *every* card in your hands – unlike being a franchisee. Both business types are based on your ability or otherwise to get sales, a necessary aspect of any form of business.

You will also require general business exposure and many of the same personal qualities needed to build your own successful conventional business, like:

- the same dedication to the core subject
- technical expertise
- appropriate attitudes and attributes (*see* Chapter 2), especially commitment, enthusiasm, drive, competitiveness
- appropriate management skills (as before) for accountancy, administration and staff management.

Be honest: if you haven't got most of the qualities for being a real entrepreneur (including an ability to get solid business), you're very unlikely to have them for being a franchisee either. So, turning to a franchise alternative as an escape route is not really a substitute.

Bear in mind, too, that the franchise might not come up to your expectations for reasons that are *genuinely outside your control*, such as a poor-quality franchise in the first place or the particular allocated territory – and there is not much in practice that you can do about that. As a result of poor achievement, the franchisor might penalize you by deliberately leaving and exercising loopholes in the Agreement for making changes to the 'rules', like lack of exclusivity, designated areas, remuneration terms and so on. You only find out about them afterwards, when it's too late.

Your freedom will be further curtailed to some extent by virtue of the franchise Agreement, and the conditions it imposes, and the fact that the franchisee will be closely monitored by the franchisor or an intermediate regional manager.

Own Business vs. Franchise
If you really have the qualities and commitment for setting up your own venture of *some* sort, you will probably derive considerably more enjoyment, freedom and income levels working for yourself in the first place.

CONTACTS

There are legal and other professionals who specialize in franchises, if you are interested in exploring matters more. There are magazines, books, trade associations, exhibitions and trade fairs. You should be able to meet the franchisor or his/her representatives, explicitly, and find out everything you need to know. Remember, that everything is ultimately governed by the Agreement (or Contract) and law; not by glossy publicity information and vague written or verbal promises. Have the draft Agreement checked by an independent lawyer. If hesitations are met with at this point, the writing should be clearly on the wall.

Questions For the Franchisor

When you contact the franchisor (and others), you should enquire about, and get satisfactory responses to the points listed below, and others. Don't be fooled by superficially likable, pleasant and endearing personalities from the franchisor or his or her representative. Seek permission to visit, and talk to references *unhindered and unaccompanied by the franchisor* – like bankers and other random franchisee premises.

Keep an open mind, and look for genuine franchise confidence-builders, credibility factors generally and any hesitation in answering questions. You should be alert to your questions being sidestepped; and very wary of unsatisfactory replies. Be on you guard if you do not get credible concise answers about:

- precise nature of the franchise
- product or service features, benefits and *so what's*
- knowledge of competition
- realistic expansion plans
- directors' and other key executives' business experience
- franchise company's track record and history: length of operating time
- number of existing franchises and their success rates
- financial data on franchisor and the franchise company
- realistic profit and loss figures, and Annual Accounts
- franchisor's bankers and other professional advisors
- restrictions of franchisor's personal involvement – ivory tower syndrome
- long-term viability of franchise company, its products or services
- obvious and clearly visible central support facilities, and the nature of precise training offered
- specific details of the central marketing activities – for example, not zero or weak advertising
- specific details relating to territory, commission, bonuses, and so on
- operating restrictions and opening hours/days
- launch assistance
- franchisor's rights to choose/approve sites
- the total franchise cost, including 'extras' – and a breakdown of that amount

- precise price, covering the initial investment, commissions, royalties, management fees, licence costs, rental fees and other monies due to the franchisor
- what is and what is not covered by the above
- whether training or anything else costs extra
- working capital needed
- data and help on raising finance

Your meeting should be at a respectable address like the headquarters – a tangible, geographically convenient, contact point offering credibility – not a hotel meeting room. It should be with the franchisor directors and key personnel.

Further Points To Watch
Watch out for:

- denial of accessibility to, and immediate availability of, the directors or key personnel
- matters that are deliberately not mentioned at all in the Agreement
- the multitude of small-print items in the draft Agreement and elsewhere
- brilliant, but independently unsubstantiated, claims and statistics
- exceptionally tempting promises
- huge profits promises, but from very minimal investment
- phrases like *easy sales*, *leads provided* or *no selling required*
- discounted franchise offers
- stocking plans – buying quantities of possibly useless stock
- vague definitions or phrases
- recruiting subcontractors and then subcontracting for profits
- effective 'pyramid selling' – which is illegal in this country
- very short-term Agreement
- oversold recruitment phrases
- phrases like, *act now to get in on the ground floor*, *work from home* or *it will cost more later.*

The Agreement
There are so many legal points the novice franchisee should look out for and be exceptionally concerned about. Ask for a sample Agreement to take away, read, get independent advice and have legally scrutinized. The Agreement and Prospectus should cover:

- opportunities and unhindered scope
- very precise financial requirements and obligations, with amounts and dates
- precise nature and extent of the obligations of all parties, including buying stock
- exclusivity, geographical area, boundaries, types of customer
- targets, and penalties, if any
- territorial boundaries

- timescales
- rights of all parties
- terms and conditions for terminating the Agreement
- how to get out of the franchise arrangement if it does not appear to be working out
- your right to sell/transfer franchise ownership
- your heirs' rights in the event of your death
- your right to extend or renew agreement beyond original term.

CONCLUSION

Franchises are characterized as being of somewhat lower risk, much lower reward and strongly regulated by the inflexible terms of contract between you and the true owner as laid down by the franchise Agreement. While they undoubtedly have their place for certain people, they are too tightly controlled for the true entrepreneur. They offer far less fun, excitement and financial reward, and yet significant money is still needed up front, but without a meaningful stake in the business. Your destiny is in someone else's hands again, just like an employed situation, and the life and stability of franchises are not guaranteed, nor under your full control.

So, at a stroke several of the advantages of being one's own boss (refer to Chapter 2) are eliminated. Add to that, that you will still lose all (or at least the vast majority) of your investment. Heads the franchisor wins, tails you lose.

Viewed dispassionately, franchises are not really the vehicle with which to build your own business, experiment with building your own business or become your own boss.

Although they unquestionably provide some sort of a taster, it will be for a high price. It's demonstrably a very expensive training exercise. If you follow this route you will need the prerequisite up-front franchise money, periodic payments and working capital; possibly in addition to all the conventional capital called for when a true own venture is launched.

If you are determined to have your own business one day, don't go the franchise path as a trial run and training exercise. Instead you should:

- simply get an ordinary employee position, within the desired non-franchised industry
- learn the trade from the inside to gain confidence
- establish the trade contacts, before really going freelance.

PROPOSITION

If you want to build your own business and also dabble in franchises, what's wrong with:

- creating your own conventional business in whatever field
- becoming a successful and indeed a super-brilliant entrepreneur

- setting up your *own chain of franchised businesses* – maybe as an expansion plan?

You reap the profits from others for *your* own business' and personal benefit. You becomes the franchisor, not the *franchisee*!

WHAT HAVE YOU LEARNT IN THIS CHAPTER?

★ What are the characteristics of a franchise business?
★ What are the advantages?
★ What are the disadvantages?
★ How do they sharply differ from conventional own businesses?
★ What are the best qualities, attributes and attitudes for a franchisee to have?
★ How do these differ for those required for an own-business entrepreneur?
★ How do franchises and own-businesses compare?
★ What are the points to watch in discussions about a franchise Agreement?
★ What's a brilliant way to become involved in franchises without becoming a franchisee?

Useful Contacts

Institute of Directors
116 Pall Mall
London
SW1Y 5ED

Tel: 020 7839 1233
www.IOD.com

Confederation of British Industry
Centre Point
103 New Oxford Street
London
WC1A 1DU

Tel: 020 7379 7400
www.cbi.org.uk

Companies House
Crown Way
Cardiff
CF14 3UZ

Tel: 0870 3333636
www.companieshouse.gov.uk

Forum of Private Businesses
Ruskin Chambers
Drury Lane
Knutsford
Cheshire
WA16 6HA

Tel: 01565 634 467
www.fpb.co.uk.

Federation of Small Businesses
Sir Frank Whittle Way
Blackpool Business Park
Blackpool
Lancs.
FY4 2FE

Tel: 01253 336000
www.fsb.co.uk

Advertising Standards Authority
Brook House
216 Torrington Place
London
WC1E 7HW

Tel: 020 7580 5555
www.asa.org.uk

Institute of Chartered Accountants in
England and Wales
Chartered Accountants' Hall
PO Box 433
London
EC2P PBJ

Tel: 020 7920 8100
www.icaew.co.uk

Useful Contacts

Chartered Institute of Management
Accountants
26 Chapter Street
London
SW1P 4NP
Tel: 020 7663 5441
www.cimaglobal.com

Institute of Insurance Brokers
Higham Business Centre
Midland Road
Higham Ferrers
London
NW10 8DW

Tel: 01933 410 003
www.iib-uk.com

The Law Society
113 Chancery Lane
London
WC2A 1PL

Tel: 020 7242 1222
www.lawsoc.org.uk

Business Links
Tel: 0845 600 9006
www.businesslink.org

NVQ/SVQ
Tel: 024 7660 4033
www.dfes.gov.uk

Mail Order Protection Scheme
18a Kings Street
Maidenhead
Berks
SL6 1EF

Tel: 01628 641 930
www.mops.org.uk

The Department of Trade and Industry
1 Victoria Street London
SW1H 0ET

Tel: 020 7215 5000
www.dti.gov.uk

ACAS
Brandon House
180 Borough High Street
London
SE1 1LW

Tel: 08457 47 47 47
www.acas.gov.uk

Office of the Data Protection Registrar
Wilmslow
Cheshire

Tel: 01625 545745
www.dpr.gov.uk

UK Patent Office
Concept House
Cardiff Road
Newport
Gwent
NP10 8QQ

Tel: 01633 814708
www.patent.gov.uk

Customs and Excise
New King's Beam House
22 Upper Ground
London
SE1 9PJ

Tel: 020 7620 1313
www.hmce.gov.uk

Inland Revenue
Tel: 0845 3021455
www.inlandrevenue.gov.uk

Telephone Preference Service
Tel: 0845 070 0707
www.tpsonline.org.uk

Tel: Direct Marketing Association
020 7291 3300
www.dma.org.uk

Index